T0394557

(Non)referentiality in Conversation

Pragmatics & Beyond New Series (P&BNS)

ISSN 0922-842X

Pragmatics & Beyond New Series is a continuation of Pragmatics & Beyond and its Companion Series. The New Series offers a selection of high quality work covering the full richness of Pragmatics as an interdisciplinary field, within language sciences.

For an overview of all books published in this series, please see
benjamins.com/catalog/pbns

Volume 344

(Non)referentiality in Conversation
Edited by Michael C. Ewing and Ritva Laury

(Non)referentiality in Conversation

Edited by

Michael C. Ewing
University of Melbourne

Ritva Laury
University of Helsinki

John Benjamins Publishing Company
Amsterdam / Philadelphia

™ The paper used in this publication meets the minimum requirements of the American National Standard for Information Sciences – Permanence of Paper for Printed Library Materials, ANSI z39.48-1984.

DOI 10.1075/pbns.344

Cataloging-in-Publication Data available from Library of Congress:
LCCN 2024002707 (PRINT) / 2024002708 (E-BOOK)

ISBN 978 90 272 1462 1 (HB)
ISBN 978 90 272 4704 9 (E-BOOK)

John Benjamins Publishing Company · https://benjamins.com

Table of contents

CHAPTER 1

Toward the interactional relevance of (non)referentiality

Ritva Laury, Michael C. Ewing & Sandra A. Thompson
University of Helsinki   University of Melbourne   University of California Santa Barbara

1. Introduction

This volume brings together research focused on the ways in which participants in everyday conversation make use of the grammatical resources of a wide variety of languages to express distinctions such as referential/nonreferential, generic/particular and specific/nonspecific in the service of shaping social action. In this introductory chapter, we place the studies in this collection in their theoretical context, noting claims made in previous literature which have had an impact on subsequent thinking, including in the research presented in this volume. We then outline the key themes that arise from the novel approaches to referentiality and nonreferentiality that are taken in the chapters brought together here.

2. Prior research on referentiality

2.1 The early modern work of logicians

While questions of referentiality – in particular the relationship between language and reality – have engaged thinkers since antiquity (notably as developed in Plato's *Cratylus*), we will begin our discussion with work by late modern European scholars. This work on referentiality was largely undertaken by logicians such as Frege (1892) and Russell (1905). They focused, for the most part, on singular, definite noun phrases – what Russell called 'denoting phrases'. Their studies were largely concerned with the truth conditionality of hypothetical examples in English with little bearing on actual language use. Nonetheless, these logicians made important baseline observations by exploring multiple senses of referring expressions and the complex relationships between referentiality, definiteness, and specificity – key issues that researchers have continued to grapple with from

https://doi.org/10.1075/pbns.344.01lau
© 2024 John Benjamins Publishing Company

various perspectives over the decades. In broad terms, these more traditional approaches to referring expressions often queried the existence 'in the world' of some entity which was being referred to and saw referential features as properties of noun phrases and deictics.

An early observation made by Frege (1892: 214) was that the use of referring expressions generally assumed the existence of the referent. A slightly different point was made by Russell (1905): he claimed that definite noun phrases, such as, famously, *the King of France*, implied both the existence of that entity and its uniqueness. Russell distinguished between the meaning and denotation of such a phrase (a distinction already made by Frege), and he claimed that while *the King of France* has meaning, it has no denotation, since France is not a monarchy. For that reason, according to Russell, we cannot in fact speak of *the present King of France*, since no such person exists, and in a similar vein we cannot speak of *the inhabitant of London*, since there is more than one inhabitant of London (1919: 176).

2.2   Reference in context

Controversially, Russell had claimed that since denoting phrases such as *the man* can be true of any individual matching the description, they do not refer directly; that is, unlike proper names, they do not directly pick out particular referents (1919: 173). This claim was contested by Strawson (1950) who argued that definite (and indefinite) noun phrases are in fact used to refer, and also that, in contrast to what Russell had claimed, their use does not imply existence, but only presupposes it. Strawson makes the important point that mentioning or referring is not something that expressions do, but rather something expressions can be *used* to do: "it is people who mean, not expressions" (1950: 328). The separation of the referential potential of definite expressions and the *use* of such expressions is similar to Guillaume's (1919) distinction between *le nom en puissance* 'the potential noun' and *le nom en effet* 'the actual noun' (see also Hjelmslev 1928). This allows Strawson to make the crucial point that what an expression refers to, and indeed whether it refers at all, is a function of the context in which it is used. He also brought up the role in meaning of what he called "language habits" (1950: 329), noting that the meaning of expressions is "the set of rules, habits, conventions for its use in referring" (1950: 328) and that "the problems of use are wider than the problems of analysis and meaning" (1950: 337).

Another early work which focused on the role of context is Bühler (1934), which took language as an instrument used in the communicative act; Bühler was the first to classify deixis based on type of context and on the nature of the referent. Along these lines, later scholars further developed the distinction between the referring and descriptive or attributive use of noun phrases (Searle

1958; Donnellan 1966). This distinction had already been explored by Strawson, who noted that it is "primarily one between different rôles or parts that expressions may play in language, and not primarily one between different groups of expressions" (1950:337). Strawson does not make entirely clear how one could tell the difference between the two uses, but he does imply that the distinction has to do with the kind of sentence the expression appears in, as well as the type of expression used, suggesting that when definite expressions appear as subjects of "singular subject-predicate sentences", they exemplify the referring use, and also that pronouns are mainly used referentially (1950:337).

Donnellan (1966), on the other hand, makes a clear distinction between definite noun phrases (or 'definite descriptions' in his terms) that are used referentially – picking out an entity in order to say something about it – and those used attributively – characterizing an entity in some way. Crucially, he points out that the distinction does not depend on the structure or semantics of sentences in isolation, but must also take into account the speaker's intentions within "a particular occasion on which [a definite description] is used" (Donnellan 1966:110). In influential and forward-looking work, Silverstein explored the role of indexicality and showed that particular forms not only reflect their context, but that "reference itself [can be] seen to be an act of creation, of changing the contextual basis for further speech events" (1976:34). Further work at this time examined the grammatical status of the NP, the modality of the clause in which it occurs, and the speaker's commitment to the existence of the entity being mentioned (see especially the crosslinguistic work of Givón 1978). Despite their emphasis on context, these scholars, like the earlier logicians, were still concerned with theorizing about hypothetical speakers and their intentions. Nonetheless, their insights helped pave the way for much subsequent research on reference, including the chapters in this volume, which aims to empirically examine what real interactional participants do with language in their everyday social encounters.

2.3 Reference in discourse

In the later part of the twentieth century a number of researchers began to approach referentiality and Strawson's "problems of use" (Strawson 1950:337) through the empirical examination of actual discourse data, deepening our understanding of identifiability and the tracking of referents. Du Bois (1980), in his insightful account of definiteness, identifiability, and referentiality in narrative data, suggests that referentiality involves continuity of identity over time, and that exact identifiability of referents is not always required, but that identifiability is only required to be close enough to be accepted in its context. One strand of discourse-oriented research has examined the match between the form of referring expressions and the cognitive status of the referent. In such an approach, referentiality might be tacitly assumed (Prince 1981) while in other approaches, definite forms are thought to refer, and indefinite forms could be used either referentially or non-referentially (see, e.g., Gundel, Hedberg & Zacharski 1993).

Givón (1983) is an attempt to quantify the referential dimensions of topic continuity and discourse prominence in a scalar fashion and to examine these issues cross-linguistically. A key finding is that grammatical realization of reference shows a certain degree of iconicity, whereby mentions of highly topical or prominent referents tend to be realized by reduced forms whereas mentions of less topical or less prominent referents tend to be realized by more elaborated NPs. Chafe (1994) sees referentiality as part of the flow of language and consciousness. He examines several discourse functions of referring expressions including contrastiveness, starting points, and identifiability, but pays particular attention to activation, the processes by which information to brought into consciousness. This involves not only the speaker's consciousness, but importantly the speaker's model of the listener's shifting state of consciousness. Du Bois and Thompson (1991) further develop a multidimensional theory of "information flow", which includes the concepts of givenness, identifiability and identifiability pathway along with the referential-specific concepts of generality (involving generalizing and particularizing uses of NPs) and discourse referentiality (involving whether or not a referent is tracked through discourse). Key to the work of Givón (1983), Chafe (1994), and Du Bois and Thompson (1991) is the multidimensional approach that each brings to issues of referentiality. This contrasts with work such as Prince (1981) and Gundel et al. (1993) who conflate these related but essentially orthogonal dimensions into single dimensional scales. While this work has produced important insights, it has been primarily speaker-centered, focusing on the speaker's intentionality in the production of meaning.

2.4   Interaction

Another strand of discourse-oriented studies of reference has prioritized everyday talk-in-interaction, examining what speakers of a range of languages actually accomplish when they use referring expressions (e.g., Auer 1984; Fox 1987; Hanks 1990; Fox 1996; Enfield & Stivers 2007). Focus on participants' authentic usage raises issues such as the interactional negotiation of referents. Examples of such negotiation include the ways in which the form of an expression is motivated by attention to particular addressees and shaped by addressees' actions and reactions (Ford and Fox 1996). In her groundbreaking work on anaphora, Fox (1987) presents a general pattern in which subsequent mentions in the same interactional sequence are coded with pronouns, while mentions that are not in the same sequence are coded with full noun phrases. She introduces the concept of the 'return pop', in which a pronoun can be used in a first mention in a sequence to return to an already closed sequence, and that even recently mentioned entities can be referred to with full lexical NPs to open a new sequence (see also Chafe (1994: 296–300) on new "paragraphs"). An important generalization from these findings is that "an anaphoric choice at once is determined by and itself determines the structure of the talk" (Fox 1987: 17). Ford and Fox (1996) and Lerner (1996) show that the form of a mention can be used to attract a particular recipient, and speakers can be seen to shape the form accordingly; forms are tailored to who among potential addressees is attending to the speaker, and speakers can be seen to be monitoring this from moment to moment. In addition, forms can be used to project the action that an utterance in progress is intended to accomplish. Consequently, speakers may shift the referential form in mid-utterance to deal with "audience diversity" (Goodwin 1986).

Particularly influential to studies of referential practice has been Hanks's work on Mayan deixis (1990, 1992), which concerns the dynamic creation of contexts and ultimately speakers' lifeworlds through the use of indexical expressions. Like Ford and Fox (1996), Hanks shows how indexical reference both reflects and shapes the context in which it is performed. For Hanks, the context is dynamic and sociocentric, and thus deictics, such as demonstratives, are tools for reflecting and creating indexical contexts for reference in real time. Speech is "situated" by preexisting linguistic and non-linguistic forms and categories available to the speaker, and also by "the highly particular inferences that arise in conversational contexts as well as the specific objects denoted" (Hanks 2005: 196), created by talk itself. Thus, for example, there is a 'common sense' appeal to thinking of the semantics of deictics such as *here* in terms of proximity and contiguity, but such thinking obscures other "critical aspects of deixis, including the mutual orientation of interactants, all nonperceptual modes of access such as background knowledge, memory, and anticipation, and all that is part of a social setting and the relations between participants but not embodied in physical objects" (Hanks 2005: 196). Hanks points out that social facts can constrain what a person can and cannot say: a Maya farmer may say "I am opening a ditch here", even if he is himself not engaged in labor, but his sons are, while a non-landowning laborer may not say so if he is not concretely engaged in the work. Thus, what can and cannot be said, or what is actually said, is constrained by more than the resources of the language and the concrete situational facts of proximity and accessibility, namely by the social structure of the situation itself.

Much work in Conversation Analysis has centered on the use of inherently referential expressions, such as person reference in a range of languages (e.g., Enfield and Stivers 2007), an extremely rich area of study. Early work in this area found that reference to persons is governed by preferences for recognitional forms and for minimization; obviously, these two preferences may be in conflict, in which case recognizability is argued to take priority (Sacks and Schegloff 1979). Schegloff (1996) distinguishes between the use of forms in initial and subsequent position (a point also made earlier by information flow theorists), and suggests that when an 'initial' type is used in 'subsequent' position, more than just referring is being done. There is, of course, much variation among languages in terms of whether the unmarked referring term is a name or a possessed kinterm, and whether the preference for minimization is similarly operative in all languages (see papers in Enfield and Stivers 2007).

3.   Key themes emerging from investigating reference in conversation

Still largely underexplored in the work cited above are questions of how and whether distinctions around referentiality are interactionally relevant to participants from their point of view – a central focus of this volume, which can be viewed as an exploratory venture into the issues which emerge when referentiality and nonreferentiality are examined in everyday talk from a variety of languages. Four key themes run through these studies and help to further broaden our understanding of reference as an interactional phenomenon. Collectively, the chapters develop insights showing that reference is often fluid, dynamic, and indeterminate, that referential indeterminacy is typically unproblematic for participants, that shifts in referentiality are often tied to specific social goals, and that reference and referentiality emerge dialogically and interactionally. These themes cut across the various contributions to this volume in complex ways, making it difficult to group the studies by topic. We have therefore chosen to arrange the chapters alphabetically by author and we highlight the thematic threads running between them in the following discussion.

For the chapters in this volume, the theme of referential fluidity is based on evidence from conversational data, which shows that speakers often do not appear to require a referent, whether 'in the world' or 'in their minds', to be clearly and uniquely formulated, nor do they require referents to maintain continuity of identity through the course of interaction. This point is made in several of the chapters, including those by Ono and Thompson and by Laury, who demonstrate how speakers can seamlessly move between referencing parts or individuals, and referencing wholes or aggregates, without overtly marking the shift. Speakers are shown to rely only on pronouns without explicit antecedents in the case of English or to shift to a specific mention in a generic frame of reference in Finnish. Indeterminacy is illustrated by Helasvuo and Suomalainen, where the Finnish use of impersonal forms can be heard to refer either generically, to a co-participant, or to both simultaneously. These findings support the notion that referents do not exist a priori as fixed entities, but rather are socially constructed. They can shift without being explicitly reconfigured and may not need to be made entirely clear to interactants even as interaction progresses successfully.

That the potential for indeterminacy is generally unproblematic for speakers suggests that detailed notions of referentiality as outlined by philosophers and linguists may often be largely irrelevant to speakers. Ewing discusses this for Indonesian conversation in which referents are frequently unexpressed and only alluded to, such that precise identification of who or what is being discussed is not possible, yet again interaction progresses smoothly. Matsumoto finds a similar situation in Japanese, where participants do not require that referents be made explicit for the purpose of the ongoing conversation. Suzuki shows that an onomatopoeic item can be collectively restructured as a nominal referential form and then tracked by several participants simultaneously as a resource for playfulness. In this way speakers can accomplish particular interactional ends which would not be available if strict referential determination was required. Ono and Thompson show that when a demonstrative does not have a clear referent, it can have the important interactional purpose of serving as an invitation to 'go along with' the action being carried by that turn. This again underscores the importance of progressivity for interactants, even in the face of indeterminacy.

Many of the studies demonstrate that shifts in referentiality are often tied to specific social goals. Ewing discusses this in terms of a change in footing, often moving between generalization and example or between narration and reported speech. Helasvuo and Suomalainen show that shifting changes in non-specific reference can be used to modulate participation frameworks, bringing outside voices into the interaction. Tao's analysis of generic reference in conversational Mandarin shows that generic formulations play a key role when relatively complex or controversial subject matter is involved and where incongruent stances are often negotiated. Laury examines how the distinction between specific and generic can be a manipulable resource to be exploited for interactional purposes, in particular to create shifts in stance.

A central point made in all of the chapters of this volume is that referents and referential properties emerge dialogically and intersubjectively through interaction; that is, rather than being a property of forms used, reference is something achieved by the participants in conversation, for their purposes and from their perspective.[1] As mentioned above, referring is often not a matter of explicitly

---

1. This is reminiscent of Strawson (1950), who noted that forms themselves do not refer, but rather speakers use them to refer. However, as noted above, Strawson's claims were not based on conversational language, nor did he address the role of dialogicality in reference.

stating a referent, but rather inviting a coparticipant to engage in referent creation. For example, Suzuki demonstrates how conversationalists can use a non-canonical Japanese postposition to creatively and humorously collaborate in the construction of a referent through the use of overlap, gaze, and bodily behavior, including smiling and laughter. Le Mené et al. outline the ways referentiality emerges dynamically in the context of French child-adult interaction, where input from adults is varied, children's reference is often indeterminate, and adults take up and negotiate referentiality in different ways. Tao shows how potential ambiguities in referentiality can be negotiated through multimodal contextualization cues, such as temporal displacement, semantic incongruity, and intonation. Matsumoto highlights the importance of interaction for establishing shifts in referentiality, even when no referent is explicitly mentioned. The shifts in specificity discussed by Laury and by Ewing are also contextually embedded. For Helasvuo and Suomalainen, the intersubjectivity of referent co-construction is a crucial part of participants' movement between real and imagined spatio-temporal frames.

4.   Conclusion

The chapters in this volume complement each other by providing evidence, from a number of different languages and very different contexts, of the ways speakers make use of the resources of their language in the domain of referentiality. The four themes discussed above – referential fluidity, the unproblematic nature of indeterminacy, (non)referentiality and social goals, and emergence through interaction – work together in important ways, as evidenced by the fact that several chapters in this volume develop more than one of these themes. Taken together they make the case that referentiality emerges through interaction from a coalescence of multiple semiotic, grammatical, and discourse factors.

References

Auer, Peter. 1984. "Referential Problems in Conversation." *Journal of Pragmatics* 8 (5–6): 627–648.
Bühler, Karl. 1934. *Sprachtheorie. Die Darstellungsfunktion der Sprache.* Jena: Fischer.
Chafe, Wallace. 1994. *Discourse, Consciousness, and Time: The flow and Displacement of Conscious Experience in Speaking and Writing.* Chicago: University of Chicago Press.
Donnellan, Keith. 1966. "Reference and Definite Descriptions." In *Semantics*, ed. by Danny D. Steinberg & Leon A. Jakobovits, 100–114. Cambridge: Cambridge University Press.

Du Bois, John W. 1980. "Beyond Definiteness: The Trace of Identity in Discourse." In: *The Pear Stories: Cognitive, Cultural, and Linguistic Aspects of Narrative Production*, ed. by Wallace Chafe, 203–274. Norwood, NJ: Ablex

Du Bois, John W. & Sandra A. Thompson. 1991. Dimensions of a Theory of Information Flow. Unpublished Ms. University of California, Santa Barbara.

Enfield, N. J. and Tanya Stivers, eds. 2007. *Person Reference in Interaction: Linguistic, Cultural and Social Perspectives*. Cambridge: Cambridge University Press.

Ford, Cecilia and Barbara Fox. 1996. "Interactional Motivations for Reference Formulation: *He had. This* guy had, a beautiful, thirty-two O:lds." In *Studies in Anaphora*, ed. by Barbara Fox, 145–168. Amsterdam: Benjamins.

Fox, Barbara A. 1987. *Discourse Structure and Anaphora: Written and Conversational English*. Cambridge: Cambridge University Press.

Fox, Barbara A., ed. 1996. *Studies in Anaphora*. Amsterdam: Benjamins.

Frege, Gottlieb. 1892. "Über Sinn und Bedeutung." *Zeitschrift für Philosophie und philosophische Kritik* 100 (1892): 25–50.

Givón, Talmy. 1978. "Definiteness and Referentiality." In *Universals of Human Language, Vol. 4, Syntax*, ed. by Joseph Greenberg, 292–330. Stanford: Stanford University Press.

Givón, Talmy, ed. 1983. *Topic Continuity in Discourse: Quantitative Cross-language Study*. Amsterdam: John Benjamins.

Goodwin, Charles. 1986. "Audience Diversity, Participation and Interpretation." *Text* 6 (3): 283–316.

Guillaume, Gustave. 1919. *Le problème de l'article et sa solution dans la langue française*. Paris: Hachette.

Gundel, Jeanette K., Nancy Hedberg and Ron Zacharski. 1993. "Cognitive Status and the Form of Referring Expressions in Discourse." *Language* 69: 274–307.

Hanks, William. 1990. *Referential Practice: Language and Lived Space Among the Maya*. Chicago: The University of Chicago Press.

Hanks, William. 1992. "The Indexical Ground of Deictic Reference." In *Rethinking Context: Language as an Interactive Phenomenon*, ed. by Alessandro Duranti and Charles Goodwin, 43–76. Cambridge: Cambridge University Press.

Hanks, William. 2005. Explorations in the Deictic Field. *Current Anthropology* 46 (2): 191–220.

Hjelmslev, Louis. 1928. *Principes de grammaire générale*. Copenhagen: Bianco Lundo.

Lerner, Gene. 1996. "On the Place of Linguistic Resources in the Organization of Talk-in-Interaction: 'Second Person' Reference in Multi-Party Conversation." *Pragmatics* 6 (3) 281–294.

Prince, Ellen. 1981. "Toward a Taxonomy of Given–New Information." In *Radical Pragmatics*, ed. by Peter Cole, 223–255. New York: Academic Press.

Russell, Bertrand. 1905. "On Denoting." *Mind* 14 (56): 479–493.

Russell, Bertrand. 1919. *Introduction to Mathematical Philosophy*. London: Allen & Unwin.

Sacks, Harvey and Emanuel A. Schegloff. 1979. "Two Preferences in the Organization of Reference to Persons in Conversation and Their Interaction." In *Everyday Language: Studies in Ethnomethodology*, ed. by George Psathas, 15–21. New York: Irvington.

Schegloff, Emanuel A. 1996. "Some Practices of Referring to Persons in Talk in Interaction: A Partial Sketch of a Systematics." In *Studies in Anaphora*, ed. by Barbara Fox, 437–485. Amsterdam: John Benjamins.

Searle, John R. 1958. "Proper Names." *Mind* 67: 166–173.

Silverstein, Michael. 1976. "Shifters, Linguistic Categories, and Cultural Description." In *Meaning in Anthropology*, ed. by Keith Basso and Henry Selby, 11–55. Albuquerque: University of New Mexico Press.

Strawson, Peter F. 1950. "On Referring." *Mind* 59: 320–344.

CHAPTER 2

Elusive referentiality and allusive reference in Indonesian conversation

Michael C. Ewing
The University of Melbourne

This chapter examines referential practices in a corpus of colloquial Indonesian conversation and attempts to address the question: "Does referentiality matter to speakers?" I take referentiality to be a multi-dimensional phenomenon involving (at least) whether referents are construed as general or particular and whether they are tracked through discourse. Through close examination of excerpts from conversational interaction, I show that there is often a blurring between the general and the particular, that referents are often indeterminate, and that referentiality as a discrete and classifiable linguistic property often does not seem to be relevant to participants in ongoing interaction. In this sense, referentiality does not always appear to matter to speakers. At the same time, referential practices do appear to be exploitable by speakers as resources for social action. Specifically, I show that a shift in referential practices regularly coincides with a shift in alignment, understood in terms of footing. These may involve shifts between generalising and exemplifying or moving from narratorial to quoted speech. To the extent that shifts in referentiality coincide with shifts in footing, then it can be said that referentiality does matter to speakers.

Keywords: interactional linguistics, referentiality, conversation, Indonesian

1. Introduction

This chapter examines referential practices in a corpus of colloquial Indonesian conversation and attempts to address the question: "Does referentiality matter to speakers?" In the next section, I present the theoretical framework of this study, which approaches referentiality as a social phenomenon, emerging through interaction and the wider interactional context (Laury, Ewing, and Thompson, this volume). After briefly discussing possible approaches to analysing referentiality, I find that rather than viewing referentiality in binary or scalar terms, a multi-

https://doi.org/10.1075/pbns.344.02ewi

dimensional approach is more useful. I use the information flow dimensions of generality and tracking to analyse referential practices in excerpts from a corpus of Indonesian conversational interactions. These data are introduced in Section Three. The first set of excerpts, examined in Section Four, involve examples in which instances of (possible) referring are not explicitly expressed, that is, cases of ellipsis, or as I prefer, cases of allusive reference. The second set of excerpts, examined in Section Five, involve instances of explicit reference, that is, cases where referents are expressed via pronouns or lexical noun phrases. A discussion is provided in Section Six which further explores the links between referentiality, indeterminacy and social action. In the case of both referring practices – allusive and explicit – referentiality is shown to be often fluid or indeterminate, indeed elusive. While in many cases such indeterminacy does not seem to matter for speakers, it is also apparent that shifts in referentiality often accompany shifts in alignment or footing (Goffman 1981). This connection between referentiality and footing seems to indicate that referentiality, despite its indeterminacy and fluidity, can indeed be a useful resource for speakers in interaction.

2.   Theoretical background

Referentiality is often discussed as if it is a binary characteristic, frequently attributed to noun phrases. For example, a noun phrase might be classified as either referential or nonreferential. One difficulty of this approach is that different researchers will draw the line between referential and nonreferential in different places. For example, in his discussion of Tagalog articles, Nagaya describes referential phrases as having "definite, indefinite or generic reference" (2011: 593). Other nominal expressions, such as property-denoting nominals, are nonreferential. This is an understanding of referentiality which he says is common across Philippine linguistics. Chen (2009), however, in a paper contrasting referentiality in Chinese and English, asserts that referential expressions must have three characteristics: (1) they must presuppose an entity; (2) that entity must be unique and individuated; and (3) the speaker uses the expression with the intention of referring to that presupposed, unique entity. Noun phrases that fail on any of the three criteria are considered nonreferential NPs. We can see that some of Nagaya's (2011) referential entities, such as those expressing indefinite or generic reference, would be considered nonreferential by Chen (2009). In both cases a binary distinction is made, although it should be noted that both researchers do also recognize several subcategories.

In whatever way a divide between referential and nonreferential is made, a number of factors are involved including (among those mentioned above) existence, definiteness, and specificity, as well as speaker intention. Other researchers have dealt with these factors in a scalar fashion, for example through a Givenness Hierarchy (Gundel, Hedberg & Zacharski 1993: 274–276; Gundel 2010). Alternatively, a multidimensional approach to referentiality would let us tease apart a variety of different factors, allowing the dimensions to vary independently and allowing for the emergence of patterning across dimensions, without presupposing binary or scalar (linear) relationships. One such approach, and the one which I adopt in this chapter, is that of Du Bois and Thompson (1991), which places referentiality within a multidimensional theory of information flow. The five dimensions they propose are *givenness, identifiability, identifiability pathway, generality*, and *discourse referentiality*. The latter two – generality and discourse referentiality – are the most relevant to our discussion of (non)referentiality. Generality involves the way a nominal expression refers, which can be *particular* or *general*. Discourse referentiality involves the role of a nominal expression at the point at which it occurs in discourse and whether a nominal expression is intended to be *tracking* or *non-tracking*. Nominal expressions that are tracking are those whose referents have a continuity of identity within discourse (see Du Bois 1980). In a broad sense, tracking nominal expressions refer to the entities that speakers are talking about. The role of non-tracking nominal expressions, in contrast, can be to characterize, orient, or predicate something of other entities and events in the discourse.

The concepts of generality and discourse referentiality will be used in the following analysis. It will be shown that in colloquial Indonesian conversation, the dimension of generality is not categorically binary and there is often fluidity or indeterminacy between whether an instance of referring may be interpreted as particular or general. This fluidity and indeterminacy can give a sense, at least to analysts, that referentiality in conversational interaction can be elusive. It can seem difficult to pin down. Yet as shown in this study and the other contributions to this volume, this apparent elusiveness of referentiality does not generally seem to be problematic to speakers themselves.

With regard to discourse referentiality it will be shown that nominal expressions, and indeed instances of allusive referring practices, can be successful in either tracking or non-tracking roles, even when the entity being referred to may be indeterminate or its generality status fluid. This study (like Matsumoto, this volume), then, departs from much of the earlier work on referentiality, in that it is not focussed primarily on nominal expressions. Earlier work on referentiality has concentrated on understanding how nominals refer (e.g., Frege 1892; Russell 1905) or how nominals are used by speakers to refer (e.g., Strawson 1950; Donnellan 1966). The Dimensions of Information Flow approach (Du Bois & Thompson 1991) adopted here also concerns characteristics of nominal expressions. In this study I show that referents are not only referred to by explicit nominals. When not explicitly mentioned with nominal expressions, referents may be alluded to through other linguistic and non-linguistic cues, and at the same time, the referential properties of generality and discourse referentiality may also be alluded to. A combination of structural, semantic, and contextual cues combine in the service of referring and referentiality – at least to extent necessary for interaction to progress.

3.   The data

The data used in this study are from a corpus of spoken colloquial Indonesian recorded in Bandung in 2014. Included are audio recordings and transcripts of nine separate conversational events. They range in length from seven minutes to thirty-three minutes and involve from two to five speakers, including all-female conversations and mixed male-female conversations. All the participants were young adult speakers, ranging in age from 18 to 25, with at least secondary education and many attending or recently completing tertiary education. This is augmented by the extract in Example (2), which is from a corpus of data collected in East Java in 2008 by Howard Manns. All recordings were made with the informed consent of the participants and transcripts are presented using pseudonyms. Transcripts are segmented into Intonation Units using the conventions of Du Bois et al. (1993).

4.   Allusive reference and indeterminacy

The first set of examples presented here involve referring practices in cases without an explicit referring expression. In Indonesian, as in many languages of the region, it is common for arguments of a clause not to be explicitly expressed, especially in colloquial, conversational language. This practice is conventionally called ellipsis and in the case of Indonesian is regularly described as "the omission from a sentence of a word when its presence is not necessary … [because] the person or thing referred to is clear from context" (Sneddon 2006:109). Line 2 of Example (1) is a straightforward case of this.

(1) *Rapido*
         1 Faizah: *Lu gak bilang lagi Puj.*
                         2S NEG say   again Puj
                         'You didn't even say Puj.'
         2 Puji: *Lu=pa=.*
                         forget
                         '(I) forgot.'

This excerpt is from an encounter in which two friends are collaboratively constructing a narrative about a series of events they had each participated in separately. Some of the background is given in Example (6) below, in which Faizah talks about trying to get a Rapidograph pen back from her former boyfriend by eliciting help from her current boyfriend. We find out that Puji already knew something about this from the former boyfriend and the two women are comparing notes. In the excerpt in (1), Faizah is (light-heartedly) chastising Puji for not telling her earlier that she'd talked to the former boyfriend and Puji says she had forgotten. In line 1 Faizah uses the pronoun *lu* '2s' to explicitly refer to Puji, but in her response, Puji just says *lupa* 'forget', with no explicit argument. As Indonesian verbs have no person marking morphology, the hearer must infer the likely referent of any implied arguments from the interactional context. In this case it is clear that Puji herself is the one who forgot, as indicated by the parenthetical first person pronoun *I* in the free translation.

In Djenar, Ewing and Manns (2018: 105–149) we make the case that labelling a situation like (1) as "omitting a word" – say, a pronoun or noun phrase – is not analytically appropriate because it implies something existed in a specific position, which is then be omitted in the actual utterance. "Omission" is not a useful concept in this context because, among other reasons, it is not possible to reconstruct either a specific lexical item that may have been omitted nor the exact location from which it would have been omitted.[1] We prefer the term "allusive reference" based on Goffman (1983), who points out that alluding to unstated presuppositions and common ground allows for economic language and that allusive phrasing both "affirms relationships [and] organizes talk" (Goffman 1983: 42). With regard to referential practices, allusion organizes talk by allowing for both semantic and information flow inferences about possible referents that are not explicitly mentioned. As discussed in Djenar et al. (2018), allusive reference affirms relationships by relying on a certain level of common ground between interactants, and in so far as referring is successful (to the extent necessary in the given moment), then this common ground and the relationship implied by it are both affirmed. This is true whether the common ground that underpins successful allusion is

---

1. Even in the "clear" case of Example (1), Puji, like all Indonesian speakers, has access to a variety of first-person referring expressions that she can choose from according to various social and intersubjective considerations. Indeed, speakers may use different first-person referring terms in the same event and with the same interlocutor (Ewing and Djenar 2019) and we cannot say for sure which pronoun would have been "omitted". Additionally, word order is relatively flexible in conversational Indonesian so we could not say whether the first-person referring expression was omitted from pre-predicate or post-predicate position (Ewing 2005). Ono and Thompson (1997) and Ono and Suzuki (2020) make similar points about so-called "zero" or "ellipsis" in Japanese.

actual shared knowledge and experience or "fictive" common ground, assumed and accepted in the moment of interaction. (See Wouk (1999, 2001) on fictive common ground in the context of Indonesian pragmatic particles.)

Applying the concept of allusion to reference highlights that in an utterance like that in line 2 of Example (1), when Puji says *lupa* 'forgot', she is saying exactly what she has intended to say without omitting anything and that her utterance alludes to the understanding that it is she herself who has forgotten – an allusion which in this context is easily and successfully understood by Faizah (and analysts).[2] When a potential argument is not explicitly mentioned, rather than the referent being simply "clear from context", a mutual understanding of what is being alluded to emerges between interlocutors in a way that is "inherently collaborative, requiring as it does active work on the part of both speaker and hearer to arrive at an interpretation that is shared (as Garfinkel would say, 'for all practical purposes')" (Fox 1994: 2).

In Ewing (2019) I show that use of allusive reference can be considered the default for colloquial Indonesian clause structure, due to the preponderance of predicates without explicit arguments. In the data used in that study, 66% of 698 clauses consisted of only the predicate and no explicit arguments, while the remaining 33% included at least one argument. Describing allusive reference as the default in colloquial Indonesian calls attention to the fact that, rather than trying to explain why some arguments are not expressed (e.g., because they are "clear from context"), it is more fruitful to explore the motivations for the less frequent, explicit expression of arguments.[3] This point has been made for other languages as well, including Japanese (Nariyama 2003), Korean (Oh 2007) and Javanese (Ewing 2014).

In Example (1), the unexpressed referent is truly "clear from context" and with regard to the discourse referential dimensions of information flow, this is an example of particular reference to a tracked referent. Yet, despite examples like these, allusive referring practices in Indonesian conversation can disrupt the expectation that referents will generally be "clear from context." Such disruptions

---

2. Note the analogy with tense. Indonesian does not mark tense on verbs. While *lupa* might be glossed as 'forget' it can be used in situations in which the forgetting took place previously, is happening now or in the future, or may be hypothetical. Temporality is often implied by the context, although it can also be expressed explicitly with adverbs or other means if necessary. Similarly, arguments of a predicate can be contextually implied, that is, alluded to, within in a specific context of use or can be expressed explicitly by a speaker for any number of reasons. Just as it is inappropriate to talk about "omitting" tense in Indonesian, so too it is unproductive to talk about "omitting" arguments.

3. Some key interactional contexts where arguments are more frequently expressed in Indonesian include introducing new referents, making contrasts, at junctures in discourse, and in narrative.

can manifest in three ways. First, a referent may be indeterminate. Second, generality (whether a general or particular reading is intended) may be indeterminate. Finally, and closely linked to the previous two points, discourse referentiality (the way an entity is tracked (or not) in discourse) can be unclear. Examples of these disruptions are given in the following sections.

4.1 Indeterminate particular reference

This section illustrates how allusive reference can clearly be particular rather than general, yet still indeterminate as to what particular referent is being referred to. In Example (2), Karina, Firdaus, and Citra have been talking about family issues and Firdaus mentions that among all the cousins in her extended family, the children in her own immediate family are the only ones who are not yet married (lines 3–4). She is talking about this in relation to her mother, mentioning her mother's children in line 1 and comparing the situation with the children of her mother's siblings in line 2. Note the emphasis on the number of children in each family: *lima bersaudara* 'the five siblings' (Firdaus's mother and her four siblings) and *kita berempat* 'the four of us' (Firdaus and her three siblings). Karina elicits the information that Firdaus's younger sibling is in the second year of junior high school and that he is a boy. (As an aside, Citra laughs, pointing out in line 9 that being so young, he could not possibly be married in any case.)[4] Having established that the youngest sibling is a brother, Karina then asks how many of the siblings are sisters, and Firdaus replies in line 11 that there are three girls (that is, all the other, older, siblings). Karina's response in line 12 contains the example of indeterminate allusive reference that we want to focus on.

(2) *Family*

```
 1 Firdaus: Jadi anak-anak-nya   ibu-ku    tu.
             SO   child-REDUP-ASSOC mother-1S that
             'So my mother's children.'
 2           ya=,.. pokok-nya dari lima ber-saudara itu,
             yes    main-ASSOC from five MID-sibling that
             'Yes the point is from the five siblings (mother and her siblings),'
 3           .. yang belum   kawin   cuma anak-nya   ibu-ku.
                REL   not.yet married only child-ASSOC mother-1S
             'The ones who aren't married yet are my mother's kids.'
 4           … Cuma kita ber-empat.
                only 1P   MID-four
             'Just the four of us (Firdaus and her siblings).'
 5 Karina:   Lho adik-mu            kelas berapa   Daus?
             PART younger.sibling-2S class how.many Daus
             'So what grade is your younger sibling in Daus?'
```

---

4. Citra uses two Javanese words at the end of her line, including the common vocative *Mbak* 'older sister', which is metaphorical and does not indicate consanguineal kin here.

```
 6 Firdaus: SMP         kelas dua.
            middle.school class two
            '(He's in) the second year of middle school.'
 7 Karina:  .. Cowok?
            male
            '(He's) a boy?'
 8 Firdaus: [Iya].
            yes
            'Yes.'
 9 Citra:   [Terus] ga mungkin kawin   kan Mbak              @.
            then   NEG possible married PART older.sister.JAV
            'So it's impossible (he) would be married, right mbak? (laughing)'
10 Karina:  Cewek-nya berapa?
            girl-ASSOC how.many
            'How many girls are there?'
11 Firdaus: Tiga.
            three
            'Three.'
12 Karina:  Oh jadi pengen anak  cowok.
            oh so   want   child boy
            'Oh so (they/she/?) wanted a son.'
13 Firdaus: Iya=.
            yes
            'Yes.'
```

In line 12, Karina responds to Firdaus's information that the three older siblings are sisters and the youngest is a brother, by observing *Oh jadi pengen anak cowok*, literally 'Oh so wanted a son'. Who it is that wanted a son is not explicitly mentioned and so the other participants can only infer who Karina is alluding to. Before discussing who this referent might be, it will be instructive to look at the other example of allusive reference in this extract, found in lines 5–9. In line 5 *adikmu* 'your younger sibling' establishes explicitly and unambiguously who they are talking about. This is a particular referring expression, and it is tracked. Together the women then collaboratively construct (through questions, responses and comments) three points about him with allusive reference: that the younger sibling is in middle school, that he is boy and that he couldn't possibly be married. In all cases it is clear who they are referring to through these allusive practices.

Although the present study is not a systematic comparison of allusive reference across languages (which would be well beyond its scope), nonetheless it is interesting to note that English also often uses allusive reference in some similar cases. The answer given in line 6 could easily be produced in English without explicit reference and would sound completely normal. We could imagine line 7 in English either 'he's a boy?' or 'a boy?', with the latter natural, but possibly sounding clipped or reduced. In contrast, an utterance like that in line 9, which uses allusive reference and is very natural in Indonesian, would be very unlikely to occur without an explicit subject in English. This point is just meant to demonstrate that despite the fact that allusive reference occurs in both English and Indonesian, it is much more common in Indonesian. Indeed, we can even characterize it as pervasive, as seen in the examples presented here.

Returning to the issue of referentiality, the identity of the younger brother is clear and easily tracked with the use of allusive referring practices after he is introduced into the discourse. This clarity contrasts with the example of allusive reference in line 12. At first glance, line 12 may seem relatively clear and we could be tempted to say the natural English free translation would be 'so they wanted a son'. However, there are two points to keep in mind. If we look back through the discourse, the only possible referent for the argument of the clause in line 12 that is "clear from context", in the sense that there is a previously mentioned antecendent, is Firdaus's mother (*ibuku* in lines (1) and (3)). This prior mention could motivate a free translation of 'so she wanted a son'. But this is unlikely from the cultural context, which would suggest that the intended referent is not just the mother, but the parents, or even the extended family more broadly. In this case 'they' would be the better free translation. But note that English 'they' is also indeterminate here, probably referring to the parents, but also possibly the family at large. Referential indeterminacy is by no means unique to Indonesian; however, I would contend that a language like English tends to allow less indeterminacy than a language like Indonesian. This is because in English, some referent usually needs to be expressed explicitly, and in this context, there would be a choice of pronouns, whether *they* (parents, family, or some gender-neutral individual), *she* (most likely the mother who was mentioned previously), or *he* (most likely the father, a choice that would also make sense in a patriarchal society). With the use of allusive reference in Indonesian, all of these possibilities may be the case and neither speaker nor addressee needs to commit to any of them.

In any case, the allusive referent of the unexpressed argument in line 12, whoever it may be, is unambiguously particular. This is not a generic statement about what families in general want. It is a very specific statement about Firdaus's own family situation. Yet even when allusive reference is clearly pointing to a particular referent, that referent can be indeterminate. Further, and crucially, despite this indeterminacy, Firdaus unequivocally answers 'yes' in line 13, without the need for further clarification or explanation. This allusive reference is enough for interaction to proceed smoothly, despite (or because of) the indeterminacy.

4.2   Indeterminate reference in sequence

This section examines an extract with two sequences of allusive referring actions. In both sequences one speaker initiates a predicating action that alludes to an unexpressed referent. This is then confirmed by their interlocutor. The first sequence involves an indeterminate particular allusive referent, while the second involves an indeterminate general allusive referent. In Example (3), two people who have just met are chatting on a university campus. Asmita is a student studying Interior Design and Fakri is a design professional who is on campus to assist with examinations. He has been talking about his colleagues and work experiences in Bandung, the city where the recording was made. Extensive use is made of allusive reference and I have attempted to capture the feeling of this in the English free translation by avoiding reconstructed referents, unlike the reconstructed referents in brackets provided in Examples (1) and (2).

(3)   *Interior Design*

```
1 Fakri:  … Kalau Desain Interio=r,
             if    design interior
          'As for Interior Design,'
2         Eh.  Interior ya?
          REPAIR interior yeah
          'Uh. Interior right?'
3 Asmita: Iya. .. Desain Interior.
          yes     design interior
          'Yes. Interior Design.'
4 Fakri:  … Banyak,
             many
          'Many,'
5         kalau Bandung banyak,
          if    Bandung many
          As for Bandung many,'
6         .. banyak ini  kok=.
             many   this PART
          'There are many of these you know.'
7 Asmita  .. Banyak sih.
             many   PART
          'Indeed many.'
```

In line 1 Fakri presents a topic, 'interior design' (see Ewing (2015) on the use of *kalau* 'if' as topic framing device). He then checks in line 2 to make sure the topic is relevant, and Asmita confirms that it is in line 3. What is happening here is that Fakri is asking whether he has correctly remembered from a discussion earlier in the conversation that Asmita is majoring in Interior Design. In lines 1 and 2 a noun phrase is presented and then partially repeated. In line 1 Fakri is about to say something about interior design, which is why it is presented as a topic, but within his request for confirmation in line 2, '(interior) design' serves a predicating function. It is, however, not exactly clear how this predicate nominal relates to some assumed referent, which is left entirely to inference. The intention is clear to the participants: Fakri is asking something like 'Your major is interior design' or 'You are studying interior design'. The structures of these two English free translations are different, as are the roles played by the pronoun *you/r*. But in the Indonesian original, it is not possible to unambiguously reconstruct a putative structure or subject referent. The participants simply provide each other with the predicate nominal (*desain*) *interior* 'interior (design)' and this is enough for them to infer some intended subject, whether 'your major', 'you' or something else. The intention is sufficient for successful communication, without a certain subject referent being "clear form context". While indeterminate, the referent can still be understood as particular, because it is not a generic statement, but rather a comment on Asmita's specific personal circumstances.

Fakri then returns to the main point he was about to make when he presented the topic of interior design, and a new sequence of allusive reference begins. In line 4 he simply produces the predicate *banyak* 'many' without specifying what there are many of. In line 5 he specifies the location he is talking about, Bandung, but again without specifying what there are many of in Bandung. Finally, in line 6, Fakri produces an explicit S argument for the predicate: *banyak ini* 'these are many' or 'there are many of these'. Despite being an explicitly articulated form, the demonstrative pronoun *ini* 'this/these' does not actually provide any more information than the previous allusive referring moves since there is no explicit antecedent that *ini* refers to. Based on the previous discourse context, we can infer that when Fakri expresses the predicate *banyak* 'many' three times (twice without an explicit subject, that is with allusive reference, and once with the subject *ini* 'this/these'), his intention is something like 'There are many job opportunities in interior design', 'There are many people working in interior design', or 'There are many companies hiring in the field of interior design'. While the intention is clear enough, a referent remains indeterminate. And this is the point, that the most abbreviated forms, with no clear reference, can still engender successful communication. Here the allusive referent seems to be general, referring to a class of workers, jobs or companies, rather than to a particular entity, but cannot be further specified beyond that.

4.3   Referential fluidity

In this section we explore a possible shift in generality from particular to general, which accompanies a shift in verb form and clause structure. Such a shift in generality would also entail a shift in referent, but in Example (4), the use of allusive reference means that this shift remains indeterminate, and it is impossible from the data to establish whether such a shift in generality is intended by the speakers. Whether or not a shift in generality is intended, the possibility of referential fluidity allows Asmita to align with her interlocutor's shift in grammatical structures, without necessarily aligning with a shift in referentiality. Again, in this excerpt an attempt has been made at replicating allusion to certain referents in the English free translation, which is evocative of the feel of the Indonesian original, although sometimes a little awkward sounding in English.

(4) *Making cream soup*

```
1 Asmita: Nah itu=,
         PART that
         'That's it,'
2         kalau .. urang mah    bikin-nya gini.
          if     1s.SUN PART.SUN make-ASSOC like.this
          'as for me the process is like this.'
3         .. Jadi pakai air   dingin dulu.
             so  use   water cold   first
          'So use cold water first.'
4         .. Jadi misalnya     teh,
             So   example-ASSOC PART.SUN
          'So for example,'
5         .. masuk-in       [dulu].
             enter-APPL     before
          'put in first.'
6 Lani:                     [Di-larut-in]   dulu.
                            PV-dissolve-APPL before
                            'dissolve first.'
7 Asmita: Di-larut-in    dulu   semua-nya.
          PV-dissolve-APPL before all-ASSOC
          'dissolve all first.'
8 Bayu:   He=.
          Huh.
9 Asmita: Nah.
          PART
          'So.'
10        [Baru    di-panas-in].
          only.then PV-hot-APPL
          'Only then heat.'
11 Lani:  [Baru    di- ke- kompor-in].
          only.then PV-    stove-APPL
          'Only then put on the stove.'
```

These friends are discussing different ways to make cream soup, and, in this excerpt, Asmita explains her method. In line 2 she explicitly indicates that she is describing what she herself does by using the first-person pronoun *urang* (which happens to be Sundanese rather than Indonesian): *kalau urang mah, bikinnya begini* 'as for me, the process is like this'. In lines 3–5 she describes the first two steps. The key verbs, *pakai* 'use' and *masukin* 'put in' are in agent voice and there is fairly clear continuity of discourse referentiality, that is, tracking, which suggests Asmita is the agent of both clauses, in her first-person role of telling about her method.[5] I qualify this as "fairly clear continuity," because the use of verbs without explicitly agents can be heard as generic in certain contexts in Indonesian. In

---

5. While this discussion is focussed on referentiality of the agent, it should be noted that the patient of *masukin* 'put in' is also not completely clear. Earlier the friends have been talking about using a soup mix and also about using corn starch to thicken the soup (whether from scratch or a mix). Sixteen lines before this extract another speaker had mentioned soup mix and twenty-five lines before that Asminta had mentioned corn starch. But at this point it is not clear whether Asmita means she is putting soup mix or corn starch into the water.

this example, however, the introduction of Asmita as the topic in line 2 strongly suggests these clauses are not intended to be heard generically, but as being about Asmita herself.

The discourse referentiality potentially shifts subtly in line 6 when Lani collaborates in the description of the procedure. Asmita has said she puts something in the water, and then Lani clarifies in line 6 that the point is to dissolve it in the water. Asmita confirms this through repetition in line 7, adding emphasis by using *semua* 'all' or 'everything'. Grammatically, the verb in line 6, which Asmita repeats in line 7, is in the patient voice, with the prefix *di*-. This introduces a new level of indeterminacy, made possible by the referential fluidity. According to prescriptive standard Indonesian grammar, patient voice verbs with *di*- are meant to be used with third person agents or when the agent is unknown or unimportant. The use of an agentless *di*- prefixed verb is thus common in generic statements. At the same time, agentless *di*-prefixed verbs are also used as a politeness formula to avoid explicitly mentioning an agent and this is especially common when the agent is second person. Additionally, in colloquial Indonesian, choice of person for agents of *di*-prefixed verbs is not as rigid as in the standard language, and these forms can occur with first- or second-person agents, despite the "rule" of prescriptive grammar. The range of possible uses for *di*-prefixed verbs means there is a range of possible interpretations of the agent of *dilarutin* 'dissolve' and which, if any, may have been intended in this context remains indeterminate. There is a sense in which Lani's statement in line 6 feels more generic than Asmita's statement in line 5, but could nonetheless be interpreted as being specifically about Asmita's action. Asmita accommodates Lani and uses the *di*- form in her repetition in line 7.

The ambiguity continues in line 10 (Asmita: *baru dipanasin* 'only then heat') and line 11 (Lani: *baru dikomporin* 'only then put on the stove'), because as mentioned above, *di*- forms can be used informally with first-, second-, or third-person agents. Asmita is accommodating to Lani's grammatical framing of the procedure in patient voice, thus creating a strong sense of collaboratively describing the procedure. At the same time, it is impossible to say whether Asmita's intention is only to accommodate to Lani's grammatical framing, or whether she intends to shift to a generic telling of the steps. We can only note that in the process of accommodation and collaborative description, there is a shift from fairly clear expression of a particular referent (Asmita) to an indeterminate one (Asmita or generic).

In Section Four we have explored disruptions in referentiality that can occur with allusive referring practices. These include the indeterminacy of referents and indeterminacy of generality, which taken together, particularly in the context of allusive reference, highlight the fluid nature of referentiality.

5.   Changes in referentiality and footing with explicit reference

The referential indeterminacy and fluidity outlined in Section Four might be considered unsurprising, given the highly underspecified nature of allusive reference. However, Section Five illustrates that similar disruptions in referentiality can also occur in situations where some form of explicit reference is used.

5.1   General to particular reference and change of footing

When referents are explicit, indeterminacy and subtle fluid shifts in referentiality are still observable, similar to those identified for English by Ono and Thompson (this volume). These shifts in referentiality also accompany shifts in footing, similar to that observed for Finnish by Laury (this volume) and by Helasvuo and Suomalainen (this volume). In Example (5), a group of friends are talking about their experiences selling plush toys in a pop-up market. In this extract Asmita begins by saying she used to find demanding children irritating, but that she has changed her mind after selling plush toys at the market. She states this in lines 1–8 and Wida observes in line 9 that demanding children help their sales, thus explicitly expressing the point of Asmita's observation. In the remainder of the extract, the participants proceed to mimic the kind of interaction that occurs between a child and their mother at the market. While some allusive reference occurs, there are also many examples of explicit reference. The key thing to notice is the subtle shifts between particular and generic referentiality as well as the introduction of hypothetical reference presented as realis statements.

(5)   *Troublesome children / The troublesome child*
```
 1 Asmita: Eh aku kan,
              HES 1S  PART
              'Uh I you know,'
 2            sebel   yah,
              irritate yes
              'get irritated yeah,'
 3            ama= .. anak-[ana=k],
              by      child-REDUP
              'by children,'
 4 Wida:              [anak-anak].
                       child-REDUP
                       'children,'
 5 Asmita: yang .. rewel gitu      ya,
              REL     fussy like.that yes
              'that are fussy like that yeah,'
 6            tapi kayanya aku .. mulai menyukai-nya ketika,
              but like    1s     start enjoy-3s     when
              'but like I've started to like them when,'
 7            .. kita jualan <@ boneka,
                 1s/P sell       plush.toy
              'we're selling plush toys,'
```

```
8         gitu      @> @@@.
          like.that
          'like that.'
9  Wida:  Laris.
          popular
          '(our things) sell well.'
10 Asmita: <VOX Mama mau  i=ni VOX>.
               mama want this
               'Mama (I) want this.
11 Rinal:  Iyah.
           yes
           'Yeah.'
12 Asmita: [Udah    deh.
           already PART
           'Alright already.'
13         Gak usah @@@@@@].
           NEG need
           'There's no need.'
14 Rinal:  [yang rewel-rewel.
           REL   fussy-REDUP
           'The fussy ones.'
15         Jadi=,
           therefore
           'So,'
16         [bikin rezeki].
           make    earnings
           '(they) produce good money.'
17 Wida:   [Biasanya kan]?
           usually   PART
           'Usually you know?'
18 Rinal:  @
19 Wida:   Mita [..] jadi     yang kaya .. tante-tante,
           Mita      therefore REL  like    aunt-REDUP
           'Mita so the auntie-like ones,'
20 Asmita:    [@]
21            mau itu.
              want that
              '(I) want that.'
22 Wida:   Gak usah lihat,
           NEG need look
           '(You) don't need to look,'
23         gak usah lihat,
           NEG need look
           '(You) don't need to look,'
24         [<@ gak  usah lihat @>].
           NEG need look
           '(You) don't need to look.'
25 Asmita: [@@@]
26 Wida:   @@
27 Rinal:  @
28 Wida:   Giliran sekarang.
           turn    now
           '(Your/their) turn now.'
29         [@@ Ayo     ga=n].
              come.on boss
              'Come on boss.'
30 Rinal:  [XXXX].
```

```
31 Asmita: @@
32 Wida:    <@ Adi=k            @> @@.
              younger.sibling
              'Kid.'
```

Asmita's initial observations in lines 1–8 are made about a generic class – *anak-anak yang rewel* 'children that are fussy/troublesome'. While this referent is being tracked, it is general rather than particular. This is suggested by the reduplication of *anak* 'child' to *anak-anak* 'children', which as in English, can be read as either particular plural or as generic. Asmita is not (necessarily) talking about specific children that she encountered but is make a generalization based on her experience. In line 10 Asmita moves to an exemplar of these fussy, troublesome children. What is interesting is that she does not explicitly introduce a singular, particular noun phrase as a way of formally marking the shift from generic category to specific example of the category. Instead, she mimics what such a child would say, *Mama mau ini* 'Mama (I) want this', using a whining, child-like voice. Note that this is doubly allusive, in that the reported speech is not explicitly attributed (there is no 'the child said…'; see Djenar et al. (2018: 150–192) on presentation of voice in Indonesian narrative contexts), and within the reported speech itself, there is no overt subject. We infer that it is the reported (first-person) speaker that wants something (presumable a plush toy), as well as that the reported speaker is a child of the type who whines and makes their parents buy them toys. It is the content of the demand, the use of *Mama* as a vocative (indicating the recipient within the narrative world) and the child-like voice, that all point to this implied referent. Asmita then continues her dramatization by imitating the mother's reaction in lines 12–13 (cf. Helasvuo & Suomalainen, this volume, on *Deixis am Phantasma*). While both the child and the mother are presented as specific examples, it remains indeterminate is whether they represent an actual mother and child Asmita is remembering or are just hypothetical constructs. However, such a distinction does not seem to be relevant to the speakers, who continue to enjoy the dramatization through the remainder of the excerpt. Rinal and Wida (lines 14–17) then re-establish generic referentiality through reduplication – *yang rewel-rewel* 'the fussy ones' (line 14) – and the use of *biasanya* 'usually' (line 17). Wida continues this generic presentation in line 19 with *yang kaya tante-tante* 'the ones who are like aunties', while in line 21 Asmita seamlessly moves back to exemplification, reporting again what such a child says. At this point Wida joins Asmita in the dramatization, mimicking how such a mother would respond in lines 22–24.

After they all laugh, Wida then says in line 28, *giliran sekarang*, literally 'turn now', meaning something like, it is now this mother's turn to experience what several other mothers have experienced – a child whining to buy one of the toys this group of friends sells. In this way the implied discourse referentiality has shifted from general (what this type of mother experiences) to particular (what this particular, collaboratively constructed and possibly fictional mother is experiencing). While it is clear whose turn is being referred to, it is not clear how Wida intends this utterance to be framed. Is she making the observation as a member of the group that is collaboratively dramatizing the situation ("It's her turn now"), or is she quoting an observation she would have made while watching such a scene play out at their pop-up kiosk ("It's your turn now")? In both cases the referent remains the same: it is the mother's turn. In such a context, the structural conventions of English would force a decision about how to frame the utterance, resulting in the choice of "her turn" or "your turn". The convention of regularly relying on allusion in Indonesian means Wida does not have to make this choice. What she says can be heard simultaneously as an observation made in the moment of speaking to her friends and also representing what she could have said in the narrative moment of the dramatization. In line 29, the use of hortative *ayo* 'come on' makes it much more likely she is now quoting what she would have said directly to the mother. While this suggests an "in narrative" understanding of Wida's utterance in line 28, this is not definitive. There is laughing and a prosodic reset at line 29, so change in footing is also plausible, but ultimately indeterminate. Finally, Asmita simply calls out *adik* 'kid' while laughing in line 32.[6] Again, while the referent of *adik* 'child' is the (possibly hypothetical) exemplar of a troublesome child in the dramatization, Asmita's footing, and so the question of who is voicing this, is not clear. She could be exclaiming about the child to her current interlocutors, she could be reporting what she might have said (or thought) when she witnessed such an occurrence in the kiosk, or she may even be reporting what the mother might have said or thought. Again, the identity of the purported the speaker of the line is indeterminate and could be any of the players simultaneously.

What we have observed here is that during the exchange, the participants move seamlessly between generalizations about these kinds of mothers and children and exemplars of these types of customers – similar to the situation discussed in Ono and Thompson (this volume), where a customer and a salesperson move seamlessly between the class of tape recorders and a hypothetical exemplar of such tape recorders. In this example the fluid referentiality involves not just those referents expressed or implied as part of the propositional content of the utterances, but also those who are implied as speaking characters within the dramatization.

---

6. *Adik* 'younger sibling' is an address term commonly used for young children, regardless of the relationship to the speaker. It can be used by older siblings to their younger siblings, but is also commonly used by parents to younger children in the family, or by adults to any child (e.g., a teacher to primary school students).

5.2   Change of footing through fluid generality

In this section referential fluidity is observed as shifts in form imply possible shifts in generality. These shifts are also associated with shifts in footing. In Example (6) Faizah is presenting the initial part of a complex story that she is telling collaboratively with her friend Puji (first seen in Example (1)). In the story, Faizah tries to get a Rapidograph pen back from her former boyfriend, Abang. The pen was an expensive one given to her by her father, and she enlists the aid of her current boyfriend, Obed, in order to arrange a meeting with Abang. In the first extract Faizah recounts in lines 1–6 how her father had asked what happened to the pen. In the thirty-two lines not included here, Faizah describes the pen, repeating that her father asked about it, adding that the pen is with her former boyfriend, but she hasn't told this to her father. In the extract in lines 41–48, she explains why she hasn't told her father and then begins to talk about enlisting Obed's help to retrieve the pen. The first thing to notice is that Faizah refers to herself with three different first-person pronouns, as well as allusively. As explained below, these three pronouns indicate different types of social indexicality, while at the same time indicating shifts in footing that also imply subtle movement between particular and general referentiality.

(6)   *Rapido*

```
      1 Faizah: .. Ayah   aku tuh  ngomong gini      ka=n,
                  father 1s  that say    like.this PART
                  'My father said this you know,'
      2         … E=h,
                  hey
                  'Hey,'
      3         .. Mana  rapido=?
                  where Rapidograph.pen
                  'where's the Rapidograph pen?'
      5         .. Eh rapido       kamu mana=?
                  hey Rapidograph 2s    where
                  'Hey where's your Rapidograph?'
      6         katanya gitu      kan.
                  say-3s  like.that PART
                  'He said that you know.'
      7         .. Ayah   aku kan,
                  father 1s  PART
                  'My father you know,'
      8         dulu    pernah ngasih rapido.
                  before ever   give   Rapidograph
                  'had given (me) a Rapidograph pen.'
                  32 INTERVENING LINES
     41 Faizah: Yah gak enak juga.
                  yes NEG nice also
                  'Yeah (it's) really not nice.'
     42 Puji:   [He-em].
                  Uh-huh
                  'Uh-huh.'
```

```
43 Faizah: [Kita kan] udah     dikasih gitu,
           1S/P  PART already PV-give like.that
           'I/we/you were given (a/the pen) you know,'
44            terus,
              then
              'then,'
45 Puji:   [Iyah].
           yes
           'Yes.'
46 Faizah: [terus] barangnya gak ada  kan?
           then    thing-DEF NEG EXIST PART
           'then the thing is lost right?'
47            .. Terus gua cerita      ni=h yah?
              then 1S  tell.story this yes
              'Then I told the story, right?'
48            ke Si Obed kok.
              to DEF Obed PART
              'to Obed, you know.'
```

The first-person pronoun *aku* 'is' (lines 1 and 7) is a familiar form commonly used among family and friends, especially by younger women. The pronoun *kita* 'is/p' (line 43) is classified as first person plural inclusive in standard Indonesian grammar and is also used generically (similar to 'one' or generic 'you' in English). Colloquially, *kita* 'is/p' is also used for first person singular and first person plural exclusive reference (Ewing 2005). Finally, *gua* 'is' (line 47) is familiar but carries a more coarse or assertive feeling than *aku* 'is', being associated with the cosmopolitanism of the capital city, Jakarta, and also commonly used by both men and women. (See Djenar et al. 2018 for a more detailed discussion of social indexicality in Indonesian pronouns.) What is happening as Faizah shifts between *aku* (lines 1 and 7), *kita* (line 43), and *gua* (line 47)? In the two sections presented in (6), Faizah is speaking directly to Puji (in contrast to much of the narrative which recounts conversations with Abang and Obed). In terms of referentiality, both *aku* and *gua* are unambiguously first person singular and refer to Faizah herself. The difference lies in subtle shifts in social indexicality, which relate to shifts in the relationship of Faizah (and possibly also Puji) to the contexts and characters being talked about in the narration. In lines 1–8, Faizah is talking about her father and highlights her relationship with him by discussing the expensive gift he had given her. In this context the more intimate *aku* highlights this familial connection. In lines 47–48 Faizah introduces her boyfriend Obed into the narrative. While we do not necessarily know how she refers to herself when speaking directly to Obed, we can see from her use of *gua* a more assertive stance, one that indexes the more boisterous sociability of the young people in this friendship group, in contrast to the more intimate and possible acquiescent stance of her family relationships.

Referential ambiguity appears when Faizah uses *kita* during the segment in lines 41–46. She first makes an evaluative statement in line 41: *Ya gak enak juga* 'Yeah (it's) really not nice'. She then explicitly states in lines 43–46 what the situation is that she evaluates as not nice. Because she chooses *kita* here, rather than continuing her use of *aku* or beginning her use of *gua* (which starts four lines later), her statement becomes ambiguous between a particular and a generic reading. Conversationally, *kita* '1s/p' is often used to refer to first person singular and also as a generic pronoun. Thus, her statement in this segment can be heard as either a generic statement 'It's not nice – one is given something / a pen and then loses it' or as a particular statement 'It's not nice – I was given the pen and then lost it'. This ambiguity is augmented by the use of allusive reference. Because the object which was given is not explicitly stated, it can also be understood as generic (any gift) or it could be the particular pen in question. In other words, Faizah's statement is ambiguous between a generic comment, which is used to evaluate the circumstances she is describing (It's not nice if someone gives you something and you lose it) or as a commentary on the specific event she is talking about (It's not nice because my father gave me the pen and I lost it)

Note that an explicit object, either *rapido* 'a Rapidograph' or *rapido itu* 'the/that Rapidograph', could help disambiguate. Compare: *Kita kan udah dikasih rapido gitu* 'I/you/one was given a Rapidograph you know' and *Kita kan udah dikashi rapido itu gitu* 'I was given the Rapidograph you know'. There are two points to be made here. The first is that referentiality is not simply a property of a noun phrase (or an instance of allusive reference), but rather emerges from the overall format, content and context of the utterance. The second point is that this fact should not be interpreted to mean that, if only we could figure out which direct object Faizah intended, then we would know whether *kita* was generic or particular. Rather, the entire utterance as whole is produced indeterminately, with all components working together to produce this indeterminacy, which allows either a particular reading or generic reading. However, what seems even more likely in actual interaction is that neither and both readings are possible simultaneously. That is, the utterance as produced is completely interpretable for Faizah's interlocutor and delivers interactional progressivity: Puji responds *iya* 'yes' as Faizah continues.

In Faizah's use of three different first-person pronouns, we see a shift in footing. She is the focus of her story about her father, indexed by the pronoun *aku*. The focus goes blurry with the use of *kita*, and then things come back into focus with a different footing and different alignment towards her social network of peers, indexed by the pronoun *gua*. While first person reference shifts between particular and (possibly) general, at the same time tracking occurs throughout. As Faizah herself is clearly the most salient exemplar of a generic reading of line 43, a single human being in the real world (and in the discourse world being collaboratively constructed) is being tracked both in her social representations as a daughter and as a friend, and also possibly as an exemplar of a class of individuals who feel bad if they lose a valuable gift.

6.   Discussion: Referentiality, indeterminacy, and social action

In this study, I have approached referentiality through the information flow dimensions of generality and tracking, and have shown that in Indonesian conversation, referentiality can be indeterminate and fluid, a finding similar to those from other chapters in this volume. The indeterminacy of referentiality has to do with instances of (potential) referring, the extent to which a referent can be determined, and whether that referent is being construed as particular or general. Examples were provided which illustrated cases where there was no clear evidence for what referent speakers had in mind or whether interlocutors had the same referent in mind in any given point in interaction (Examples (2), (3), and (4)). Examples were also provided which illustrated cases where the general or particular nature of referents may be indeterminate (Examples (4), (5), and (6)). Yet such indeterminacy need not cause interactional difficulties for speakers. Despite this apparent indeterminacy of referentiality, in these examples referring has emerged in a way that has been successful, in that the progressivity of the interaction continues smoothly.

In contrast to indeterminacy, which may be about any one instance of emergent referring, fluidity has to do with how the stability (or not) of referential qualities shift over time, either within the utterances of a single speaker or across speaker turns. This fluidity involves whether the same referential qualities are maintained or whether there are shifts in how speakers appear to understand and deploy referents. Examples were provided showing shifts in generality (Examples (4), (5), and (6)). These shifts were not necessarily marked explicitly in the grammar of the noun phrase or larger construction, but rather can often only be surmised by the broader discourse and interactional context.

Indonesian makes extensive use of allusive reference. There are two points to make about this in relation to referentiality. First, referentiality is still potentially relevant with allusive constructions; that is, referentiality is not exclusively a property associated with explicit noun phrases. Aspects of the utterance other than an explicit noun phrase – for example, discourse context and common ground between speakers – allow for referentiality to emerge. When an utterance in context alludes to a referent, it also alludes to its (possible) referential properties. Second, it might be surmised that the referential indeterminacy found in Indonesian conversation can be attributed to the frequent occurrence of allusive reference. That is to say, when a referent is only implied and not explicitly expressed, this sets up a situation in which differing inferences can be made, thus causing referential indeterminacy or fluidity. Allusive reference can indeed heighten indeterminacy through the underspecification of resources that might contribute to precise determination of referentiality, but it should be remembered that explicit reference does not guarantee precise referentiality nor does allusive reference prohibit it. The degree of referential indeterminacy and fluidity might increase with allusive reference, but indeterminacy and fluidity can also be found when referents are explicit.

The lack of interactional consequences when referentiality is indeterminate or fluid suggests that referentiality might not be something speakers attend to. Yet there are also occasions when referentiality, even when indeterminate, does seem to align with important social actions. This is especially the case when shifts in referentiality align with shifts in footing, which play an important role in the interactional organization of talk. This is not to suggest a causal relationship between referentiality and footing, but rather a correlation where referentiality coalesces with footing. While indeterminacy and fluidity of reference are by no means unique to Indonesian, the nature of Indonesian grammar, usage styles, and the frequency of allusive reference make such indeterminacy a common practice in informal conversational interaction, and thus provides a clear case for demonstrating not only the indeterminacy and fluidity of referentiality, but also its relevance to speakers.

Acknowledgements

I am grateful for the input on early versions of this study from the participants at the 2018 Referentiality workshop at the University of Alberta, Edmonton, and the Nonreferentiality panel at the 2019 International Pragmatics Association conference. I would especially like to thank my coeditor, Ritva Laury and two anonymous referees, whose comments and suggestions have greatly improved this work. I also greatly appreciate the long hours poring over Indonesian conversational data with Novi Djenar and Howie Manns, which have helped me refine my thinking on these topics. All shortcomings are of course my responsibility.

References

 Chen, Ping. 2009. "Aspects of Referentiality." *Journal of Pragmatics* 41, 1657–1674.

 Djenar, Dwi Noverini, Michael C. Ewing and Howard Manns. 2018. *Style and Intersubjectivity in Youth Interaction*. Berlin: De Gruyter.

Donnellan, Keith. 1966. "Reference and Definite Descriptions." In *Semantics*, ed. by Danny D. Steinberg & Leon A. Jakobovits, 100–114. Cambridge: Cambridge University Press.

Du Bois, John W. 1980. "Beyond Definiteness: The Trace of Identity in Discourse." In *The Pear Stories: Cognitive, Cultural, and Linguistic Aspects of Narrative Production*, ed. by Wallace L. Chafe, 203–274. Norwood, N.J.: Ablex.

Du Bois, John W. and Sandra A. Thompson. 1991. "Dimensions of a Theory of Information Flow." Unpublished Ms. University of California at Santa Barbara.

Du Bois, John W., Stephan Schuetze-Coburn, Susanna Cumming, and Danae Paolino. 1993. "Outline of Discourse Transcription." In *Talking Data: Transcription and Coding in Discourse Research*, ed. by Jane A. Edwards and Martin D. Lampert, 45–89. Hillsdale, N.J.: Lawrence Erlbaum Associates.

Ewing, Michael C. 2005. "Colloquial Indonesian." In *The Austronesian Languages of Asia and Madagascar*, ed. by Alexander Adelaar and Nikolaus P. Himmelmann, 227–258. Routledge: London.

Ewing, Michael C. 2014. "Motivations for First and Second Person Subject Expression and Ellipsis in Javanese Conversation." *Journal of Pragmatics* 63: 48–62.

Ewing, Michael C. 2015. "The *Kalau* Framing Construction in Indonesian Comics." *NUSA: Linguistic Studies of Languages in and around Indonesia* 58: 51–72.

Ewing, Michael C. 2019. "The Predicate as a Locus of Grammar and Interaction in Colloquial Indonesian." *Studies in Language* 43 (2): 402–443.

Ewing, Michael C., and Dwi Noverini Djenar. 2019. "Address, Reference and Sequentiality in Indonesian Conversation." *The Social Dynamics of Pronominal Systems: A Comparative Approach*, ed. by Paul Bouissac, 253–287. Amsterdam: John Benjamins.

Fox, Barbara A. 1994. "Contextualization, Indexicality, and the Distributed Nature of Grammar." *Language Sciences* 16 (1): 1–37.

Frege, Gottlieb. 1892. "Über Sinn und Bedeutung." *Zeitschrift für Philosophie und philosophische Kritik* 100 (1892): 25–50.

Goffman, Erving. 1981. "Footing." In *Forms of Talk*, ed. by Erving Goffman, 124–159. Oxford: Blackwell.

Goffman, Erving. 1983. "Felicity's Condition." *American Journal of Sociology* 89 (1): 1–53.

Gundel, Jeanette K. 2010. "Reference and Accessibility from a Givenness Hierarchy Perspective." *International Review of Pragmatics* 2: 148–168.

Gundel, Jeanette K., Nancy Hedberg and Ron Zacharski. 1993. "Cognitive Status and the Form of Referring Expressions in Discourse." *Language* 69 (2): 274–307.

Nagaya, Naonori. 2011. "Rise and Fall of Referentiality: Articles in Philippine Languages." In *Nominalization in Asian Languages: Diachronic and Typological Perspectives*, ed. by Foong Ha Yap, Karen Grunow-Hårsta and Janick Wrona, 549–626. Amsterdam: John Benjamins.

Nariyama, Shigeko. 2003. *Ellipsis and Referent Tracking in Japanese*. Amsterdam: John Benjamins.

Oh, Sun-Young. 2007. "Overt Reference to Speaker and Recipient in Korean." *Discourse Studies* 9 (4): 462–492.

Ono, Tsuyoshi and Ryoko Suzuki. 2020. "Exploration into a New Understanding of 'Zero Anaphora' in Japanese Everyday Talk." In *Fixed Expressions: Building Language Structure and Social Action*, ed. by Ritva Laury and Tsuyoshi Ono, 41–70. Amsterdam: John Benjamins.

Ono, Tsuyoshi and Sandra A. Thompson. 1997. "Deconstructing 'Zero Anaphora' in Japanese." *Proceedings of the Twenty-Third Annual Meeting of the Berkeley Linguistics Society: General Session and Parasession on Pragmatics and Grammatical Structure* (1997): 481–491.

doi Russell, Bertrand. 1905. "On Denoting." *Mind* 14 (56): 479–493.

Sneddon, James N. 2006. *Colloquial Jakartan Indonesian*. Canberra: Pacific Linguistics.

doi Strawson, Peter F. 1950. "On Referring." *Mind* 59: 320–344.

doi Wouk, Fay. 1999. "Gender and the Use of Pragmatic Particles in Indonesian." *Journal of Sociolinguistics* 3 (2): 194–219.

doi Wouk, Fay. 2001. "Solidarity in Indonesian Conversation: The Discourse Marker *ya*." *Journal of Pragmatics* 33 (2): 171–91.

CHAPTER 3

First and second person forms as resources for open reference and participation in Finnish everyday conversations

Marja-Liisa Helasvuo & Karita Suomalainen
University of Turku   Åbo Akademi University

Based on data from Finnish conversational interaction, this article explores the use of 1st and 2nd person forms in creating deictically non-specific, open reference. We focus on the linguistic and embodied features of turns that contain these open personal forms and examine their sequential positioning. We show that the 1st and 2nd person forms that receive a deictically open interpretation typically occur in assessments, accounts of personal experience, and imaginary descriptions. They function as deictic displacements, shifting the origo of the speech situation, and causing a change of footing in the discourse roles, thus modulating the participation framework of the speech situation.

Keywords: Finnish, everyday conversation, first person singular, open reference, person expressions, participation framework, second person singular, referential index, deixis

1. Introduction

First and second person forms (e.g., personal pronouns, verbal person markers) are typically described as referring to speech act participants, i.e., to the speaker, and the addressee (Siewierska 2004:1–2). It is well known, however, that second person forms can also be used more openly, so that they do not refer exclusively to the addressee, but rather, are less referentially specific (Kitagawa & Lehrer 1990; Kluge 2016; for an overview, see Suomalainen & Varjo 2020:100). First person forms can also be used for creating non-specific reference (Helasvuo 2008; Zobel 2016; see also Kitagawa & Lehrer 1990:741–742 on the "impersonal I").

Our study explores the use of 1st and 2nd person forms in creating deictically non-specific reference – or, as we call it, *open reference* – in conversational interaction, focusing on how these forms modulate the participation framework and

https://doi.org/10.1075/pbns.344.03hel

how the reference they create is interpreted intersubjectively by the participants. This interpretation is based not only on the immediate syntactic context but also on the larger sequential context, including the co-participants' responses to the turns that contain the reference forms.

In previous studies, various terms have been used when referring to the deictically non-specific use of person forms; the terms used have included, for example, "generic" (e.g., Jensen & Gregersen 2016) and "impersonal" (e.g., Kitagawa & Lehrer 1990), which imply that these forms point to referents that are outside of the immediate speech context. As our study shows, however, even the so-called generic expressions may find their referent(s) in the speech situation. In this sense, they are open to different interpretations and carry the potential not only to refer non-specifically to people in general but also point to specific referents in the immediate speech context (see also Laitinen 2006: 216; Varjo & Suomalainen 2018: 335–337; Suomalainen & Varjo 2020: 98–99, 115–116). Therefore, we have chosen to use the term "open reference" to describe the referential potential of the deictically non-specific use of personal forms.

Using data from everyday Finnish conversations, our study aims to provide answers to the following questions: (1) In what kind of sequential contexts do the deictically open 1st and 2nd person forms occur? Are they part of certain interactional practices? (2) Are there any special linguistic features and embodied conduct in the composition of turns that contain open 1st or 2nd person forms? (3) How do the open 1st and 2nd person reference forms modulate the participation framework of the ongoing speech situation?

This article is organized as follows. Section 2 discusses our theoretical framework. We first discuss open reference forms as grammatical resources, placing the Finnish open reference forms into a cross-linguistic perspective (Section 2.1), and as interactional resources for creating reference and modulating the participation framework (Section 2.2). We then introduce the data and methods that we used (Section 3). In our analysis (Section 4), we focus on the interactional functions of the open reference forms as well as on the linguistic features and embodied conduct that accompany them. We also show how open reference forms can be used to modulate the participation framework. Section 5 presents our concluding discussion.

2.   Theoretical background

In this section, we examine open reference forms as part of the person system in Finnish and compare them to similar forms in other languages. We also discuss 1st and 2nd person forms as referential indices used for modulating the participation framework.

2.1 Open reference forms in grammar and interaction

In Finnish, the category of person is expressed through verbal person markers (suffixes), personal pronouns, and possessive suffixes. In the person system, 1st person singular forms primarily serve to refer to the speaker, and 2nd person singular forms refer to the addressee. 2nd person forms can, however, be used in reference to somebody other than the addressee (see Suomalainen 2020; Suomalainen & Varjo 2020; Uusitupa 2017), and similarly, 1st person forms can be used so that they do not index the speaker but are rather used more openly in reference to anybody or humans in general (Helasvuo 2008). The Finnish person marking system does not make a formal distinction between the deictically specific and open 1st and 2nd person singular forms. Instead of formal coding, the interpretation of a certain form as being specific vs. open is based on the context.

In addition to the open use of 1st and 2nd person forms, Finnish has other means of creating an open reference. Among these, the most frequent is the so-called zero-person construction, which involves a third-person verb form that has no overt subject (see Laitinen 2006; Varjo 2019). The use of the zero person is a conventional way to construe generic statements concerning human beings, but in certain contexts, the zero person may also get a more specific interpretation; it can, for example, be used when the speakers talk about their own experiences or feelings (Laitinen 2006; Suomalainen & Varjo 2020).

Besides Finnish, the open usage of 2nd person forms has been recognized in a wide variety of languages (for Danish, see Nielsen et al. 2009; for English: Kitagawa & Lehrer 1990; Kamio 2001; for French: Williams & Compernolle 2009; for German: Bredel 2002; Kluge 2016; Auer & Stukenbrock 2018; for Mandarin, Biq 1991, Tao, this volume; for Swedish: Fremer 2000). There has been much less research interest concerning the use of 1st person forms for creating a deictically non-specific, open reference (for German: see Zobel 2016). Previous studies have shown that open personal expressions are used for certain interactional goals; they can be used for construing involvement and inviting the addressee to join in the perspective that is being offered (Auer & Stukenbrock 2018; Jensen & Gregersen 2016; Nielsen et al. 2009; Stirling & Manderson 2011; Suomalainen & Varjo 2020).

Interestingly, when used for creating open reference, the 1st and 2nd person forms may nevertheless carry certain features of their deictically specific meaning (Helasvuo 2008; Kluge 2016; Laitinen 2006; Suomalainen 2018; Stirling & Manderson 2011; Zobel 2016), as we will show in Section 4 (below). This means that their referential scope may to some extent also cover the point of view of the speaker (in the case of 1st person singular) or invite participation from the recipient (in the case of 2nd person singular). For 2nd person forms, this procedure has been described by Sacks (1992, part 1: 163–168, 348–353), according to whom the English second person pronoun *you* is referentially ambiguous: when the recipients hear 'you', they go through a procedure to define how broad a scope the expression has in its context of use (for a further exploration of this procedure in Finnish, see Suomalainen 2018). In case the recipients do not interpret *you* to refer exclusively to them, *you* receives an ultimately open interpretation. As Sacks (1992, part 1: 350) puts it: "'You' as it expands and eventually meets 'everyone', excludes no one. It comes to mean 'me', indeed, also."

2.2   Reference and participation

In previous studies, 1st and 2nd person forms have been described as *referential indices* (Silverstein 1976) or *shifters* (Jakobson 1971 [1957]). The idea behind these terms is that 1st and 2nd person forms have a conventional meaning that indexes the interactional role of the participant being referred to: *I* indexes the role of the speaker, and *you* the role of the recipient (Goffman 1981: 47; Linell 2009: 69; see also Buber 1962 [1923]). In everyday interaction, the speaker is the one who utters *I*, and the recipient is the other, addressed party. However, 1st and 2nd person forms can also be understood as indicating discourse roles (Levinson 1988: 164; Siewierska 2004: 1; see also Ochs, Gonzales & Jacoby 1996); as such, they represent the roles of the interaction's two crucial parties: 'Self' and 'The Other' (cf. Linell 2009: 69, 77, 109–110; see also Buber 1962 [1923]). By indicating discourse roles, 1st and 2nd person forms do not always refer to physical entities "in this world", as we will show in our analysis in Section 4.

Indexing participant roles, 1st and 2nd person singular forms can be employed in the course of interaction to modulate the *participation framework*. The participation framework is a concept that was developed by Goffman (1981; for its application in linguistics, see Levinson 1988). Originally, Goffman (1981) used the idea of the participation framework to decompose the concept of *addressee* and to describe the different roles that so-called "hearers" have: there are both ratified participants (e.g., addressed recipients and other "official hearers") as well as unratified participants (e.g., over-hearers or eavesdroppers). The roles of the speaker were further analyzed using the concept of *production format* (Goffman 1981: 226). The concept of participation framework has been further developed within conversation analytic research so that it covers both the role of the speaker and that of an addressee, articulating all interactional, transitional positions that the interaction's different parties take up and orient to on a moment-by-moment basis (see Goodwin & Goodwin 1990; for Finnish, see Seppänen 1996, 1998).

According to Goffman (1981: 128), the changes that take place within the participation framework are called *changes of footing*. Such changes can happen, for example, when a turn is addressed to a certain recipient and he or she is chosen as the next speaker. However, a change of footing can also be carried out within the turn of an individual speaker and in the form of reported speech through which the current speaker brings in another voice.

In this paper, we argue that the open use of 1st and 2nd person forms affects the participation framework and leads to changes of footing. Open personal expressions shift the perspective of the subject matter that is under discussion to that of a more abstract level, indicating a transfer outside of the here-and-now of the current speech situation. When the participants use the open 1st or 2nd person forms, they no longer refer directly to themselves as speakers, or to their interlocutors as hearers. In open use, they primarily come to index the participant role of 'Self' or 'Other' that is associated with the person form in question, hence dissolving the referential relation to the participants who utter them, or to whom they are uttered.

3.   Data and methods

Our data come from the Arkisyn corpus of conversational Finnish compiled at the University of Turku (see Arkisyn in References). It currently contains data from 27 different conversations that in total comprise approximately 30 hours. For this current study, we extracted all 1st and 2nd person singular forms (personal pronouns, verbal person suffixes, and possessive suffixes) from seven conversations (8.5 hrs.). We also used additional data from another interaction (1.5 hrs.) that is not included in the Arkisyn corpus. The data include both video and audio recordings. For all data included in the corpus, the participants have signed a consent according to which the data can be used for research purposes. All data have been anonymized. In Section 4, we present one still picture (Figure 1) which has been taken from a video recording of our data and further processed to ensure anonymity.

Table 1 shows the data that were selected from the Arkisyn corpus. It compares deictically specific and open personal forms in the data. This table shows that 2nd person forms are much more frequently used for open reference than are 1st person forms (11.3% vs. 0.04%, respectively). The additional data we have used is not included in Table 1.

The additional data (recording of one conversation (1.5 hours) from the Archive of Finnish and Finno-Ugric languages, University of Turku) contains 6 additional cases of deictically open singular 1st person. So, all in all, we have analyzed 26 cases of singular 1st person and 199 cases of singular 2nd person forms

Table 1. Deictically specific and open personal forms in the data

Personal reference form	N of occurrences with deictically specific reference	N of occurrences with deictically open reference	N of all occurrences
SG1	4,874 (99.6%)	20 (0.04%)	4,894 (100%)
SG2	1,560 (88.7%)	199 (11.3%)	1,759 (100%)

with deictically open reference. The analysis we present in Section 4 below is based on careful microanalysis of these data.

In our analysis, we utilized conversation analytic (Sidnell & Stivers eds 2012) and interactional linguistic methods (Selting & Couper-Kuhlen eds 2001; Couper-Kuhlen & Selting 2018). The conversation analytic approach provides us with tools to analyze how the interpretation of the personal reference form is created turn-by-turn, sensitive to the current interactional context, and in cooperation between the participants. Our analysis of linguistic practices in their contexts of use is based on interactional linguistics. We analyze the relationship between the linguistic forms that are used in these contexts and the paradigmatic and syntagmatic options that are available.

4.   Analysis

In this section, we analyze the open use of 1st and 2nd person singular forms in our data. We devote particular attention to the sequential positioning of the target constructions as well as the linguistic practices and bodily cues that are related to the composition of the turns that contain the target constructions (cf. Lerner, 1996: 285–291).

We start our analysis by describing the sequential contexts in which open 1st and 2nd person singular forms occur and their interactional functions (Section 4.1). We then investigate the implementation and functions of certain linguistic and embodied features that co-occur with open 1st and 2nd person forms, after which we discuss what effect these features have in relation to deictic shifts that happen when open personal expressions are used (Section 4.2). Finally, we discuss how the use of open personal expressions modulates the participation framework (Section 4.3).

4.1   Sequential contexts and interactional functions

As we mentioned earlier in Section 2, the Finnish person marking system does not make a formal distinction between the open and deictically specific 1st and 2nd person singular forms; instead, the open interpretation is primarily based on the context of use. As for this context, the sequential features are especially important; these features include the interactional practices and the action and activity type in which the person form occurs.

It has been shown that deictically specific 2nd person forms are common in the first turns of adjacency pairs, such as questions or requests as well as in turns that describe or evaluate the addressee or their actions (Suomalainen 2018; 2020: 50). Deictically specific 2nd person forms typically select somebody else as the next speaker; as a response, these turns receive a second pair part in which the addressed recipient orients to the use of 2nd person singular form, for example, by using 1st person singular forms. This is demonstrated by the following example in which 1st and 2nd person singular forms are deictically specific, occurring in a question-answer adjacency pair. The 2nd person forms (verbal person suffix and pronoun) occur in Salla's turn (line 1: *haluut sä* 'do you want') in which she poses a question to the recipient, Janna, who is also addressed by name.

```
(1)   SG123
      01 Salla: haluut  sä  Janna nyt kirjottaa
                want-2SG 2SG NAME   now write-INF
      02        siihen mun     kave[rikirjaan. ].
                DEM-ILL 1SG-GEN friendship.book-ILL
                do you want to write in that friendship book of mine now, Janna.
      03 Janna:                    [voim  mä] kirjottaa,
                                    can-1SG 1SG write-INF
                                    sure I can write,
      04 Salla: >hyvä,< *
                good
                great,
                         *goes to get the friendship book
```

In her turn, Salla uses the 1st person singular pronoun form to refer to something she possesses (line 2: *siihen mun kaverikirjaan* 'to that friendship book of mine'). As a response, Janna provides an answer to Salla's question by using the 1st person singular forms (verbal person suffix and pronoun; *voim mä* 'I can') and repeating the verb *kirjottaa* 'to write' when referring to her own action (line 3).

In contrast to deictically specific 1st and 2nd person singular forms, the open person forms are not typically found in adjacency pairs in which the first turn projects a specific type of second turn. Instead, the 1st and 2nd person forms used for open reference in our data are commonly found in lengthy narrative sequences that involve actions such as assessments, accounts of personal experience, and descriptions of states of affairs. Quite often, the personal experiences or states of affairs that are discussed are of a hypothetical or imagined nature or otherwise expand beyond the here-and-now of the speech situation, which, for the participants, makes the open interpretation natural.

Different open personal expressions frequently occur in the same sequential contexts and form clusters (for Danish, see Nielsen, Fosgerau & Jensen 2009: 125, and for Mandarin, see Tao, this volume). In our data, the open 1st person singular forms almost always co-occur with the open 2nd person forms or the so-called zero-person construction, which is a construction that creates open reference that is formed with 3rd person forms. The open 2nd person forms show more varied clustering as they may co-occur not only with the open 1st person forms or the zero-person construction, but also, they may form their own clusters (see Suomalainen & Varjo 2020).

Example (2) below demonstrates, in a typical sequential context, the co-occurrence and clustering of open 1st and 2nd person singular forms. It is taken from a conversation involving three young adults – Toini, Kaisa, and Masa – who know each other through their church activities. Before the excerpt that is shown in the example, one of the participants, Toini, has told the others that it has been hard lately for her to participate in church meetings because she has gone through some difficult phases in her life and has not felt like talking about this with others in church meetings. In the excerpt shown below, Toini moves from the description of her personal experience to a more general evaluation of the situation.

(2)   SG440

```
01 Toini: [ov   vähäv vaikee   sillei:] tullas  seurakuntaaj
          be-3SG a.bit difficult like    come-INF congregation-ILL
          it's a bit difficult to come to church
02        ja ollas <sillee et> hei mä haluun  olla
          and be-INF like   COMP PTC 1SG want-1SG be-INF
          and be like hey I wanna be
03        yks(h)[in he niin, .hhhh
          alone       PTC
          alone, .hhhh
04 Kaisa: [nii, niin nii[j joo.
          PTC  PTC  PTC    PTC
          yeah yeah yeah I see.
05 Toini:          [se ov    vähäv vaikee   seurassa  sillei,
                   DEM be-3SG little difficult company-INE like.that
                   it's like a bit difficult in company,
06        (1.2)
07 Kaisa: niim mä tiiän  se on    oikeestikkik #ku#.
          PTC  1SG know-1SG DEM be-3SG really-CLT  when
          yeah, I know it's really (like that).
08        (0.8) #va-,# (0.2) tai sillee et vois    olla et
              dif-        or like  COMP could-3SG be-INF COMP
          dif- (0.2) I mean it could be that
09        jos meet jonnekki iham   muuhun
          if  go-2SG somewhere totally another-ILL
          if you go to some completely different (church)
```

```
10        ku ọmaa   seuraku[ntaan   ni sit voi    ollakki
          than own-ILL congregation-ILL PTC then can-3SG be-INF-CLT
          than your own church then (one) can be
11 Toini:                    [nii.
                             PTC
                             Yeah
12 Kaisa: (.) saa    ọllakki   enemmär <raahas>
               get-3SG be-INF-CLT more      peace-INE
               one can have more peace
13        °mut sit° kuitenkik kaikki    tulee   kỵse#leej ja#;
          but then still     everybody come-3SG ask-INF    and
          but then still, everybody comes and asks and;
14        (0.2)
15 Toini: mmmmmm?
          PTC
          mm?
16        (0.2)
```

In Example (2), Toini's first turn (lines 1–3) elaborates her feelings by presenting an imaginary situation in which a person participates in a church meeting but says to everybody that he or she wants to be alone. This situation is framed by a zero-person formulation *ov vähäv vaikee sillei: tullas seurakuntaaj ja ollas <sillee et>* 'It's a bit difficult to come to church and be like' (lines 1–2) without specifying to whom it is difficult. The zero-person construction is often used in tellings of personal experience to introduce a topic that is later illustrated, for example, with the use of open 2nd person singular forms (Varjo & Suomalainen 2018: 355). In Example (2), the zero-person construction is followed by the use of open 1st person singular (pronoun and verbal suffix): *hei mä haluun olla ỵks(h)[in he niin,* 'hey, I wanna be alone' (lines 2–3). The utterance in which the open 1st person singular occurs is presented as direct reported speech, the source of which, however, remains open, or at least implicit, due to the preceding use of zero-person forms.

In Example (2), the open 1st person singular forms have a twofold function. On the one hand, the imaginary line in a hypothetical dialogue, produced from the 1st person perspective, is used to demonstrate the feelings of the speaker or whoever goes to church and does not feel like talking to others there. On the other hand, the use of the 1st person singular introduces a "new" voice in the situation in question and thus makes Toini's turn become polyphonic. With the 1st person singular form, it is possible to give an individual voice to a generic, yet very personal, experience.

In Example (2), the introduction of a new voice calls for mutual negotiation of the ongoing referential framework, as the use of an open personal expression provides a potentially relatable perspective to the situation at hand for the other participants. In her response, which consists of agreeing response particles (lines 3–4: *nii niin niij joo*), Kaisa displays that she recognizes the experience that is being talked about and affiliates with the previous speaker (see Sorjonen 2001: 133).

After having shown recognition of the experience that Toini was describing (lines 3–4), Kaisa explicitly states that she knows what Toini is talking about (line 7: *niim mä tiiän* 'yeah I know'; see Couper-Kuhlen 2012:122–126 and Mikesell et al. 2017:281 on the English *I know*; cf. Vatanen 2018:204) and then goes on to present her perspective on the matter (*se on oikeestikkik #ku#* 'it's really (like that)'). After this, however, she slightly changes the direction of her turn, indicated by the particle *tai* 'I mean; or' (Sorjonen & Laakso 2005) and starts to describe a hypothetical situation, where a person goes to a church that is not her usual one. It is in this context that the use of open 2nd person singular verbal suffix occurs (lines 9–10: *jos **meet** jonnekki iham muuhun ku omaan seurakuntaan* 'if you go to some completely different church than your own'). Similar to the open 1st person singular form in line 2, the open 2nd person singular form illustrates the situation that is being discussed, and, with it, Kaisa demonstrates a certain way of acting. Interestingly, the open 2nd person singular is followed by zero-person forms *voi ollakki* '(one) can be' (line 10) and *saa ollakki enemmä <raahas>* '(one) can have more peace' (line 12). The change to the zero person might be motivated by the perspective change: Kaisa moves from describing a way of acting to elaborating an individual's inner feelings, a context in which zero-person construction is more common than the open 2nd person singular (Suomalainen & Varjo 2020).

Similar to the open 1st person form earlier in Example (2) (line 2), the use of open 2nd person singular in the example has a twofold function: The 2nd person forms paint a picture of an objectified agent who performs the described action, but, at the same time, the 2nd person singular also addresses the other participants and thus invites them to recognize the described situation. Here, the display of recognition from the other participants' side comes from Toini and immediately follows the introduction of the 2nd person form, even though this display is rather minimal (line 11: *nii*).

Comparing the use of open 1st and 2nd person singular forms in this extract, we can see that they are both part of a sequence in which participants intersubjectively evaluate a specific yet hypothetical experience. The open 1st and 2nd person singular forms are used in rather similar parts of the sequence, namely in passages in which the hypothetical experience is exemplified. However, the local contexts of occurrence are different; the open 1st person singular form in Example (2) occurs in a context where an individual's inner feelings are described, whereas the open 2nd person singular illustrates a presumably shared way of acting.

4.2   Linguistic features and embodied conduct

In our data, we have identified several linguistic features that are often present in conjunction with the open 1st and 2nd person singular forms and add to the interpretation of these forms as not (only) referring to the current speaker or the interlocutor. These include the presence of markers of reported speech or dialogue (e.g., *olla sillee* 'be like,' Example (2) above: lines 2–3) or other indexical elements that indicate a change of footing, often into an imaginary or hypothetical situation and spatio-temporal frame. In addition, there might be some embodied markers of spatio-temporal shifts in turns with open 1st and 2nd person singular forms, such as illustrative hand movements or enacted voice. We will now discuss these linguistic and embodied markers.

A common verbal means of indicating a change to an imagined situation is the presence of an *if–then* frame. It is used to create a hypothetical world, such as in Example (2) (lines 9–10, 11–12). The *if–then* frame indicates a deictic shift in which the origo (i.e., the situation's vantage point) is no longer in the here-and-now of the speech situation but is instead in an imaginary or at least irrealis spatio-temporal domain. However, verbal elements are not the only way to create such shifts in our data; the use of open 1st and 2nd person singular forms is often accompanied by illustrative embodied action, such as enacted prosody (e.g., voice modulation), or narrative kinesic movements. These features are illustrated with Example (3), which comes from a conversation between sisters Jaana and Tuula.

Before the excerpt that is shown below, the participants had been discussing a mutual acquaintance who has retired because of a serious illness: sclerosis. Jaana has told Tuula how their friend's family treats her, which involves not showing any understanding of her condition. Then Jaana moves the discussion to a more general level.

```
(3)  SG437
     01 Jaana: et  ku kauheen monis    perheis     on    sillai että:, (0.4)
               COMP as awfully many-INE family-PL-INE be.3SG so    COMP
               in very many families, it is so that,
     02        et  sillo et  jos tulee   niinku joku tämmönen tauti.
               COMP when COMP if  come-3SG like  some DEM-ADJ  disease
               if (one) gets some kind of disease.
     03        (0.2) ni, (0.2) .hh ta#i:# joku tämmönen tilanne.  .hhhh nin, (0.2)
                     so      or     some DEM-ADJ situation    so
               so .hh or is in some kind of a situation.  .hhhh
     04        se ettei  voida          niinku suːhtautuu sillai
               DEM COMP-NEG can-CONNEG-PASS like  behave-INF so
               that they cannot handle (it) so that
     05        että et  nyt on    näin, (.) voidaan asia
               COMP COMP now be.3SG like.this can-PASS thing
               now it is so, (.) we can (deal with) this
     06        mä voin   *niinkun, (0.2) sulle pilkkoa
               1SG can-1SG like       2SG-ALL chop-INF
```

```
                 I can like chop up for you
                            *moves hands above Tuula's plate and illustrates chopping up
                 food
07               esimerki[ks ruuan,
                 for.example food-ACC
                 for example, food,
08 Tuula:             [mm;
                      PTC
                      mhm;
09 Jaana: .hh enkä       ole      olet- (.) s:illai    että; .hhhh
               NEG-1SG-CLT be-CONNEG be        like.that COMP
               and I'm not like; .hhhh
10 Jaana: *@sun nyt vaan täytyy   olla   kunnos
               2SG-GEN now just must-3SG be-INF shape-INE
               you just have to be in shape
               *makes a fist with her hand and shakes it in rhythm with her speech
11         sun      täytyy@ olla, (.)*
           2SG-GEN must-3SG be-INF
           you have to be, (.)
           --------------------------------*
```

In Example (3), Jaana first sets up a frame that is referring to a situation that happens 'in many families' (*monis perheis*, line 1). She then construes an imaginary situation with an *if* construction (lines 2–3) within which she describes actions in general terms by using passive constructions (lines 4 and 5). In this imaginary situation, she then sets an imagined speaker who is presenting his/her speech by using 1st person singular references (pronoun and verbal suffix); the imagined speaker offers to chop food for the sick person (line 6). She contrasts this with a situation where the imagined speaker just tells the sick person to behave (lines 8–9). With the 2nd person forms, Jaana construes an imaginary addressee for the talk (lines 6, 10–11), thus creating a dialogue between 'I' and 'you,' 'Self' and 'Other' (Linell 2009).

In Example (3), it is clear that when using the 1st and 2nd person forms, Jaana is not speaking about herself or her family because no one in her family is sick. Instead, Jaana is reporting – and reproducing – someone else's speech. Her turns are thus polyphonic, which is also signaled by the several uses of *että* (lines 1, 2, 4, 5, 9) which in this context indicate that the current speaker is not the author of the words she is about to produce (see Laury and Seppänen 2008; see also Keevallik 2008). In addition, Jaana uses enacted prosody (marked with @-signs: lines 10–11) in conjunction with open reference forms. She also makes use of embodied actions to indicate that she is not herself talking but is instead giving voice to somebody else. In Goffman's words (1981), Jaana acts as an *animator*, as someone who merely produces the utterance, while the *principal* whose view Jaana's 1st person singular forms represent is to be found somewhere else. Jaana accompanies her talk (line 6) with an illustration of chopping food (Figure 1); she holds both of her hands above the plate of her co-participant, Tuula, and enacts a chopping gesture.

Figure 1. Illustrative embodied action in Example (3), line 6

In Example (3), the multimodal elements that are in connection with the use of 1st and 2nd person forms are enacted, not happening in the real world but rather in the imagined world. As such, they represent what Stukenbrock (2014) described as the multimodally-created *Deixis am Phantasma* of face-to-face interaction (see also Auer & Stukenbrock 2018). The concept of *Deixis am Phantasma* ('imagination-oriented deixis') was originally presented by Bühler (1965 [1934]) to describe deictic expressions that refer or point to non-present entities that can only be accessed in imagination. Stukenbrock (2014:71) proposes that in face-to-face interaction, such expressions are deictic displacements that shift the origo of the speech situation away from the participants' actual space of perception to that of an imaginary spatio-temporal domain within which the speakers can orient their interlocutors' attention to physically absent entities.

Bühler (1965 [1934]) distinguishes between different types of *Deixis am Phantasma*: two main types (*Hauptfälle*) and a third, intermediate type. In Bühler's first main type of *Deixis am Phantasma*, the speaker refers to physically absent objects as if they were present. In the second type, the speaker displaces himself/ herself in imagination to a place outside of the speech situation. The third type is defined as an intermediate case between remaining "here," in the speech situation, and going "there," to the imagined word outside of the speech situation. (See also Stukenbrock 2014:72–73, 89.) As Stukenbrock (2014:77) notes, typical examples of the *Deixis am Phantasma* are imagined spaces created while telling a story. This is also the case in Example (3) that is presented above: The imagined situation that is being referred to and enacted upon is purely hypothetical, but it is made accessible with the help of open personal expressions. The use of 1st and 2nd person singular forms invites the actual conversational participants, Tuula and Jaana, to see the situation as if they were experiencing it directly from the imaginary actors' point of view, first from the position of the speaker (1st person forms) and then that of the recipient (2nd person forms). Had Jaana used, for example, third person forms or the Finnish passive construction instead, the situation would not be presented as directly accessible for the participants in the same manner, but rather, they would be observing it from outside.

The use of open 1st and 2nd person forms implements deictic displacements along the dimensions of time, place, and person. They do this by blending the here-and-now vantage point of the speech situation with the vantage point in the imagined reality that they are used to describing. In Bühler's (1965 [1934]) terms, the use of open 1st and 2nd person singular forms in our data represent the intermediate case of simultaneously remaining "here," in the speech situation, and going "there," to the imagined world. In Example (3), by producing the description of the situation in the 1st person singular form, the speaker, Jaana, projects herself into the narrated 'Other' whose vantage point she takes, and supports this by embodied action enacted from the vantage point of the narrated 'Other' (see Figure 1; cf. Stukenbrock 2014: 83).

4.3   Modulating the participation framework

With the help of referentially open personal constructions, the participants can modulate the deictic field of the ongoing interaction. They can use them to shift the perspective from the immediate speech situation to a more abstract level or to make a transfer to another imaginary world outside the here-and-now of the speech situation, as demonstrated in Section 4.2. Furthermore, open 1st and 2nd person forms can also be utilized to induce a change of footing in the participation framework (Goffman 1981) and give rise to new or multiple voices and perspectives in the course of the interaction.

Example (4) illustrates the use of referentially open personal forms to modulate the participation framework. In the excerpt that is shown in this example, the participants are discussing an upcoming music festival. Some of them have participated in the festival in previous years, and they share their experiences of attending the festival. Prior to the excerpt Ina and Mikaela have complained about how crowded the festival is and how much planning it requires to attend the festival, to which another participant, Alma, has responded by stating that such planning is stressful and unnecessary. She goes on to suggest that the festival should be about hanging out together and feeling the music:

(4)   D134
```
      23 Alma:   ku      se >pitäis<,    mennä sillee    niinku,
                 because DEM must-COND.3SG go-INF like.this like
                 because it/one should go like,
      24         (0.2) ↑<hengailee,>↑
                 hang.out-INF
                 hang out,
```

```
25 Mikaela: [nii-i,
            PTC
            right,
26 Onni:    [@pitää olla   semmonen flou[siin hommas@.
            must-3SG be-INF DEM.ADJ    flow DEM.INE job-INE
            should have like a flow in that deal.
27 Alma:                       [↑fiilistelee,↑
                               have.good.vibes-INF
                               have good vibes,
28 Mikaela: nii mut [sit-
            PTC but
            yeah but
29 Alma:           [eikä m[itää    stressii  mennä sinne.
                   NEG-CLT nothing.PAR stress-PAR go-INF there
                   and no stress going there.
30 Ina:                   [>mut et    sä oikee pysty<
                          but   NEG-2SG 2SG really be.capable.of-CONNEG
                          but you cannot really
31          hengailee > jos [et   sä]<pääse    minnekää
            hang.out-INF if  NEG-2SG 2SG. get.CONNEG anywhere
            hang out if you don't get in anywhere
32 Mikaela:              [e:i. ]
                         NEG.3SG
                         no.
33 Ina:     [°kuuntelee°,            ]
            listen.INF
            to listen (to the music),
34 Mikaela: [mut jos et     sä pääse]  jos sä haluut   et,
            but if  NEG-2SG 2SG get.CONNEG if 2SG want-2SG. COMP
            but if you don't get in, if you want to,
35          @mä haluisin    ehkä nähä   vähä     tätä
            1SG want-COND-1SG maybe see-INF a.little DEM-PAR
            I would maybe like to see a little bit of this
36          ja vähä     tätä@,=
            and a.little DEM-PAR
            and a little bit of that,
37          =mut sit jos sä (.) meet   johonki. (0.2) ni sit
            but then if 2SG   go-2SG some.ILL      PTC then
            but then, if you go somewhere, then
38          sä näät   sitä vähä    jostai
            2SG see-2SG DEM-PAR a.little some-ELA
            you see a little bit of it from somewhere
39          ja sit sä oot    sillee
            and then 2SG be-2SG like
            and then you are like
40          et äh mä haluun   nähä   sitä  toistaki,
            COMP   1SG want-1SG see-INF DEM-PAR other-ELA-CLT
            I want to see the other one also,
41          (0.2)
```

In lines 23–24, 27 and 29, Alma presents a general claim regarding how one should behave at the festival. In their responses, Ina and Mikaela do not align with Alma's claim. In line 28, Mikaela tries to start a disaligning turn (starting with *nii mut* 'yeah but') but is cut-off by Alma (line 29) who continues with her claim. In line 30, Ina responds to Alma in overlap. Ina's turn (lines 30–31, 33) begins with the particle *mut* 'but' that indicates an alternative perspective (cf. Hakulinen et al. 2004: §1034); in her turn, Ina states that it is quite difficult to "hang out" if the crowd at the festival makes it impossible to access the music performances. Mikaela agrees with Ina (l. 32), and after Ina has finished the turn, Mikaela produces an account for her earlier claim (not shown here) of why it is necessary to prepare for the festival by scheduling.

Both Ina's and Mikaela's turns are disagreeing and even disaffiliating with Almas preceding turn, and accounting for the claims that the participants have presented earlier about the festival. Both Ina and Mikaela have said that they have attended the festival before, so their accounts are based on personal experiences. However, these experiences are presented with the open 2nd person singular forms (lines 30–34, 37–39), which indicates that the experiences they are talking about could potentially be recognized by the other participants. It may also be worth noting that Example (4) comes from an argumentative context, and this may have an effect on the use of open 2nd person singular forms. Here they are used to strengthen the individual participant's claims: the use of open 2nd person singular invites the participants to personally identify with the described experience and thus notice the truthfulness of it.

While Ina's turn contains only 2nd person singular forms, Mikaela alternates between 1st and 2nd person. In line 34, Mikaela produces two *jos* 'if' clauses, both with the 2nd person singular. The first one (*jos et sä pääse* 'if you cannot get (in)'), describing the action of the person attending the festival, is cut off and Mikaela starts a new one (*jos sä haluut et* 'if you want to') with which she refers to the mental process of choosing what to attend to in the festival. She uses the complement-taking predicate *haluut* 'want to' and the complementizer *et*. According to Laury and Seppänen (2008), this complementizer can be used to bring in a new voice. Mikaela continues with an alternative perspective using the 1st person singular form (line 35), which is marked as reported speech or thought by modulating the voice quality (marked with the @-sign). With the 1st person singular, Mikaela presents the inner thoughts of the person attending the festival. In line 37, she switches back to the 2nd person singular when describing the imagined actions of the person who is attending the festival. The imagined actions are set in an 'if – then' frame. In line 40, Mikaela again switches to the 1st person singular to express the inner thoughts of the one who is attending the festival. This expression is framed as reported thought or speech with the expression *sä oot sillee et* 'you are like' (line 39; for the use of the complementizer *että* for bringing in another voice, see Laury & Seppänen 2008).

In Example (4), the deictic origo is set in an imagined world amid which the participants are invited to share the experiences described by the 2nd person forms and to reflect the thoughts of an imaginary speaker who is referred to by the 1st person forms. The 2nd person singular forms are used to portray the described situation as being mutually accessible and potentially intersubjectively shared among the participants, while the 1st person singular forms give a voice to somebody who is experiencing the described situation and indicate that the one who is talking is an animator (cf. Goffman 1981). Consequently, the participation framework is modulated so that the 1st person singular does not index the actual speaker but rather an imaginary speaker or a generalized 'Self' (cf. Linell 2009: 96, 116–117). In the same manner, the 2nd person singular does not refer to one specific recipient but rather to a shared human experience to which the participants can recognize and potentially relate (see Tao, this volume, on "limited generality" of second person expressions in Mandarin).

When the open 1st and 2nd person singular forms are used, the changes in the participation framework could be described as the *layering of voices-effect* (Stukenbrock 2014: 87, 89): The participants' voices and perspectives mix with those of the actors in the imagined spatio-temporal frame. The 1st and 2nd person singular forms invite the participants to recognize the described situation by making it accessible from the perspective of the ongoing speech situation.

5. Conclusions

In this study, we have focused on the open use of 1st and 2nd person singular forms. We have investigated these forms' sequential and interactional contexts, turn-composition, as well as the linguistic and embodied features that occur in connection with them and how they modulate the participation framework.

In our data, those 1st and 2nd person singular forms which receive a deictically open interpretation typically occur in actions such as assessments, accounts of personal experience, and descriptions of hypothetical or imaginary states of affairs. In these contexts of use, 1st and 2nd person forms are used to illustrate or exemplify something that is being discussed in their context of occurrence. The composition of turns with open 1st and 2nd person forms is characterized by certain verbal and embodied conduct, such as hypothetical 'if–then' frames, markers of reported speech or dialogue, and multimodal deictic elements (e.g., enacted prosody or modulation of voice) that function as deictic displacements; this shifts the origo of the speech situation away from the participants' actual space of perception to that of an imaginary spatio-temporal frame where the described phenomena can be seen as if they were real. As such, the use of open 1st and 2nd person forms modulates the participation framework of the speech situation.

Furthermore, the participation framework can be modulated through a change of footing in the discourse roles. When used as open reference forms (i.e., non-deictically), the open 1st person singular form does not refer to the current speaker but rather to a generalized 'Self'. This gives voice to a generalized but at the same time, individualized and identifiable experience, which makes the current speaker the animator of the "voice" of this experience. The open 2nd person singular form identifies a certain experience or situation and invites the participants of the speech situation to recognize it. It is used to establish beliefs and experiences that are construed as mutual and potentially shared.

The intersubjectivity of referent co-construction is a crucial part of participants' movement between real and imagined spatio-temporal frames. Our analysis demonstrates how the open personal expressions that are produced by one speaker are interpreted and responded to by other participants. Open personal expressions tend to occur in contexts in which the participants are sharing their knowledge and experiences with others, making the matters under discussion accessible to and recognizable by others. We could say, then, that by using 1st and 2nd person forms to create open reference, the participants construe the situation as something that is shared between the participants. Our findings support the idea that person forms are not only used for creating a reference but also to implement specific social actions (also see chapters by Ewing and by Tao, this volume).

As referring expressions, open 1st and 2nd person forms do not designate an individual referent but they are rather used to describe experiences or states of affairs; in that sense one could say that they are not highly referential. However, compared to other open or generic person expressions, the experiences and states of affairs open 1st and 2nd person forms refer to are quite unique and often also personal, even if they are presented as generalizable, which signals a relatively high specificity. Our results indicate that there is no clear distinction between so-called *general* and *specific* reference (cf. Tao, this volume, on "limited generality"). Instead, these two attributes coexist in our data, as the speakers use open 1st and 2nd person forms to describe and create generalized, yet identifiable, experiences or states of affairs that are presented from the perspective of an individual.

References

Arkisyn: A Morphosyntactically Coded Database of Conversational Finnish. *Database compiled at the University of Turku, with material from the Conversation Analysis Archive at the University of Helsinki and the Syntax Archives at the University of Turku.* Department of Finnish and Finno-Ugric Languages, University of Turku.

Auer, Peter, and Anja Stukenbrock. 2018. "When 'You' Means 'I': The German 2nd Ps.Sg. Pronoun *du* Between Genericity and Subjectivity." *Open Linguistics* 4: 280–309.

Biq, Yung-O. 1991. "The Multiple Uses of the Second Person Singular Pronoun in Conversational Mandarin." *Journal of Pragmatics* 16: 307–321.

doi Bredel, Ursula. 2002. "'You Can Say *You* to Yourself': Establishing Perspectives with Personal Pronouns." In *Perspectives and Perspectivation in Discourse*, ed. by Carl Friedrich Graumann, and Werner Kallmeyer, 167–180. Amsterdam: John Benjamins.

Buber, Martin. 1962 [1923]. *I and Thou*. Edinburgh: T & T Clark.

Bühler, Karl. 1965 [1934]. *Sprachtheorie. Die Darstellungsfunktion der Sprache*. 2nd edition. Stuttgart: Gustav Fischer Verlag.

doi Couper-Kuhlen, Elizabeth. 2012. "Exploring Affiliation in the Reception of Conversational Complaint Stories." In *Emotion in Interaction*, ed. by Anssi Peräkylä, and Marja-Leena Sorjonen, 113–146. New York: Oxford University Press.

Couper-Kuhlen, Elizabet, and Selting, Margret. 2018. *Interactional Linguistics: Studying Language in Social Interaction*. Cambridge: Cambridge University Press.

Fremer, Maria. 2000. "Va e du då. Generiskt du hos ungdomar och vuxna talare [Generic use of "du" in adolescent and adult speech]." In *Ungdom, språk og identitet: Rapport fra et nettverksmøte* [*Youth, language, and identity: A report from a network meeting*], ed. by Ulla-Britt Kotsinas, Anna-Brita Stenström, and Eli-Marie Drange, 133–147. Copenhagen: Nordisk Ministerråd.

Goffman, Erving. 1981. *Forms of Talk*. Oxford: Basil Blackwell.

Goodwin, Charles, and Marjorie Harness Goodwin. 1990. "Context, Activity and Participation." In *The Contextualization of Language*, ed. by Peter Auer, and Aldo di Luzio, 77–99. Amsterdam: John Benjamins.

Hakulinen, Auli, Maria Vilkuna, Riitta Korhonen, Vesa Koivisto, Tarja Riitta Heinonen, and Irja Alho. 2004. *Iso suomen kielioppi* [*Comprehensive grammar of Finnish*]. Helsinki: Finnish Literature Society.

Helasvuo, Marja-Liisa. 2008. "Minä ja muut: Puhujaviitteisyys ja konteksti [Speaker reference and contextual interpretation]." *Virittäjä* 112: 186–206.

Jakobson, Roman. 1971 [1957]. "Shifters, Verbal Categories and the Russian Verb." In *Selected Writings of Roman Jakobson 2*, 130–147. The Hague: Mouton.

Jensen, Torben Juel, and Frans Gregersen. 2016. "What Do(es) *You* Mean? The Pragmatics of Generic Second Person Pronouns in Modern Spoken Danish." *Pragmatics* 26: 417–446.

doi Kamio, Akio. 2001. "English Generic *We, You*, and *They*: An Analysis in Terms of Territory of Information. *Journal of Pragmatics* 33: 1111–1124.

doi Keevallik, Leelo. 2008. "Conjunction and Sequenced Actions: The Estonian Complementizer and Evidential Particle *Et*." In *Crosslinguistic Studies of Clause Combining: The Multifunctionality of Conjunctions*, ed. by Ritva Laury, 125–152. Amsterdam: John Benjamins.

doi Kitagawa, Chisato, and Adrienne Lehrer. 1990. "Impersonal Uses of Personal Pronouns." *Journal of Pragmatics* 14: 739–759.

Kluge, Bettina. 2016. "Generic Uses of the Second Person Singular – How Speakers Deal with Referential Ambiguity and Misunderstandings." *Pragmatics* 26 (3): 501–522.

doi Laitinen, Lea. 2006. "Zero Person in Finnish: A Grammatical Resource for Construing Human Reference." In *Grammar from the Human Perspective: Case, Space and Person in Finnish*, ed. by Marja-Liisa Helasvuo, and Lyle Campbell, 209–231. John Benjamins, Amsterdam.

doi Laury, Ritva, and Eeva-Leena Seppänen. 2008. "Clause Combining, Interaction, Evidentiality, Participation Structure, and the Conjunction-Particle Continuum: The Finnish *Että*." In *Crosslinguistic Studies of Clause Combining: The Multifunctionality of Conjunctions*, ed. by Ritva Laury, 153–178. Amsterdam: John Benjamins.

Lerner, Gene H. 1996: "On the Place of Linguistic Resources in the Organization of Talk-in-Interaction. 'Second Person' Reference in Multi-Party Conversation. *Pragmatics* 6 (3): 281–294.

Levinson, Stephen. 1988. "Putting Linguistics on a Proper Footing: Explorations in Goffman's Concept of Participation." In *Erving Goffman: Exploring the Interaction Order*, ed. by Paul Drew, and Anthony Wootton, 161–227. Oxford: Polity Press.

Linell, Per. 2009. *Rethinking Language, Mind and World Dialogically: Interactional and Contextual Theories of Human Sense-Making.* Charlotte, NC: Information Age Publishing.

Mikesell, Lisa, Galina Bolden, Jenny Mandelbaum, Jeffrey Robinson, Tanya Romaniuk, Alexa Bolaños-Carpio, Darcey Searles, Wan Wei, Stephen M. DiDomenico, and Beth Angell. 2017. "At the Intersection of Epistemics and Action: Responding with *I Know.*" *Research on Language and Social Interaction* 50 (3): 268–285.

Nielsen, Søren Beck, Christina Fogtmann Fosgerau, and Torben Juel Jensen. 2009. "From Community to Conversation – and Back: Exploring the Interpersonal Potentials of Two Generic Pronouns in Danish." *Acta Linguistica Hafniensia: International Journal of Linguistics* 41: 116–142.

Ochs, Elinor, Patrick Gonzales, and Sally Jacoby. 1996. "'When I Come Down I'm in the Domain State': Grammar and Graphic Representation in the Interpretive Activity of Physicists." In *Interaction and Grammar*, ed. by. Elinor Ochs, Emanuel Schegloff, and Sandra Thompson, 328–369. Cambridge & New York: Cambridge University Press.

Sacks, Harvey. 1992. *Lectures on Conversation.* Vol. 1 & 2. Oxford: Basil Blackwell.

Selting, Margret, and Elizabeth Couper-Kuhlen (eds). 2001. *Studies in Interactional Linguistics.* Amsterdam: John Benjamins.

Seppänen, Eeva-Leena. 1996. "Ways of Referring to a Knowing Co-Participant in Finnish Conversation." *SKY Yearbook of the Linguistic Association of Finland*: 135–176.

Seppänen, Eeva-Leena. 1998. *Läsnäolon pronominit [Pronouns of participation].* Helsinki: Finnish Literature Society.

Sidnell, Jack, and Tanya Stivers (eds). 2012. *The Handbook of Conversation Analysis.* Chichester: Wiley-Blackwell.

Siewierska, Anna. 2004. *Person.* Cambridge: Cambridge University Press.

Silverstein, Michael. 1976. "Shifters, Linguistic Categories, and Cultural Description." In *Meaning in Anthropology*, ed. by Keith H. Basso, and Henry A. Selby, 11–55. Albuquerque: University of New Mexico Press.

Sorjonen, Marja-Leena. 2001. *Responding in Conversation: A Study of Response Particles in Finnish.* Amsterdam: John Benjamins.

Sorjonen, Marja-Leena, and Minna Laakso. 2005. "Katko vai *eiku*? Itsekorjauksen aloitustavat ja vuorovaikutustehtävät [Cut-off, the particle *eiku* and other practices for initiating self-repair, and the interactional functions of self-repair]." *Virittäjä* 109: 244–271.

Stirling, Lesley, and Lenore Manderson. 2011. "About *You*: Empathy, Objectivity and Authority." *Journal of Pragmatics* 43: 1581–1602.

Stukenbrock, Anja. 2014. "Pointing to an 'Empty' Space: Deixis am Phantasma in Face-to-Face Interaction." *Journal of Pragmatics* 74: 70–93.

doi　Suomalainen, Karita. 2018. *Sinä*, konteksti ja monitulkintaisuus: Yksikön 2. persoonan viittaukset arkikeskustelussa [*Sinä* 'you', context, and ambiguity: Second-person singular reference in everyday Finnish conversation]." *Virittäjä* 122 (3): 320–355.

Suomalainen, Karita. 2020. *Kuka sinä on? Tutkimus yksikön 2. persoonan käytöstä ja käytön variaatiosta suomenkielisissä arkikeskusteluissa* [Who is 'you'? On the use of second person singular in Finnish everyday conversations]. Annales Universitatis Turkuensis C 499. Turku: University of Turku.

doi　Suomalainen, Karita, and Mikael Varjo. 2020. "When Personal is Interpersonal: Organizing Interaction with Deictically Open Personal Constructions in Finnish Everyday Conversation." *Journal of Pragmatics* 168: 98–118.

Uusitupa, Milla. 2017. Rajakarjalaismurteiden avoimet persoonaviittaukset [Open person constructions in Border Karelian dialects]. Dissertations in Education, Humanities, and Theology 117. Joensuu: University of Eastern Finland.

doi　Varjo, Mikael. 2019. "It Takes All Kinds to Make a Zero: Employing Multiple Correspondence Analysis to Categorize an Open Personal Construction in Conversational Finnish." *Corpus Linguistics Research* 5, 55–87.

doi　Varjo, Mikael, and Karita Suomalainen. 2018. "From Zero to 'You' and Back: A Mixed Methods Study Comparing the Use of Two Open Personal Constructions in Finnish." *Nordic Journal of Linguistics* 41 (3): 333–366.

doi　Vatanen, Anna. 2018. "Resisting an Action in Conversation by Pointing out Epistemic Incongruence: *Mä tiedän* 'I know' Responses in Finnish." *Journal of Pragmatics* 123: 192–208.

doi　Williams, Lawrence, and Rémi van Compernolle. 2009. "*On* Versus *Tu* And *Vous*: Pronouns with Indefinite Reference in Synchronous Electronic French Discourse." *Language Sciences* 31: 409–427.

Zobel, Sarah. 2016. "A Pragmatic Analysis of German Impersonally Used First Person Singular 'Ich'." *Pragmatics* 26 (3): 379–416.

CHAPTER 4

The (non)referentiality of the word *raha* 'money' in Finnish conversation

Ritva Laury
University of Helsinki

This chapter concerns the use of the word *raha* 'money' in Finnish everyday conversation. The main findings are that *raha* is most often used non-referentially in singular form in predications where only the category of money is at issue. When the word is used to create referential mentions of some specific money with continuity of identity, a plural form is used. The study shows that the singular-plural distinction is a manipulable resource exploited by participants in conversation for interactional purposes to create stance and to accomplish actions.

Keywords: Finnish, divisible noun, number, specificity, stance, continuity of identity, emergence

1. Introduction

This chapter concerns the ways that participants in Finnish conversation rely on grammatical resources of the language in mentions of *raha* 'money' to make non-referential use of the word or to create referents in interaction. I will show that the noun is mostly used nonreferentially in singular form in predications where only the category of money is at issue, not any particular amount or set of money. In contrast, the plural form is used to create referential mentions of money with continuity of identity. The chapter shows that for the word *raha*, the singular-plural distinction is a manipulable resource which can be exploited for interactional purposes to accomplish actions and to create stance (Du Bois 2007; Englebretson 2007). Participants can be seen to position themselves and to create alignment with others by first evoking an imagined or generic context and then using a referential, plural form of *raha*, thereby indexing the stance object as an actual, particular situation or person, thus managing to defuse a potentially delicate situation through humor or to criticize another person covertly.

https://doi.org/10.1075/pbns.344.04lau

Grammar is viewed here not as a language-internal set of structural rules but rather as a flexible set of practices continually evolving and shifting, reflexively shaped by and shaping contexts as language is being used by real speakers in the course of their everyday lives. Thus the chapter explores the uses of *raha* with a focus on the jointly achieved, interactionally motivated emergence of what we might consider 'referentiality'.

The noun *raha* is a member of a class of nouns in Finnish where the grammatical distinction between singular and plural form is used to express the distinction between generic and particular mentions, and through that, (non)referentiality. I show that the distinction is also recruited for the creation of interactional contexts of particular kinds due to the indexical power of referentiality contrasts.

With respect to referentiality, the focus of this volume, I take the position that referents are not pre-existing entities out in the world which are linguistically evoked or brought to focus or to the awareness of the addressee. Non-referential mentions do not create referents at all but rather are involved in various kinds of predications; as suggested by Ono & Thompson (1994: 408), they resemble stative predicates, "encapsulating or specifying a situation or a referent". In contrast, referents are created through referential mentions and can then be rementioned, questioned, and otherwise manipulated and thus tracked through discourse.

After a brief discussion of the data and the methodology, the chapter starts out with a description of the diachronic development of the meaning of the word *raha* and of its grammatical features, and after that, its use in everyday Finnish conversation.

2.   Data and method

The core data for this chapter are 85 uses of *raha* from Arkisyn, a morphsyn-tactically coded database of 29.5 hours of Finnish everyday conversation among groups of friends and family members.[1] The database was created at the University of Turku and consists of conversations from the Conversation Analysis Archives of the University of Helsinki Department of Finnish, Finno-Ugrian and Scandinavian Studies and from the Archive of Finnish and Finno-Ugric Languages at the University of Turku. All the proper names in the data, including place names, are anonymized, and standard written permissions were obtained from all the participants in the conversations.

---

1. I thank Mikael Varjo for his help with the Arkisyn database and Marja-Liisa Helasvuo for providing access to the audiofiles and transcripts of the conversations collected in Arkisyn.

The uses of *raha* focused on here are examined in their larger conversational contexts using the methodology of Interactional Linguistics (IL), an approach according to which the primary function of grammar is to serve the needs of interaction. IL combines insights from the discourse-functional research tradition, which holds that grammatical forms of human languages are best examined in actual use by real speakers rather than based on invented examples, and from Conversation Analysis, which examines the organization of everyday interactions (Couper-Kuhlen & Selting 2018; Selting & Couper-Kuhlen 2001). Central to the way grammar is conceived of here are usage-based models of grammar (Laury & Ono 2019), especially the theory of Emergent Grammar (Hopper 1987; Hopper 2011), which claims that grammar originates as people use language in their ordinary interactions rather than existing *a priori* in the minds of speakers before they say anything. Grammar is seen here as not only shaped by but also shaping context.

3.   *Raha* in Finnish grammars

In Finnish reference grammars, the word *raha* is considered a 'divisible' noun, a class similar to but not identical with English mass nouns. Finnish divisible nouns, unlike English mass nouns, easily pluralize. When divisible nouns are pluralized, they are understood as referring to bounded, quantitatively definite units, while singular divisible nouns are usually in the partitive case and have referents that are unbounded, thus quantitatively indefinite (Siro 1943; Vilkuna 1992: 40–76; Hakulinen et al. 2004: § 1421–22).[2] For example, if I were to say that I cleared all the snow off the roof, using the divisible noun *lumi* 'snow', I could simply use the nominative plural form, *lumet* 'snow-PL', thus referring to a bounded entity. On the other hand, if I wanted to express that I cleared only some of the snow, I could use the singular partitive *lunta* 'snow-PAR'.[3] The distinction also interacts with verbal aspect (Siro 1957; Hakulinen et al. 2004: § 555). Consider the following two sentences.

(1)   Constructed example based on (2)
```
He joivat      kaakaota
3PL drink-PST-3PL cocoa.SG-PAR
They were drinking cocoa/they drank some cocoa
```

---

2. It should be noted that quantitative definiteness and indefiniteness is not to be equated with identifiability. It is quite possible to make a mention of something quantitatively indefinite using a form that is marked for identifiability with, say, a demonstrative.

3. I am simplifying the issue here for expository purposes. Case interacts with this issue so that by using the singular accusative form *lumen*, I would also be implying that I cleared all the snow.

(2)   Hakulinen et al. 2004 § 555, from a fiction corpus
```
He joivat        kaakaot
3PL drink-PST-3PL cocoa-PL.NOM
They drank cocoas/they each drank a cocoa/they drank the cocoa
```

In (1), with a singular object noun *kaakaota* in the partitive case, both the drinking and the amount of cocoa drunk are unbounded, or to use the terminology of Siro (1957), quantitatively indefinite: some nonspecific quantity of cocoa was drunk, and there is no implication that the drinking was completed; the action is viewed as being ongoing, or 'imperfective'. In contrast, in (2), the drinking is quantitatively definite, that is, bounded, unitized, and distributed: each drinker had their cocoa, and the drinking is viewed as completed, or 'perfective'. Consider also that in the Finnish equivalent of the demand *your money or your life*, the word for 'money' is in the plural, *rahat tai henki*, implying that you are to hand over all the money you have.

There is very little previous work on the word *raha*. Etymologically, the word is thought to be an early loan into Baltic Finnic from North Germanic **skrayō* 'dried animal skin, pelt' (Tunkelo 1915:98; see Häkkinen 2004 and references therein), represented by Old Norse and Icelandic *skrá* and Old Swedish *skrā* 'document made of animal skin, parchment'. Since animal skins, particularly squirrel skins, were used as mediums of exchange, the meaning of *raha* gradually developed its modern meaning of 'coin or note; medium of exchange, measure of economic value; particular sum of money' (NS 4:611; KTS). It is already found in this use in the earliest Finnish written texts from the 16th century (Tunkelo 1915:92). Over time, the concept of money has further become more abstract, developing from reference to actual physical coins to virtual existence online as purchase power (Nurminen 1998:235–236).

In contrast to work on the word *raha* and its uses, the distinction between divisible and indivisible nouns and the connection of this distinction to definiteness and aspect is an important, much researched topic. Standard references include Siro (1943) and Vilkuna (1992). A concise account can be found in Hakulinen et al. (2004 § 555).

A bit of background on Finnish noun morphology may be helpful to those readers who are not familiar with the language. Finnish nominals (both nouns and adjectives as well as numerals and pronouns) are inflected for number and case. Nominative, genitive and partitive are the grammatical cases; nouns do not have separate accusative forms but pronouns do. Nominative is unmarked. There are eleven additional, oblique cases, including three internal and three external local cases as well as abessive, essive, translative, comitative and instructive (see Table 1). Instructive and comitative only have plural forms and comitative is always accompanied with the possessive suffix, which is optional with other cases.

Table 1 shows all the case forms of *raha*. I have not given translations for the cases since it is very difficult or even impossible to provide accurate translations without exemplification. Some cases are much more productive and used much more than others; for some cases, there are adpositions that have approximately the same meaning as the case form; for example, the meaning of the abessive can also be carried by the preposition *ilman* 'without', and the meaning of the comitative is more commonly expressed with the postposition *kanssa* 'with'. The meaning of the instructive 'with; through the use of' is more commonly expressed with the adessive case, although there are fixed usages such as *käsin* 'by hand'. There are also possessive suffixes. These are compulsory with comitatives, and in my data, there were uses of the second person possessive suffix in the colloquial form of a word-final -*s*.

Table 1. Singular and plural forms of the noun *raha* in all Finnish cases

Case	Singular	Plural
NOM	raha	raha-t
GEN	raha-n	raho-j-en
PAR	raha-a	raho-j-a
INE	raha-ssa	raho-i-ssa
ELA	raha-sta	raho-i-sta
ILL	raha-an	raho-i-hin
ADE	raha-lla	raho-i-lla
ABL	raha-lta	raho-i-lta
ALL	raha-lle	raho-i-lle
ABE	raha-tta	raho-i-tta
ESS	raha-na	raho-i-na
TRA	raha-ksi	raho-i-ksi
COM + 2SGPX		raho-i-ne-si
INS		raho-i-n

In this study, I examine the use of *raha* as a singular and plural noun and consider how this grammatical distinction relates to referentiality and features connected with it, such as specificity and generality and continued identity of a particular referent over time, as opposed to the use of the noun for category mentions. I will argue that specificity and genericity, and ultimately, (non)referentiality are interactionally motivated and emerge through negotiation among participants in conversation.

4.   *Raha* in Finnish everyday conversation

In my Finnish conversational data, *raha* is most often used in the singular partitive form *rahaa*, not to create referents but rather to build predications involving
the category of money in a generic or irrealis context. When the word is used to
refer to some particular money, that is, particular sums or amounts or concrete
coins or bills, it is usually plural, often comes with a determiner, and can be subsequently tracked in discourse (cf. Ono & Thompson 1994). However, as we will
see, participants in conversation exploit the distinction for their own purposes, so
that plural, referential mentions are made even in generic contexts for particular
interactional goals, and singular forms are used for specific references, showing
that genericity, specificity, and, ultimately, referentiality are created, negotiated
and maintained in interaction. In what follows, in Section 4.1, I will first discuss
the nonreferential use of *raha* as a singular noun in predications involving the category of money. In Section 4.2, I will discuss referential uses of *raha*.

4.1   *Raha* in non-referential use

In my data, *raha* is most frequently used non-referentially, in the singular. In these
uses, it is most often in the partitive case. Singular, partitive mentions of *raha*
occur most commonly in irrealis contexts, in conditional and negated clauses. In
such mentions, no money is being referred to; most often its existence is explicitly
denied. Consider the following excerpt.

(3)   SG 123
      mut mul   ei   oo   rahaa
      but 1SG-ADE NEG.3SG be-CONNEG money.SG-PAR
      but I don't have money

In my data, the most common single expression containing a token of *raha* was
the type we see in Excerpt (3), where the speaker claims not to have money;[4]
such an expression appeared seven times in the data. Vilkuna, in her influential
treatment of referentiality in Finnish, has two examples containing the word *raha*
(1992:56–57). In both of the examples, the word is in singular partitive form, and
one of them is a negated interrogative:

---

4. Of course, the speaker is not claiming here, or in other examples of this type, that s/he is
entirely impecunious. The claim instead seems to be that the speaker lacks funds for some particular purpose, in this case, for going out with her friends. I thank Mikael Varjo for this observation.

(4) Vilkuna 1992:56
Miksei sinulla koskaan ole   rahaa?
why-NEG 2SG-ADE ever   be-CONNEG money.SG-PAR
Why don't you ever have money?

Vilkuna notes that in both examples she gives, the singular partitive *raha* is used non-referentially as well as non-specifically, not to refer to any particular sum or unit of money (1992:56, 57), but rather for predicating something about a referent, here a person. Here, as in (3) above, the speaker is using the word *raha* to build a predication which expresses or presupposes the non-existence of money.

In the next excerpt, three young women are having coffee and talking about haircuts. Susa has just explained that she has had two bad haircuts where she really did not feel comfortable about the result.

(5) SG151
11 Susa: *et ↑nyt mie niinku käsitän sen tai siis sillee et*
          so now I kind of understand it or I mean like
12   *vaik mie o ite monta kertaa kans sanonu sitä et*
          although I have said many times myself that
13   → *ei   viittis   nii hirveesti #kampaajaa   laittaa rahaa#,*
          NEG.3SG care.to-COND so terribly hair.dresser-ILL put-INF money.SG-PAR
          it's not worth it (lit. (one) would not care to) to spend a lot of money on
          a hairdresser
14 Jossu: *mm?*
15 Susa: *.hh mut se et jos sit laittaa vähä   rahaa*
   →   but DEM COMP if then put-3SG little money.SG-PAR
          but the thing is if (you) spend (only) a little money
16   *ja sit siit tukast tulee   hirvee*
          and then DEM-ELA hair-ELA come-3SG terrible
          and then (your) hair comes out terrible
17   *ni sekää ei   o   kiva.*
          so DEM-CLT NEG.3SG be-CONNEG nice
          then that's not nice either.
18 Jossu: *[°e:i°,*
          (no it is)n't
19 Susa: *[ja sit seki maksaa ku sitä yrittää laittaa sit niinku kuosiin*
          and then it also costs when (you) try to get it back in shape
20 Jossu: *mut se vituttaa   enite et   laittaa*
          But DEM cunt-CAUS.3SG most COMP put.3SG
          but it pisses (you) off the most that (you) spend
21   → *paljor rahaa   ja siit   [tulee sit huano.]*
          much   money.SG-PAR and DEM-ELA come.3SG then bad
          a lot of money and then it comes out bad
22 Anu: *[nii just ↑niin o.]*
                                   yeah exactly how (it) is
23 Susa: *[(--) no] se o iha totta,*
          well that's really true

Susa first claims that after two bad experiences with cheap haircuts (not shown), she now realizes 'it', and then goes on to explain in a complex extraposed construction what it is that she realizes: although she has herself claimed many times that *ei viittis niin hirveesti kampaajaa laittaa rahaa* 'it is not worth it to spend a lot of money on a hairdresser' (line 13), spending only a little money and getting a bad haircut is not a good idea either (lines 15–17). The first mention of money, *rahaa* in line 13, is housed in a 'zero person' construction (Hakulinen et al. 2004: §1347; Laitinen 1995; Helasvuo & Laitinen 2006; Suomalainen & Varjo 2020; Helasvuo and Suomalainen this volume), with no overt mention of who it is who *ei viittis* 'would not care to' do so. In zero person constructions, the verb is in the third person with no overt subject, and the implication is that whatever is being predicated applies generically not just to the speaker and the addressee, but anyone; the reference made by the zero person has been called 'open'. In this way, Susa is inviting her addressees to take her statement as one that would potentially also apply to them, or anyone. The mention of money is entirely nonspecific and non-referential; no particular money is being referred to. The word is part of the predication *laittaa rahaa* 'spend money'.

After a brief response from Jossu, Susa continues with another generic statement. In line 15, the predication *jos sit laittaa vähä rahaa* 'if (you) spend (only) a little money', and the contrasting and dialogically resonating (Du Bois 2014) but upgraded worst-case scenario *et laittaa paljor rahaa* 'that (you) spend a lot of money', provided by Jossu (lines 20–21) are both done with zero person constructions, that is, formatted as generic statements. Moreover, the mention in line 15 is in an irrealis context, in a conditional *jos* 'if' clause. Again, the mentions of *rahaa* 'money' are nonspecific, and they are also nonreferential. The nonreferentiality of these mentions of *raha* is reflected in the fact that although money is mentioned three times in this short excerpt, each mention is done as a full lexical mention – no referent which could be anaphorically referred to is created. Instead, all three mentions participate in the predication *laittaa rahaa* 'spend money', a rather fixed expression here being used generically. Although we could consider money to be topical here, in terms of spending only a little or a lot of it, it remains nonreferential.

The singular, partitive form of *raha* tends to appear with certain verbal expressions in my data. Especially common is *olla* 'be', as in Excerpt (3), which appears 20 times in the corpus, most commonly in the possessive construction (17 times), in the negative form (11 times) and often with a first person singular (non)possessor (6 times). Also common is *saada* 'get', which appears 14 times in the corpus, with only one negated use.

Two fixed expressions involving singular *raha* were found in the data, *ei oo rahasta kiinni* 'money is no object, lit. (it) does not depend on money' and *rahalla saa,* 'with money (one) gets (things)', perhaps best translatable as 'money talks', both clearly nonreferential uses.

(6) SG446
```
Niil ei     oo    sillee  rahasta    kiinni
3PL  NEG.3SG be.CONNEG like.that money.SG-ELA attached
for them, money is no object (lit. 'for them, it is like not about money')
```

(7) SG444
    No rahalla   saa
    PTC money.SG-ADE get.3SG
    well money talks (lit. 'well (one/you) can get (things) with money')

Notably, these were the only oblique case mentions of *raha* in my data.

We have seen that the most common way to talk about money in Finnish is in predications about not having money and about getting money. In these uses, the word *raha* is in the singular and in the partitive case and is used non-referentially. No referent that could be referred to anaphorically with a pronoun is created; the word merely participates in predications, and notably with particular types of expressions. This is in keeping with what Ono and Thompson found in their English data, where non-referential mentions did predicating work. Helasvuo (2001) had similar findings from her Finnish data.

The non-referential, singular partitive use of *raha* illustrated in this section is the most common type found in the data. Of the 85 tokens of the word *raha* in my data, most uses, 67/85 (79%), were singular. Singular mentions were most commonly in partitive form; of the 67 singular mentions, the large majority, 53, or 79%, were partitive and overwhelmingly non-referential.[5]

Singular mentions of *raha* were common as objects (24) and as complements of possessives (17). They were less commonly used as subjects; there were only ten subject mentions of singular *raha*. Although Finnish is predominantly SV(O) (Helasvuo 2001), most of the subject mentions of *raha* (7/10) were postverbal. As Helasvuo (2001:87) shows, lexical subjects are relatively rare in spoken Finnish, and are more likely to be associated with postverbal word order than pronominal subjects, especially if the referent is non-human (2001:79). Subjects in general tend to have referents that are not new to the discourse, or if they are new, they are somehow peripheral, of "trivial importance" (cf. Chafe 1994, 'light subject constraint'), This is the case with singular subject mentions of *raha*. Most of the postverbal subject mentions of *raha* were non-referential. Postverbal complements of existential and possessive constructions have sometimes also been classified as subjects in Finnish grammars, but as Huumo and Helasvuo (2015) point out, they would be atypical subjects: they are usually new to the discourse and are not rementioned; they also do not trigger verbal agreement. For these reasons, Huumo and Helasvuo term them e-NPs. However, the e-NPs in Huumo and

---

5. One possible exception to this was found in the data. This was a mention of a particular sum of money someone had in his pocket, *sillähä oli kuus ja puolsataa rahaa siellä taskussa* 'he did have six hundred fifty (worth of) money in his pocket'. Quantifiers such as numerals require a noun they modify to be in the singular partitive form. In these mentions, only roughly translatable into English, the quantified noun functions in a way similar to classifiers in languages that have such a category. Most of the quantified uses were non-referential.

Helasvuo's were typically referential. In contrast, e-NP uses of *raha*, as shown, were typically non-referential, as were the postverbal subject mentions of *raha*.

The following is an example of a typical subject mention of *raha*. It is a postverbal, non-referential, predicating use.

(8)   SG 440

> *(0.4) siel   pyörii   niiv vähär **rahaa**,*
> DEM.LOC-ADE circulate-3SG so   little money-SG-PAR
> so little money is going around there

The speaker is discussing the unlikely possibility of getting a position working as a youth counselor in his congregation, which might qualify as national service for him as a conscientious objector to replace military service. Here he is expressing doubts about this working out since there is very little money available. The mention of money is postverbal and made in the partitive singular. It is a non-referential mention: it does not refer to any particular money or create a trackable referent but rather it is involved in a predication concerning the lack of money in general.

Let us now consider *raha* in referential use.

4.2   Referential uses of *raha*

In contrast to nonreferential uses of *raha*, which are done in the singular, are non-specific, and mostly occur in generic or irrealis contexts, referential uses of *raha* are mostly done in the plural, refer to particular amounts or sets of money, and become manipulable discourse referents which can be, and often are, subsequently mentioned and in such uses, can be referred to with a pronoun.

Although plural mentions of *raha* were much less frequent in the data than singular uses, we might note that they seemed slightly more likely to occur as subjects than the singular uses; out of the 18 plural, referential uses of *raha*, three were in subject position, and all were preverbal and referential; recall that most of the subject mentions of singular *raha* were postverbal and non-referential (see Example (8) above), not referring to any particular amounts or sets of money. Unlike the singular, non-referential mentions, plural mentions of *raha* were unlikely to be complements of possessives; there was only one such use of plural *raha*, while 17/67, almost one fourth of the singular, non-referential mentions of *raha* were complements of possessives.

In Finnish, the most common object case is partitive, although objects can also be nominative. Transitive clauses with partitive objects are low in transitivity; negated clauses require objects to be partitive. While object uses of singular *raha* were overwhelmingly partitive, with only one nominative use, only three of the ten object uses of plural *raha* were partitive ((9a) below is an example). This pattern of use is different from overall tendencies of case marking of singular vs.

plural objects. Plural objects in the Arkisyn database of conversational Finnish are more likely to be partitive than singular ones.[6] The tendency of plural mentions of *raha* to occur in subject position, and their low likelihood to occur in in low transitivity constructions and as complements of possessives, may be connected to their referentiality. The fact that singular, nonreferential mentions of *raha* occur in low transitivity clauses is to be expected given what we know about transitivity in discourse and conversation. Objects in low transitivity clauses tend to be non-individuated and non-referential (Hopper & Thompson 1980; Thompson & Hopper 2001). In our data, the singular mentions of *raha* also are associated with frequently occurring V-O compounds involving low-content verbs such as *olla* 'to be', and as predicate nominals, also typical for low transitivity contexts. The opposite is true of plural mentions of *raha*. The association of low transitivity with irrealis and high transitivity with realis is also consistent with the use of *raha* which we find in our data.

Plural mentions of *raha* often occurred in tellings of different kinds. Consider the next excerpt, which comes from a conversation between a hairdresser (H) and her client (C). They have been discussing the slippery winter weather, and the hairdresser has just reported having fallen down while walking outdoors. The client starts to tell about a recent occasion when she also fell on an icy road.

```
(9a)  SG108
      01C:  kyl mäki    kaaduin    ku: tota:
            I fell down too when um
      02    mä  viel  ajattelin    just sillon ku .hh
            I was even thinking right then when
      03    mä menin     sinne poliisiasemalle
            1SG go-PST-1SG DEM.LOC police-station-ALL
            I was going to the police station
      04  → Th(h)ak(h)een niitä    rahoja       niin,
            fetch-INF-ILL DEM.PL-PAR money-PL-PAR SO
            to fetch that money so,
```

The client starts what is a second story about falling down on ice by first providing a temporal setting: the incident happened when she was on her way to the police station to fetch *niitä rahoja* 'that money' (line 4). This mention is made in the plural,[7] and the mention, like the mention of the police station, is marked with the demonstrative *niitä*, a plural form of *se*, which marks referents identifiable to the addressee (Laury 1997). The speaker is assuming that the hairdresser is familiar with both the police station and the money she is going to get there. The mention

---

6. I thank Marja-Liisa Helasvuo for this information.

7. This mention is partitive, due to the action of going to get the money being viewed as incomplete, still in process, or imperfective. See also the use in Example (9b); the hairdresser matches the form of her mention to the form the client used.

of money is referential here: the client is talking about some particular money, which she moreover expects the hairdresser to be able to identify.

However, this does not appear to be the case. After the client is done with telling about falling down on a slippery road (see (8a), which initiates the story), the hairdresser returns to the topic of the money.

(9b) SG 108
```
16 H: → hh äh mitä [(-)  (.)   ] rahoja      sä hait.
         PTC what-PAR          money-PL-PAR 2SG fetch-PST-2SG
         um what money were you fetching.
   17 C:        [kastu vaa]
                just got wet
   18      no mä hain sillon ku (se) ryöstö oli
           well I fetched (it) when the robbery happened
   19      niin tota .hhh vaik se saatii se kundi kiinni nii ne
           so like although he was that guy was caught so they
   20 →    =sillähä   oli   kuus ja puolsataa       rahaa
           DEM-ADE-CLT be-PST six  and half-hundred-PAR money.SG-PAR
           he did have six hundred fifty (euros)
   21      siellä     taskussa?
           DEM.LOC.ADE pocket-INE
           there in (his) pocket
```

Although the client had indexed the money as identifiable, in slight overlap with the last part of the client's story (line 17), the hairdresser asks what money the client was fetching (line 16). This shows that the identifiability of the money is relevant, and thus that the money is being treated as referential. The way the hairdresser refers to it, in the plural, and asks about its identity, shows that she expects the money mentioned earlier to have continuity of identity, and that the client has referred to some particular money.

The client responds by explaining that she went to get the money when there was a robbery, and that when *se kundi* 'that guy' was captured he had money in his pocket (lines 18–20). Note that the mention of money in line 20, although referential, is done in the singular and in the partitive case, required here by the numeral modifier; the numeral is the head of the phrase. In such uses, *rahaa* is used in a way similar to classifiers in languages that have them. That is, after numerals, the counted entities are always in the singular and partitive, whether they be divisible nouns or non-divisible, referential or non-referential.

After this, the client tells about the robbery at her place of employment. After the story is brought to an end, the hairdresser brings up the matter of the money again.

(9c)
```
29 H: → ja sä sait      rahas      p[ois,
        and 2SG get-PST-2SG money-2SGPX away
        and you got your money back,
   30 C: →                  [↑mä: sain     ne    pois kyllä ihan heti
                            1SG  get-PST-1SG DEM.PL away PTC   quite right.away
                            I did get it (lit.them) back right away
```

The hairdresser provides a candidate understanding in line 29, seeking confirmation that the client got her money back. Here the nominative form of the word *raha* is followed by the second person possessive suffix: the distinction between singular and plural is neutralized in this form. However, in her response (line 30), the client uses the plural pronoun *ne* 'them' to refer to the money anaphorically. We can see that here, the mentions of the money in lines 29 and 30 are referential and the referent has continuity of identity. Some particular money, that which was stolen from the client, is being referred to, and the form used is plural.

4.3   Shifting uses of *raha* in conversation

In conversations about money, the uses of singular and plural forms reflect the shifting types of meaning. Speakers use different forms depending on how the mention is to be understood, whether some specific, referential money is being referred to, or whether money is being talked about in general, nonspecifically and nonreferentially.

Consider the following excerpt from a telephone conversation between a mother and a daughter. The daughter, Heta, has announced that she is intending to take a short trip to Stockholm on a popular overnight cruise. The mother, Irja, is concerned about her use of money.

```
(10a)   SG 124
    01   Irja: >joo. .h sittek< ku sä lähet sinne laival[le]
               yeah. .h then when you leave to go on the boat
    02   Heta:                                        [mm]::?
    03        (.)
    04 → Irja: niin <muista       pitää   rahoistas      huoli?>
               PTC   remember.IMP2SG hold-INF money-PL-ELA-2SGPX care
               so remember to take (good) care of your money
```

In line 4, Irja issues a warning: she urges Heta to be careful with her money when she gets on the boat. Here, the mention of money is specific. Through the use of the plural form and the possessive suffix, Irja indicates that she is referring to the particular money of Heta's that she is going to take with her on the trip. As is common in my data, the entirety of some particular, possessed money is mentioned in the plural and is referential. Note that this use is creative and presupposing: since Heta has not even left on her trip, the particular money she will take on the trip does not exist at the point of speaking. Rather, Irja's mentioning it creates it as a referent. Next, Irja provides a motivation for the warning by telling a cautionary tale about the theft of money on a cruise boat that she has heard from an acquaintance that has recently stopped by at the family home.

(10b)   SG 124

```
10 Irja: se oli kahvilla, >ja sano et< sen vaimo oli,
         he came over for coffee and said that his wife was
11        .hh vaimo oli siellä Sinderellalla?
          wife was on the Cinderella
12 Heta: nii?
         so?
13 Irja: ja tota noin sielt    oli (.) ainakin kolmeky-
         and PTC  PTC  DEM.LOC-ABL be-PST  at.least thirt-
         and um there at least thirt-
14        kolmeltkymmenelt naiselta varastettu
          thirty-ABL       woman-ABL steal-PASS-PPLE
          thirty women had (money) stolen
15 →     (0.8).hh rahaa        käsilaukusta
                  money.SG-PAR purse-ELA
                  money from the purse
16        kun ne oli    tanssinu.
          when 3PL be-PST dance- PPPLE
          while they had been dancing
```

Irja is talking here (line 15) about some particular money that had a physical existence in a realis context. Nevertheless, the mention is singular and partitive, associated with nonreferential mentions. Semantically, a plural form, *rahat*, would
imply that all the women's money was stolen. Although Irja is thus not talking
about money in general, what is being mentioned here is a theft of some quantitatively indefinite, non-unitized, non-individuated amount of money from the
purse while the women were dancing. Prosodically, the mention of the money
seems to form a unit with the mention of the purse, as one might expect since the
two words form one syntactic unit.[8] In other words, what was stolen was *rahaa
käsilaukusta* '(some) money from the purse' of thirty women. Note that the mention of the women's purses is done in the singular, although there were surely multiple purses just as there were multiple women. Therefore, it seems that although
the mention is realis, no particular referent is created, only a predication, and the
singular partitive form is thus motivated both semantically and pragmatically.

However, when Heta's money is discussed, the pattern is different. Irja coun-
sels Heta not to take along her bank card, and she especially objects to Heta's idea
of leaving her bank card in her cabin.

(10c)   27 Irja: (.) suosittelisin ettet pankkikorttia ainakaan
                 I would recommend you at least not your ATM card
         28   otam [mukaan.]
                 take along.
         29 Heta: [.hh] >no< täytyy varmaa hhh heittää (se)
                    well ok (one/I) should probably leave
         30   vaikk' se sitte hyttiin tai jo[tain.   ]
                 it in the cabin then or something

---

8. As pointed out by one of the anonymous reviewers.

```
31 Irja:                          [E:T.  NO]
                                  NEG-2SG PTC
                                  no you don't.

32  SINNE    EI NYT AINA[KAAN.]
    DEM.LOC.ILL NEG PTC at.least
    definitely not there.
33 Heta:                    [hmfhh,] .f he he he
34 Irja: sieltä ne sev varas[taa. ]
         they will steal it from there.
35 Heta:                       [Jaha.]
                                I see.
36 Irja: nii.
         yeah.
37 Heta: no ehä   mä nyt osaa (.)    arvioida paljon
         PTC NEG-CLT 1SG now be.able-CONNEG estimate much
         well I can't estimate how much
38 →  mul   menee fyrkkaa    mihinki   [sie]llä.
      1SG-ADE go-3SG money.SG-PAR any-ILL-CLT DEM.LOC.ADE
      money I will (need to) spend for whatever there.
39 Irja:                              [nii.]
                                       PTC
                                       yeah.
40  tai pistääs sitte .h taskuun  tajo[honkin.]
    or  put-INF then    pocke-ILL or.some-ILL-CLT
    or put (it) in your pocket or somewhere then.
41 Heta:                             [nii.  ] .h
                                      PTC
                                      yeah
42 →  täytyy tehä  sellanen vanha
      must  do.INF DEM-ADJ  old
      (one/you/I) will have to do that kind of old
43 →  rahat   @tissiliivissä temppu@
      money-PL bra-INE       trick
      the money in the bra trick
44  [Etiedät] sä niin[ku kaikisE] EleffoissaE[.h] aina
    you know like in all the movies all the time
45 Irja: [nii joo.]      [nii joo.]        [j]oo.=
         ok  yeah        ok  yeah.         yeah.
46 Heta: [et sitte ni]
         so that then
47 Irja: =[ainaki sit ] jos farkut laitat jalkaas ni .hh
         at least if you put on jeans so
48 →  sinnehä  voi   tunkee  rahat   tas[kuu.]
      DEM-ILL-CLT can.3SG stuff-INF money-PL pocket-ILL
      there (you/one) can stuff money in the pocket
49 Heta:                              [nii.]
                                       yeah.
```

In response to Irja's advice not to take along a bank card, Heta suggests she could leave it in her cabin (29–30). Irja objects vociferously, in a loud voice (lines 31–32). Heta receives Irja's objection to leaving her bank card in her cabin with laughter, but she responds to Irja's suggestion that it would be stolen from there (line 34) with the news receipt *aha* (Koivisto 2016), to which Irja responds with the particle *nii*, which confirms her earlier claim and may also implicate epistemic primacy

(Sorjonen 2001); that is, Irja may be claiming that she is more knowledgeable than Heta about bank cards in cruise boat cabins. However, Heta still returns to the issue of the means of payment she would take along, complaining that she does not know how much money she would be spending, implying that a card would be more convenient than cash (lines 37–38). She uses here a singular form of the colloquial word for money, *fyrkkaa* 'dough'. This lexeme seems to function the same way as its standard language synonym, *raha*: the use is partitive, quantitatively indefinite, non-specific, non-individuated and nonreferential, a predicating use in a negated irrealis context, and does not create a referent.

In her next turn (line 39), Irja seems to agree with a *nii* particle, but then suggests that Heta could put something in her pocket (line 40). This utterance begins with *tai* 'or', but it is not at all clear what Irja is proposing this as an alternative to. Certainly this advice does not follow from Heta's previous complaint turn. Moreover, the object of *pistää* 'put' is not expressed. One way to understand this is that Irja is ignoring Heta's just preceding turn by proposing her suggestion as an alternative, perhaps to placement in the cabin, and not specifying what it is that could be put in the pocket, or *johonkin* 'somewhere'. In her next turn, Heta agrees with *nii* (line 41), and going along with Irja's suggestion of putting a zero-mentioned referent 'somewhere', she suggests doing 'the old trick' of putting her money in the bra (lines 42–43). Here she is presumably talking about cash money, since it does not seem very likely that one would insert a bank card in a bra, especially in an old movie. Heta displays this proposed placement of money as a joke, given her laughter voice (line 44) just after. The mention of money is housed in the construction *sellanen vanha rahat tissiliivissä temppu* 'like that old money in the bra trick', and thus is not referring to any particular money, but the reference to money is still done with the plural form *rahat*. I suggest that in this utterance, Heta is going along with her mother's suggestion, taking a humorous stance already hearable in her laughter in line 33, and playfully setting up a scene (cf. Helasvuo & Suomalainen, this volume, on *Deixis am Phantasma*) where she is the one putting her money in her brassiere, just like is done in the movies. In other words, she is using the plural form associated with referentiality as a means of placing herself and her money as a proxy on the scene she creates, using the old trick, and at the same time, aligning here with her mother. By taking a humorous stance, she manages to defuse a potentially delicate situation, since she has been, albeit gently, rejecting her mother's advice. Notice also that this is the only use of the plural form of money Heta makes (the other mention she made was the singular, non-referential use of *fyrkkaa* 'dough; money'), while Irja consistently treats the money as referential.

Irja receives this joke with two *nii joo* combinations, showing agreement and recognition, ending with *joo*, expressing understanding and perhaps marking the preceding unproblematic but backgrounded (Sorjonen 2001). Thus the two participants have achieved alignment. Irja then adds another piece of advice, returning to the pocket placement theme (lines 47–48). Again in a future, irrealis context, *raha* is here in the plural form, creating the impression that while the suggestion is done with a zero person construction and presented as a potential situation through the modal *voi* 'can, may' (line 48), Irja is speaking about Heta's actual money, which she could put in her actual pocket. This is made obvious in the second person reference in the *jos* 'if' clause (l. 47) setting up the frame of the suggestion. The zero person is handy in this context, as Irja is giving advice, only suggesting a way to deal with the situation, but still speaking about a particular referent by using a plural form to make a referential mention, showing that she is speaking about Heta's money. Note that this is an object use of plural *raha* in the nominative case,[9] used in high transitivity contexts and implying total affect-edness of the individuated, referential object, and for divisible nouns, bounded-ness; the accusative creates a meaning where Heta is to put all her actual money in her jeans pocket. In that way, Irja's turn continues the theme of placement of money somewhere in one's clothing, here in Heta's jeans, if she will be wearing jeans, again using the plural form to refer to her actual money in an otherwise irrealis context in a generic zero person construction.

We can see that the grammatical distinction between singular and plural can be put to use in creative ways, so that even in generic and irrealis contexts, such as advice and suggestions, the plural form of money can be used to create certain kinds of effects and scenes of certain kinds. In this way, Irja and even Heta in her joke can index that the hypothetical, imaginary money being discussed is actually Heta's money, while the actual money stolen from the women on the cruise boat is semantically unbounded, indefinite, and merely participating in a predication non-referentially (cf. Example (10b)). In this way, they also create agreement: Irja is concerned about the safety of Heta's money, Heta uses a humorous stance to defuse the situation, and they arrive at a shared understanding of a jeans pocket as a safe place for Heta's actual money.

In the next excerpt, several friends are discussing a common acquaintance who is planning to purchase a house in the country in order to start farming. Speaker Salla (S in the transcript) knows the acquaintance, Nipa, better than the others and is aware of his circumstances. She is the main speaker in this segment.

---

9. Finnish objects are nominative in the plural, and genitive in the singular in high transitivity clauses. Only personal pronouns retain separate accusative forms, as noted.

(11a)   SG123

```
01 J: → miten sil   Nipal   on      rahaa      ostaat talo.
         how   DEM-ADE NAME-ADE have.3SG money.SG-PAR buy-INF house
         how come that Nipa has enough money to buy a house.
         (1.2)
02       voittik se lotos.
         did he win (it) in Lotto.
03 S:    ei kun,(0.6)ku se on niinku kauheen rikkaasta perheestä
         no,(0.6) because he's like from a really wealthy family
         [...]
07       mut ei ne oo [£kumpikaa
         but neither one has
08       k(h)oskaan opisk(h)ellu m(h)itäänf]?
         ever studied anything?
09 P:           [ hah hahh ha ha hah hah ha hah]
10 J:           [he he heh heh heh]
11 S: → ne    on     ryypänny  kaikki rahat,
         DEM.PL be.3SG drink-PPLE all    money-PL
         they have drunk all the money,
12       ja [kaikkee niinku oikeesti tosi tyhmää] tehny,
         and done all kinds of really stupid things,
13 J:    [heh    he    heh   he    heh   he]
14 P:    [hah   hah   hah    ha    ha    ha]
15 S:    mistä (.) käy sääliks sen vanhempia sillee et et,
         which really makes (you) feel bad for his parents like
16       niin[ku miten ne ↑SUree] sitä, £älkää N(h)Aurakof,
         like they are really sad about it, don't laugh,
         [...]
23       =mut kuitenki: #nn# nyt Nipa haluu myydä ne
         but anyway: now Nipa wants to sell those
24       .hhhhh osakkeet ja sen isä on luvannu ostaa ne
         stocks and his father has promised to buy them
25       ja sit siit  sais,
         and then DEM-ELA get-COND.3SG
         and then from that (one/he)'d get
26 → (0.4) niin kauheestir rahaa      et se vois
              so   terribly  money.SG-PAR COMP DEM can-COND
              such a huge lot of money that he could
27       ostaa  talom    maalta    ja mennäs sinne.
         buy-INF house-ACC country-ELA and go-INF DEM.LOC-LAT
         buy a house in the country and go there.
```

Speaker Jaakko (J) asks (line 1) how Nipa can afford to buy a house. Here the mention of *raha* is housed in the construction *rahaa ostaa talo* '(enough) money to buy a house', in an interrogative clause where no particular money is being mentioned, but rather the condition of having sufficient money to buy a house is being questioned.

After Jaakko's guess about Nipa having won a lottery, Salla then explains that Nipa comes from a wealthy family and he and his brother have inherited stocks to enable them to go to school and to study (not shown). She then launches into a background explanation illustrating the brothers' character and lifestyle: although the money Nipa and his brother inherited was meant to be spent on their education, they have not studied anything (lines 7–8) but rather spent all their money on drinking and have done other *oikeesti tosi tyhmää* 'really quite stupid (things)'. This causes some hilarity. Yet although Salla's mention of the brothers' not having studied anything is done through laughter, and her telling that the brothers drank all the money is also met with laughter, she nonetheless then expresses that she feels sorry for Nipa's parents and asks the others not to laugh (line 16), in spite of her own smile voice in this utterance. After discussing her many telephone conversations with Nipa's mother (not shown), Salla then explains that Nipa plans to sell the stocks to his father, and that the sale would yield enough to buy a house (23–27).

Contrast the mentions of *raha* in lines 11 and 26. In line 11, the mention is plural, specific and referential in an indicative, past tense clause: Nipa and his brother have drunk *kaikki rahat* 'all the money', the entirety of the already mentioned inherited money. Although Nipa still clearly has more financial resources left in the form of stocks, enough to buy a house, this mention is designed to express the brothers' proclivity and is intended to mean something like, 'all the money they could get their hands on', all the money available.[10] On the other hand, selling the stocks would yield *niin kauheesti rahaa* 'such a lot of money' (line 26) that Nipa could purchase a house. This mention of money is nonspecific and non-referential, done in a conditional clause that is moreover in a zero person construction, with a third person verb *sais* 'would get' with no overt subject (line 25), and is also irrealis, as it projects into the future.

The participants then spend some time speculating about Nipa's plans and the possibility of his renting out part of the house he would buy (not shown). Salla then expresses her doubts about Nipa's ability to manage the project he is planning.

(11b) SG 123
```
     01 S: se on   kyl kauheen ahdistavaa ajat- puhua sillee
           it's actually really distressing to thi- talk like that
     02   ku, .hh mul   on    niin suuret  epäilykset sitä  kohtaan,
          because 1SG-ADE be-3SG so    large-PL doubt-PL   DEM-PAR toward
          because I have such great doubts about it,
     03   et, niinkuh, jos ei      ihminen tiiä mitään
          COMP PTC    if  NEG.3SG person  know any-PAR
          so, like, if a person does not know anything
     04 → maanviljelyksestä eikä      rahojen     käytöstä?
          agriculture-ELA    NEG.3SG-CLT money-PL-GEN use-ELA
          about agriculture nor the use of money?
     05   eikä      talojen     kunnostuksesta?
          NEG.3SG-CLT house-PL-GEN repair-ELA
          nor repairing houses?
```

---

10. This is another example of the fluidity of the concept 'money'. Consider the fact mentioned earlier in fn 4 that 'not having money' is a relative statement.

```
06   .h eikä      mistään ni, #ee#,
       NEG.3SG-CLT any-ELA SO
       nor anything so,
07 J: £(h)ei m(h)istään£,
       NEG-3SG any-ELA
       not about anything,
08 S: se on      tosi epä- (.) niinku,
       DEM be-3SG true un-      like
       it's truly un- like,
09 P: mm
10 J: mm
11 S: epäonneen   tuomittu hanke
       un-luck-ILL doom-PPLE project
       a project doomed to fail
```

Salla states that she finds it distressing to talk like this, because she has great doubts *sitä kohtaan* 'about it' (lines 1–2). She does not make it explicit what she has great doubts about; the demonstrative she uses, *sitä*, could potentially refer to either Nipa or his plans. She then makes a statement (lines 3–6) about a certain kind of situation, housed in a conditional *jos* 'if' clause concerning a generic *ihminen* 'person'. This form is useful in this context. As is well known, in many languages, the word meaning 'person' or 'man' has developed into an impersonal or generic expression, such as *man* expressions in Germanic, the French *on* from Latin *homo*, as well as the Portuguese *uma/a pessoa* 'person' which may be grammaticizing in a similar direction, but at this point can refer generically but also specifically to a person, even to the speaker herself (Posio 2021). This way, Salla is able to speak generically, although she chooses a term that can also apply to Nipa, whose plans have just been discussed.

Salla's *jos* clause is made up of a four-part list (Jefferson 1990; Selting 2007) of things that the non-specific *ihminen* 'person' would not know anything about, ending with *eikä mistään* 'and nothing else', functioning here as a 'general extender' (Overstreet 2014). The second item in the list is *rahojen käytöstä* 'about the use of money' (line 4). Somewhat incongruously, given the irrealis context in a conditional clause, the mention of money here is in the plural, which, as we have seen, is ordinarily associated with referentiality. My suggestion is that this form is a contextualization cue: the addressees are to understand this as suggesting that the mention of money here is referential and particular, and intended to convey that it is Nipa who does not understand anything about the use of (his) money, as well as agriculture or repairing houses, or in fact anything else. This may be confirmed by Jaakko's echoing of Salla's general extender (line 6) *eikä mistään* 'nor about anything' as *ei mistään* 'not about anything' (line 7), indicating that he well understands that Salla's description applies to Nipa, who, in Jaakko's estimation, does not know anything. The plural form of money is useful here since the context is delicate. Thus, although there has been plenty of discussion already about Nipa's handling of money and lack of education, here

Salla manages to speak generically, in irrealis, about a situation where a person is not knowledgeable about a series of things. Her critical stance is thus indexed through the plural, referential form referring to money, which also in this case makes clear the stance object, Nipa, whose lack of experience with money is being discussed in a covert way.

This protasis, the 'if' clause containing the four-part list, is then followed by an apodosis, a consequent clause projected by *ni* 'so' at the end of line 6, where Salla again, in lines 8 and 11, using an anaphoric form *se* 'it', predicates that it is a project doomed to fail. Since the only project discussed in the preceding sequence has been Nipa's planned purchase of a house in the country, here Salla overtly expresses that she has doubts about it. The more delicate issues of Nipa's knowledge about money, farming and home repair are instead addressed less directly, but still Salla's meaning is made clear through the referential use of the word *raha*, which is consistent with and helps create the stance she is taking.

In other words, here the use of an irrealis clausal format and the use of the potentially generic form, *ihminen* 'person' allow the speaker to accomplish in a covert way the somewhat delicate action of criticizing a mutual acquaintance as someone lacking the skills to manage a farm, without specifically attributing such shortcomings to him. Here the form usually associated with particular mentions, the plural form *rahojen*, is used as a resource to create a critical stance, the implication that Salla is in fact attributing the lack of these abilities to a particular person whose use of money has just been discussed. The aligning responses of the other participants confirm these allusions (lines 9–11).

In this section we have seen that although the singular form of *raha* is ordinarily used to create predications in non-referential contexts, and the plural form is used to create referents, these forms are available to speakers to make creative use of the grammatical distinction. Thus even mentions of actual money in realis contexts can be made in the singular, and predications in irrealis contexts can be made in the plural, in order to create particular effects and to express stances.

5. Conclusions

An examination of the use of the word *raha* in everyday conversations has shown that the singular form is most often used nonreferentially for making predications in which no particular money is being referred to and no referent is created. In contrast, plural mentions are most often used to create referents with continued identity that can be questioned and referred to anaphorically with a pronoun. However, this distinction can be put to use by speakers in more creative ways, for example as shown here, to place themselves in an imaginary scene, taking a humorous stance, and to thereby align themselves with another speaker in an advice-giving sequence, and taking a critical stance, covertly attributing negative features to someone without direct reference to the person in question. This shows that in the case of *raha*, the number distinction is a manipulable resource which can be exploited for interactional purposes. Thus referentiality is shown to be a jointly achieved, interactionally motivated, emergent feature which participants use to form actions and stances in conversation.

Acknowledgements

I am grateful of the comments I received on the early versions of this study from the participants at the 2018 Referentiality workshop at the University of Alberta, Edmonton, at the Coffee seminar at the University of Turku the same year, and at the Non-referentiality panel organized at the International Pragmatics Conference in Hong Kong in 2019. I would especially like to thank my coeditor, Mike Ewing, as well as Marja-Liisa Helasvuo and Tsuyoshi Ono, and the Benjamins anonymous referees, for their helpful comments and suggestions on earlier versions of this article. All remaining shortcomings are of course my responsibility.

References

Chafe, Wallace. 1994. *Discourse, Consciousness, and Time: The Flow and Displacement of Conscious Experience in Speaking and Writing*. Chicago: University of Chicago Press.

Couper-Kuhlen, Elizabeth, and Margret Selting. 2018. *Interactional Linguistics: Studying Language in Social Interaction*. Cambridge: Cambridge University Press.

Du Bois, John W. 2007. "The Stance Triangle." In *Stancetaking in Discourse: Subjectivity, evaluation, interaction*, ed. by Robert Englebretson, 140–182. Amsterdam: Benjamins.

Du Bois, John W. 2014. "Towards a Dialogic Syntax." *Cognitive Linguistics* 25 (3): 359–410.

Englebretson, Robert. 2007. "Stancetaking in Discourse. Introduction." In *Stancetaking in Discourse: Subjectivity, Evaluation, Interaction*, ed. by Robert Englebretson, 1–25. Amsterdam: Benjamins.

Häkkinen, Kaisa. 2004. *Nykysuomen etymologinen sanakirja* [*The etymological dictionary of modern Finnish*]. Juva: WSOY, electronic version retrieved 11/15/21 at https://www.sanakirja.fi/fin_etymology/finnish-finnish/raha

Hakulinen, Auli, Maria Vilkuna, Riitta Korhonen, Vesa Koivisto, Tarja Riitta Heinonen, and Irja Alho. 2004. *Iso suomen kielioppi* [*The comprehensive grammar of Finnish*]. Helsinki: Suomalaisen Kirjallisuuden Seura.

Helasvuo, Marja-Liisa. 2001. *Syntax in the Making: The Emergence of Syntactic Units in Finnish Conversational Discourse*. Studies in Discourse and Grammar 9. Amsterdam: John Benjamins.

doi Helasvuo, Marja-Liisa, and Lea Laitinen. 2006. "Person in Finnish: Paradigmatic and Syntagmatic Relations in Interaction." In *Grammar from the Human Perspective: Case, Space and Person in Finnish*, ed. by Marja-Liisa Helasvuo, and Lyle Campbell, CILT 277, 173–208. Amsterdam: John Benjamins.

doi Hopper, Paul J. 1987. "Emergent Grammar." *Berkeley Linguistic Society* 13: 139–157.

doi Hopper, Paul J. 2011. "Emergent Grammar and Temporality in Interactional Linguistics." In *Constructions: Emerging and Emergent*, ed. by Peter Auer and Stefan Pfänder, 22–44. Berlin: De Gruyter.

doi Hopper, Paul J., and Sandra A. Thompson. 1980. "Transitivity in Grammar and Discourse." *Language* 56: 251–99.

Jefferson, Gail. 1990. "List Construction as a Task and a Resource." In *Interaction Competence*, ed. by George Psathas, 63–92. Lanham, MD: University Press of America.

Huumo, Tuomas, and Marja-Liisa Helasvuo. 2015. "On the subject of subject in Finnish." in *Subjects in Constructions - Canonical and Non-Canonical*, ed. by Marja-Liisa Helasvuo, and Tuomas Huumo, 15–42. Amsterdam: John Benjamins.

Koivisto, Aino. 2016. "Receipting Information as Newsworthy vs. Responding to Redirection: Finnish News Receipts *aijaa* and *ahaa*." *Journal of Pragmatics* 104: 163–179.

KTS. *Kielitoimiston sanakirja*. [Dictionary of Modern Finnish] 2021. Helsinki: Kotimaisten kielten keskus. URN:NBN:fi:kotus-201433. https://www.kielitoimistonsanakirja.fi/#/raha ?searchMode=all, retrieved November 19, 2021.

Laitinen, Lea. 1995. "Nollapersoona [Zero Person]." *Virittäjä* 99 (3): 337–358.

doi Laury, Ritva. 1997. *Demonstratives in Interaction: The Emergence of a Definite Article in Finnish*. Amsterdam: John Benjamins.

doi Laury, Ritva, and Tsuyoshi Ono. 2019. "Usage-Based Grammar." In *Current Approaches to Syntax: A Comparative Handbook*, ed. by András Kertész, Edith Moravcsik, and Csilla Rákosi, 241–262. Berlin: Walter De Gruyter.

Nurminen, Tuula. 1998. "Sähköisen rahan kuvaus sanomalehdissä." [Description of electronic money in newspapers]." In *Puolin ja toisin* [*On both sides*], AFinLA Yearbook 1998, ed. by Minna-Riitta Luukka, Sigrid Salla, and Hannele Dufva, 235–246. Jyväskylä: Finnish Linguistics Society.

NS = *Nykysuomen sanakirja*. [The dictionary of Modern Finnish], v. 4, ed. O–R. 1956. Porvoo/Helsinki: WSOY. https://www.kotus.fi/nykysuomensanakirja

doi Ono, Tsuyoshi and Sandra A. Thompson. 1994. "Unattached NPs in English Conversation." *Proceedings of the 20th Annual Meeting of the Berkeley Linguistic Society*, 402–419.

Overstreet, Maryann. 2014. "The Role of Pragmatic Function in the Grammaticalization of English General Extenders." *Pragmatics* 24:1.105–129.

doi Posio, Pekka. 2021. "*A pessoa* and *uma pessoa*: Grammaticalization and Functions of a Human Impersonal Referential Device in European Portuguese." *Journal of Portuguese Linguistics*, 20 (2):1–21.

doi Selting, Margret, and Elizabeth Couper-Kuhlen. 2001. *Studies in Interactional Linguistics*. Amsterdam: John Benjamins.

doi Selting, M. 2007. "Lists as Embedded Structures and The Prosody of List Construction as an Interactional Resource." *Journal of Pragmatics* 39 (3):483–526.

Siro, Paavo. 1943. "Jaolliset ja jaottomat substantiivit. [Divisble and non-divisible nouns]." *Virittäjä* 47:276–290.

Siro, Paavo. 1957. "Suomen kielen subjektista kielen rakenteen osana. [The Finnish subject as part of the structure of the language]." *Virittäjä* 61:181–190.

Sorjonen, Marja-Leena. 2001. *Responding in Conversation: A Study of Response Particles in Finnish*. Amsterdam: John Benjamins.

Suomalainen, Karita, and Mikael Varjo. 2020. "When Personal Is Interpersonal. Organizing Interaction with Deictically Open Personal Constructions in Finnish Everyday Conversation." *Journal of Pragmatics* 168: 98–118.

Thompson, Sandra A., and Paul J. Hopper. 2001. "Transitivity, Clause Structure, and Argument Structure: Evidence from Conversation." In *Frequency and the Emergence of Linguistic Structure*, ed. by Bybee, Joan Bybee and Paul J. Hopper, 28–60. Amsterdam: Benjamins.

Tunkelo, Eemil Aukusti. 1915. "Vanhaa ja uutta *raha* sanasta [Old and new about the word *raha*]." *Virittäjä* 19 (6):91–99.

Vilkuna, Maria. 1992. *Referenssi ja määräisyys suomenkielisten tekstien tulkinnassa. [Reference and definiteness in the interpretation of Finnish language texts.]* Helsinki: Suomalaisen Kirjallisuuden Seura.

CHAPTER 5

Young children's experience of referentiality and nonreferentiality in dialogue

Marine Le Mené,[1] Anne Salazar Orvig,[2]
Christine da Silva-Genest[3] & Haydée Marcos[2]
[1] Université du Québec à Montréal   [2] Université Sorbonne Nouvelle
[3] Université de Lorraine

This chapter focuses on young children's experience of referential and nonreferential uses of noun phrases (NPs) in everyday dialogues. Our study of a corpus of interactions between adults and children aged 1;10 to 2;6 showed that the indeterminacy and instability that might characterise children's uses can also be found in adults' discourse. Not only are (non)referential values co-constructed, but children are also not exposed to clear-cut contrasts between the uses or values of NPs. On the contrary, both in the adults' discourse and in the way adults react to children's utterances, they seem to experience the fact that noun phrases potentially present various facets, which can be successively or simultaneously activated in dialogue.

Keywords: dialogue, indeterminacy, labelling, language acquisition, noun phrases, referentiality

This study aims to explore the way young children experience referential and non-referential uses of noun phrases (NPs) in everyday dialogues. As Laury, Ewing and Thompson showed in their introductory chapter to this volume, the field of reference studies is far from being homogenous. If referentiality may appear as a fuzzy concept when dealing with adult language, the challenge is even greater when it comes to child language. Not only do children not fully master adult forms and meanings but adult-child dialogues also show a certain amount of indeterminacy and uncertainty in the use of noun phrases. One possible (quite classical) way to address this issue would be to track children's development from indeterminate uses to a clear contrast between referential and nonreferential uses. However, such a stance implies the assumption of a linear development from an initial point to an ending point, that is, from a lack of referential skills to a clear

https://doi.org/10.1075/pbns.344.05lem

distinction between specific reference, non-specific uses, generic uses, labelling uses, etc. However, as shown in other chapters in this book (see *inter alia* Thompson and Ono's work on the fluidity and indeterminacy of reference in everyday conversation), there are probably not such clear-cut boundaries in everyday dialogues. In that case, what do children acquire: a semantic/pragmatic contrast or the dynamics of fluctuation and fuzziness? We address this issue from an interactionist and dialogical approach (Bakhtin 1979/1986; Bruner 1983; Vygotsky 1934/1962).[1] According to this approach, children's discursive and pragmatic early skills are built from their "communicative experience", that is, both from their exposure to forms and meanings in adult discourse (frequent occurrences and unique events) and from their *in situ* involvement in the construction of a discursive space emerging from the participants' utterances and actions (see Salazar Orvig *et al.* 2021).[2]

1. Referentiality and nonreferentiality

Whereas referring may be one of the main functions of nominal expressions, it is a known fact that nouns are also produced in undisputable nonreferential uses (see among others Du Bois 1980). Beyond this first distinction, consensus about where to draw the boundaries between referential and nonreferential uses of linguistic expressions fades out (see Abbot 2014; Chen 2009; Du Bois 1980; Laury *et al.* this volume, *inter alia*). Among other dividing lines, studies on decontextualized examples tend to think of referentiality and nonreferentiality as a semantic or pragmatic property of the noun phrase whereas studies dealing with spontaneous data consider them as values that are actually built in discourse and interaction. Let us consider the case of indefinite noun phrases, which we will discuss later in this work. Indefinite NPs tend to be considered nonreferential in the classic philosophical or semantic approaches. Even when individuals are concerned, the speaker "is merely indicating that he has a certain unspecified individual in mind. That is, he is not referring but merely alluding to that individual" (Bach 2008: 28) or identifying he or she only by the denotation of the noun (what Gundel et al. (1993) call

---

1. In this text, "interactionist/interactionism" corresponds to the Vygotskian (Vygotsky, 1934/1962) and Brunerian (Bruner 1983) conceptions of language and cognitive development. In that sense, the scopes of "interactionist" and "interactional" (as in interactional linguistics, Ochs *et al.*, 1996; Ford *et al.*, 2003) partially overlap.

2. The use of "emerge" and "emergent" (as in Hopper 1998, 2015, *inter alia*) aims at insisting on the fact that speakers do not deal with *a priori* values but with values under construction in the here and now of dialogue.

"type identifiable"). Depending on the authors these uses can fall either side of the boundary between referential and nonreferential uses. However, this feature is not in the NP *per se*. It is the result of the interaction with other features in the utterance, such as the verb's action accomplishment. For instance, a modal construction will contribute to a non-specific interpretation of an indefinite NP (*I wanted to eat an ice cream*) whereas a verb at the past perfect tense points to an accomplished action, which dealt with concrete entities (*I ate an ice cream*). Therefore, even if the entity is poorly identifiable it has a concrete existence (the ice cream that was actually eaten). The verb contributes therefore to a referential reading of the indefinite NP. Moreover, this referential potential is enhanced when the indefinite NP contributes to tracking a referent in the ongoing discourse, and appears as the head of a co-referential chain (Chastain 1975; Du Bois 1980; Thompson 1997).

Until now we have considered the construction of meaning as a static phenomenon, one that would be induced by the meaning of units or their interactions. However, as research on discourse and interaction shows, the potential meanings of referring expressions are above all resources for participants to play with the different perspectives from which referents and notions may be considered in the dialogue (Laury 2001, *inter alia*). This is the perspective we will adopt to address the issue of (non)referentiality in adult-child dialogues. Before presenting our data and method, we will recall how referential and nonreferential uses of NPs have been tackled in language acquisition studies.

2.   (Non)referentiality in child language

Concerning referentiality and nonreferentiality, language acquisition shows an even more complex landscape that adult language. When children begin to acquire their first words, they are involved in a complex process: while grasping words as means to achieve pragmatic goals (for instance, asking for food, showing an object or playing), toddlers are discovering and constructing both the act of reference (using language to represent an entity) and the communication means to refer. Reference and denotation are therefore deeply intertwined both in children's discursive productions and within the activities they are involved in, where adults frequently label objects before referring to them (Bruner 1975, 1983).

Previous studies on the acquisition of referential expressions did not directly address the issue of referentiality/nonreferentiality. They rather focused on when and how children become able to use determiners (and pronouns) in accordance with their language rules, as part of the acquisition of grammatical paradigms (see for instance Bassano *et al.*, 2011), and then, from a pragmatic perspective, regarding the newness/givenness of the referent, and/or its specificity/non specificity

(Salazar Orvig *et al.* 2013). The question of (non)referentiality is primarily related to this last aspect (see also Kupisch 2007).

Two types of studies on children's use of determiners can be distinguished: those adopting experimental methods and those working on natural data. Experimental methods (Bresson 1974; De Cat 2013; Karmiloff-Smith 1979, 1985; Maratsos, 1974, Schaeffer & Matthewson 2005; Schafer & de Villers 2000) are based on the presentation of controlled stimuli. In production tasks, children are asked to produce or complete narratives, describe experimenter's actions, or encode specific referents; in comprehension tasks, children are asked to follow instructions or identify referents. Studies using natural data (Le Mené-Guigourès 2017; Rozendaal & Baker 2008; Salazar Orvig *et al.* 2013) are based on the analysis of corpora collected in everyday interactions. Some differences may be observed between both types of studies as regards to the theoretical perspectives and the age at which indefinite and definite determiners begin to be used according to their functions.

The authors of experimental studies explain this acquisition process in terms of cognition and memory, whereas corpora studies emphasize the role of interaction, as it is the case in our own studies. An example of the first type is Karmiloff-Smith's research (1979, 1985), one of the most influential works in this perspective. According to this author, determiners (and pronouns) are cohesive devices and the changes in their uses can be understood only under a theoretical model that "focuses on internal processes and representations" (Karmiloff-Smith 1985: 62). For instance, in the 1985 study, children aged 4 were not yet able to organize their discourse by means of the contrast between definite/indefinite articles because the process is still stimulus driven and the definite determiners and pronouns had a deictic value. Yet, some – but not all – experimental studies also show that children as young as 3;6 can use indefinite determiners for specific reference (Schafer & de Villiers 2000).

In contrast, studies on corpora show that at the age of 2–3, children are able to make adult-like use of determiners as specific/non-specific reference (and newness/givenness of the referent) is concerned. In a wide review, Allen *et al.* (2015) consider these abilities as the outcome of the interplay between a plurality of factors: discourse-based and perceptually-based factors as well as communication demands. We propose that these (and possibly other) factors function within the framework of adult scaffolding and co-construction in the dialogue. This could explain the earliness of skills observed in studies on corpora compared to experimental ones.

We make the hypothesis that indeterminacy in children's first uses of nouns does not only reflect limitations on a reliable interpretation of children's utterances, but that it corresponds to the actual status of noun phrases in early adult-child dialogues and that referentiality (and nonreferentiality) precisely emerge from the dynamics of these dialogues in which children are involved. However, to our knowledge, there are no studies about (non)referentiality in the adult uses of NPs when talking to children. Two different questions can arise from the previous observations. First, the issue of (non)referentiality partly overlaps that of (in)definiteness: to which extent do children possess a contrast between specific and nonspecific reference? Second, considering labelling, to what extent do children experience a clear-cut difference between referring to an entity and labelling this entity?

This chapter aims to fill a gap in studies on early referential behaviors by providing a first description of the way children experience these values in dialogue and considering some hypothetical paths for the development of (non)referential uses of language.

3.   Studying (non)referentiality: Data and method of analysis

3.1   A corpus of adult-child interactions

The study was conducted on a corpus of video-recorded adult-child interactions involving 28 French-speaking children aged from 1;10 to 2;6. The recordings[3] were made during everyday activities (meal, snack), reading or playing activities (construction or symbolic games), and non-narrative activities with iconic material such as jigsaws or memory games.

The data collected were fully transcribed taking into account the interactions' multimodal dimension, and thus focused on verbal productions and also including gestures, gaze, body moves and orientations. In order to provide a faithful representation of the ongoing construction of children's linguistic system, their utterances were phonetically transcribed. The whole set of transcribed data was made up of 18045 utterances (adults' and children's productions together).

3.2   Identifying dialogical sequences to examine (non)referentiality

In order to examine the way the dialogical and discursive context contributes to the construction of the value of a NP, be it referential or not, we set up a four-step procedure.

---

3. The corpus was gathered from various research projects (see Le Mené-Guigourès 2017; Salazar Orvig et al. 2021). In all these occasions parents and children were duly informed of the type of investigation conducted and gave their consent.

As a first step, we identified among the children's productions all the utterances (N=389) containing only one isolated NP, whether it was preceded with a determiner (Example 1) or a filler (Example 2),[4] or produced without any pre-nominal form (Example 3). We excluded any other combination of two words or more.

For readers unfamiliar with the French grammatical system, note that in French, the noun should, in most cases, be preceded by a determiner. Determiners are morphologically complex: the category is a relatively heterogeneous paradigm, made up of several subsets of determiners most often organised into two main categories: definite and indefinite determiners. It may be useful to specify here that grammars tend to establish that definite NPs present the referent as identifiable by the interlocutor, either through the linguistic context, the situational context or shared knowledge (or supposedly shared) between the speaker and the interlocutor. As opposed to definites, indefinite determiners would be used in cases where the referent of the noun could be any one of its category, cannot be identified by the interlocutor, when the information is new or when the speaker does not consider it useful to give the information. In addition, definites are the most typical form for generic values, both in singular (*la compote est un aliment sain*) and plural forms (*les compotes sont saines*) and indefinites can only be used for generic values in dislocated constructions (*une compote c'est sain*), whereas English will use bare nouns (*compot is a healthy aliment; compots are healthy*).

(1) [Lisa, 1;11: *Determiner + Noun*][5]
    ((Lisa and her father are playing with a small farm. Lisa picks up the farmer character.))
    LIS9: [la dam] *la dame*
          the lady
    FAT9: *tu crois que c'est une dame ça ?*
          you think this is a lady?

---

4. Filler syllables are pre-nominal or pre-verbal syllables, which are precursors of grammatical morphemes (*inter alia* determiners, pronouns, auxiliaries) both in pre-nominal and pre-verbal positions (see for instance Peters 2001; Veneziano 2003). In the examples, 'F' stands for a filler syllable.

5. Example captions indicate the name of the child, his/her age (years; months). The first three letters of the child's first name are given in uppercase (*e.g.* LIS for Lisa), MOT stands for mother, FAT for father and ADU for another adult participant interacting with the child. The children's utterances are transcribed phonetically (between square brackets [ ]), the interpretation in French is given in italics. For both the adults and the children an approximate English translation is given in the next line. '/' stands for a pause, { } braces indicate an uncertain interpretation and 'xxx' is used to translate unintelligible productions. The interrogative sign ('?') codes a question and '!' codes an exclamative utterance. Indications about gestures and the situation are between double brackets (( )) and in italics.

(2) [Madeleine, 1;09: *Filler + Noun*]
     ((Madeleine and her mother are jointly telling a Mr. Men story: Mr. Bump
     meets Mr. Forgetful.))
     MOT15: *mais le problème c'est qu'il est étourdi !*
            but the matter is that he is dizzy!
     MAD15: [ʒ bys] *F bus*
            F bus

(3) [Clément, 2;03: *Noun*]
     ((Clément is playing with a jigsaw and pointing at one of the pieces.))
     CLE40: [vwaty]? *voiture ?*
            car?

The use of isolated NPs, with or without a determiner or filler, is a particularly distinctive feature of children's first stage of linguistic development, and of the transitional stage between this first stage of one-word utterances and the following two-word utterances stage (*inter alia* Clark 2009). As no other element in the utterance may help to determine whether the NP is associated with a referential or nonreferential value, these isolated NPs are potentially subject to various interpretations and only the context (both linguistic and related to the current situation) may help favor one interpretation rather than another.

As a second step, to grasp the way (non)referentiality may emerge from the dynamics of dialogue, we also focused on the complete thematic sequences in which they appeared. Therefore, we paid attention to children's productions with regard to adults' productions and vice versa. These thematic sequences make up our data collection and the dialogical material discussed below. An example of how thematic sequences were identified is presented through Excerpt 4. First, we identified the isolated NP produced by the child (line LUB492), and then, from this NP, we selected the whole sequence concerning the same discourse object, and in this case, the same piece of the jigsaw (an elephant piece). Ultimately, these sequences may encompass several occurrences of isolated NPs as seen in Example 4.

(4) [Lubin, 1;11: *Thematic sequence*]
     ((Lubin and his father are playing with a giant jigsaw, manipulating pieces,
     and talking about the animals showing on them.))
     FAT491: *ça c'est qui lui ?*
             who is this one?
             ((pointing at the space dedicated to the elephant))
     LUB492: [fã] *(élé)phant !*
             elephant
     FAT493: *l'éléphant*
             the elephant
     FAT494 : *oui*
             yes
     LUB495 [xxx a]
     LUB496: [uʒ pa] *(b)ouge pas*
             don't move
             ((embedding the elephant piece))

```
LUB497:  [elefa] éléphant
         elephant
LUB498:  [gaje] gagné !
         well done!
FAT499:  gagné !
         well done!
```

Then, as a third step, we examined how these thematic sequences were built up, considering both utterances that preceded and followed the children's isolated NPs. In particular, we explored the values of the different NPs within each sequence, by coding them according to three different categories: REFERENTIAL, NONREFERENTIAL, and INDETERMINATE. This coding drew on a body of both verbal and/or non-verbal evidence, which allowed us to favor one category (or value) over another. These categories and the information on which we based our coding are presented below.

If we were able to pinpoint one singular object (human or not) it referred to, then we coded it as REFERENTIAL. This coding decision was made possible only when (1) we had enough verbal cues to clearly identify this singular object, in the analysed utterance itself or in a previous/following utterance (see Example 5), (2) when non-verbal resources like gestures or gaze direction allowed targeting one particular object (see Example 6), (3) when the material context and our knowledge of the situation provided a clear understanding of the participant communicative intention (see Example 7). These cues showed in the data either separately or simultaneously.

For instance, in the Example 5 below, the NP [kuku] (produced for 'crocodile') in LUB601 was coded as referential since both the father's preceding question (*tu défais le crocodile?* 'you undo the crocodile?') and the child touching the jigsaw piece with his foot provided significant information to identify the specific crocodile both participants were playing with.

(5) [Lubin, 1;11: *Referential uses – Verbal cues*]
     ((Lubin and his father have just finished the jigsaw they were playing with.))
```
FAT600:  tu défais l(e) croco(dile) ?
         you undo the crocodile?
LUB601:  [kuku] c(r)oco(dile)
         crocodile
         ((trying to take the crocodile piece out of the puzzle board with his foot))
FAT602:  mais pas avec le pied avec la main
         but not with the foot with the hand
FAT603:  c'est / c'est compliqué avec le pied
         it's complicated with the foot
FAT604:  voilà
         there you go
```

Sometimes, as just noted, it is mainly the non-verbal context that helped identifying first what participants referred to, and therefore that the mention was referential. In Example 6, Iris and her father are playing with a train, and the child says *l'autre* 'the other one', moving around looking for a train wagon she seems familiar with. The child's behavior suggests that the repeated mention *l'autre* does not refer to either a nonreferential or indeterminate object, but rather to a singular well-identified train wagon.

(6)   [Iris, 1;11: *Referential uses – Non-verbal cues*]
```
IRI127: [lot] l'autre
        the other one
IRI128: [lot e lot] l'autre [xxx] l'autre
        the other one [xxx] the other one
FAT107: là il est là
        here it's here
```

In some other instances, the coding decision was taken on the basis of our knowledge of the situation. In Example 7 below, Elodie and her mother are playing with a construction game. Both ELO4 and ELO5 were coded as referential uses of the NP *Moulin*[6] since the child is actually looking for the specific helix she played with a few minutes before.

(7)   [Elodie, 2;3: *Referential uses – Material context / Knowledge of the situation*]
```
ELO4: [a mulɛ̃] F moulin
      F mill
ELO5: [u mulɛ̃] F moulin
      F mill
MOT6: le moulin il est là + tiens
      the mill is here + here you are
```

In contrast, in other cases, the discursive or the situational context oriented towards a labelling use of the NP. This is the case in the following Example (8) where Elodie's mother offers a labelling use of the noun *barrière* ('gate'), which is repeated by the child in the following turn.

(8)   [Elodie, 2;2: *Labelling uses*]
      ((Elodie and her mother are playing with a small farm.))
```
MOT73: c'est une barrière
       it's a gate
ELO48: [bajɛʁ] ba(rr)ière
       gate
```

In the same way, some uses could be interpreted as non-specific or generic. In Example 9 below, Clémence's mother produces a generic utterance about what cows eat, and the child takes up the generic NP *'la vache'* in CLE34.

Labelling and non-specific/generic uses of NPs were both included in a NON-REFERENTIAL coding category.

---

6. Note here that both the child and the mother use the noun 'moulin' (mill) to refer in fact to the helix of a mill. In the Example (7), we decided to translate the word 'moulin' by 'mill', even though we know it is not the object that the participants are manipulating.

(9) [Clémence, 2;3: *Generic uses*]
     MOT67: *et la vache qu'est-ce qu'elle mange? de l'herbe?*
            and cows, what do they eat?[7] grass?
     CLE33: [ɛb] *he(r)be*
            grass
     CLE34: [lavaç] *la vache*
            the cow

Finally, when the participant's communicative intention was particularly difficult to grasp, and that we found no evidence enabling us to favor one of these two preceding values (REFERENTIAL or NONREFERENTIAL) over another, neither in the linguistic context nor in the current situation or personal knowledge of this situation, the NPs were coded as INDETERMINATE. Examples 11 (in Section 4) or 15 (in Section 5) provide clear illustrations of these kinds of ambiguous, indeterminate uses.

Having described both the data and the method we used to analyse these data, the next part of this study will now focus on the way children actually experience (non)referentiality. Our analysis will follow the central thread of dialogue and its role in constructing (non)referentiality, but through three different angles: first, to understand the uses children are exposed to, we had a look at the way adults use NPs in the dialogue; second, we focused on children's uses and analysed the role played by the preceding context in the construction of children's NPs values; and finally, we tried to capture what happens following children's NPs, and in particular, how the possible values of these NPs were taken up in the following turns of the sequence.

4.   Adult uses of NPs in the ongoing dialogue

As shown earlier, several studies focused on both referentiality and nonreferentiality. Yet very few of them examined the role of dialogue in the development of child's (non)referential uses of language or the type of uses children are exposed to in the language addressed to them. This is precisely what we did in this work: analysing adult uses to better understand children's uses.

Our first analysis showed that children are actually exposed to a great variety and variability of uses in everyday communication. The following example of dialogue between Serena (2 years and 3 months) and her mother provides a good illustration of how diverse and mixed adult uses can be.

---

7. As mentioned in Section 1, in French, generics are expressed with definite NPs. In the English translation, we used either a plural bare noun or a definite NP to convey this generic value.

(10)   [Serena, 2;3: *Adult's variety of uses*]
((Serena is with her mother, having a snack (compote and cookies). She starts licking the lid of the compote jar.))

```
MOT14:   oh ça tu aimes ça
         oh you like that
MOT15:   qu'est-ce que c'est ça? c'est le + ?
         what's that? it's the +?)
         ((touching the lid))
MOT16:   comment ça s'appelle ça ?
         how do you call that?
         ((Serena looks at her mother and at the lid.))
MOT17:   t'es coquine !
         you're mischievous!
SER2:    [asasela] ah ça c'est {la/là}
         ah this is there
         ((showing the lid))
MOT18 :  ouais mais qu'est-ce que c'est ça ?
         yes but what's this?
         ((touching the lid))
SER3:    [a compɔt] F compote
         F compote
MOT19:   la compote
         the compote
MOT20:   oui mais tu manges la compote dans le couvercle
         yes but you eat the compote in the lid
         ((tapping the lid))
         ((MOT puts a teaspoon in the pot of compote and brings it near SER.))
MOT21:   allez mange la compote là
         come on eat the compote there
         [...]
         ((Later, Serena pushes the pot and grabs some cookies.))
SER16:   [a zə vø lɛ kado dabɔʁ] ah je veux les gâteaux d'abord
         oh I want the cookies first
MOT 66:  tu manges les gâteaux d'abord ?
         you eat the cookies first?
         ((she takes the spoon and gives some compote to the child))
MOT67:   alors un peu de compote aussi
         then also some compote
         ((The mother makes the child eat the compote.))
MOT68:   parce que les compotes y a des fruits dedans
         because compotes have fruits inside
```

In these excerpts of an everyday activity, the mother displays two different expressions to refer to the COMPOTE (the demonstrative pronoun *ça* and the definite NP *la compote*) and, at the same time, various uses of the noun *compote*. She begins (MOT 15, 16 and 18) by asking her child to identify or label what she is eating (or licking). The child answers with a noun associated with a filler [a]. The mother takes up the noun and reformulates the filler with a definite determiner *la* (MOT 19). The next occurrences refer to the content of the lid (MOT 20) and of the pot (MOT 21), with the referential value of the NP being reinforced by the deictic *là* 'there'. In MOT 67, the bare noun in *alors un peu de compote* 'then also some compote' takes a mass value whereas in MOT 68, *parce que les compotes y a des fruits dedans* 'because in compotes there are fruits inside', *compote* has a generic value.

This example shows, in the first place, that children are, from early on, exposed to both referential and nonreferential uses of NPs. This example also highlights the fact that children do not necessarily experience, in the adults' discourse, contrasts of forms conveying contrasts of values (for instance Serena's mother uses mostly the definite determiner).

Moreover, forms in the adult discourse can be indeterminate, that is, they cannot be assigned with a given value. Their interpretation is driven by the discursive and dialogical context. Some forms, as for instance *la compote* (MOT 19) can be interpreted either as a nonreferential use (a way to label the referent) or as a referential use, introducing a referent that will be taken up in the next turns as in MOT 20 and 21.

In addition to these moves between referential and nonreferential uses, we found that some of the adult's uses may be inherently multifaceted, encompassing both referential and nonreferential potential values as in Example 11.

(11) [Lubin, 2;6: *Adult's ambiguous uses*]
((Lubin is playing a card game, whose goal is to make pairs by combining animals and their living areas.))

```
LUB138:  [ɔl e la sa mɛzɔ̃]  F est là sa maison
             his house is here
MOT139:  alors mon Lulu
             so my Lulu
ADU140:  la maison de qui ?
             whose house?
             ((Lubin assembles two cards that form a pair.))
ADU142:  oui
             yes
LUB143:  [də mutɔ̃]  F mouton
             F sheep
ADU144:  ouais la maison du mouton c'est celle-là
             yes the sheep's house is this one
```

The adult (ADU) interacting with the child (LUB) makes use of linguistic forms which are usually associated with specific uses (such as the interrogative pronoun *qui* 'who' in ADU140 and the definite NP *la maison* 'the house' in ADU144), but for uses that are more likely to be generic (referring here to the whole class of the sheep). This kind of use is frequent in the data, and in particular when participants are playing with iconic material. The pictures on the cards stand both for a specific individual (the one represented in the picture and the piece of the game set) and for the whole category. For instance, in Example 10 the adult's question in ADU 140 concerns both the specific piece to be searched for and the construction of a general knowledge about the place sheep live in. And in both cases, they can be discussed by the dyads and result in indeterminate uses.

By analysing adult's uses, to understand child's uses, we could see that in everyday conversations, child-directed speech is composed of a great diversity of uses, sometimes alternating between referentiality and nonreferentiality – and yet verbalised with the same forms – and even to indeterminate uses with potentially multiple values. In the next section, we will take a closer look at the children's uses of NPs by the children.

5.   Child uses of NPs: The role played by the preceding context

As far as (non)referentiality is concerned, we have seen that a referential or non-referential value is not given by or included in the linguistic units but constructed through the context. From this perspective, our second analysis focused on the context preceding each NP produced by the child and on the way this context may impact both its form and the value to which it may be assigned.

Two different scenarios were observed. In the first one, the child's use was framed by the ongoing dialogue – for instance by a question of the adult. This pattern may be found in MOT18 in Example 10 above, but also in FAT150 in Example 12 below. In both cases, the adult's question elicited a labelling answer.

(12)   [Lubin, 1;11: *Child's use framed by the dialogue*]
((Lubin and his father are playing with a jigsaw. The father points at one piece.))
FAT150: *c'est quoi ça ?*
        what is this?
LUB151: [a ! eokɛ !] *ah ! (p)e(rr)oquet !*
        ah! parrot!
FAT152: *oui un perroquet !*
        yes a parrot!

The child's use was also framed by the ongoing activity and the discursive routines that are associated with the activity. In Example 13, the child and her mother were playing with a picture lotto game. Before placing the pictures on her lotto board, the child asked what was on the card she had picked up (cf. OLG12, OLG13b or OLG14b). The mother answered these labelling questions by naming what was shown on the pictures, and the child then repeated the mother's utterance. These NPs (OLG13a, OLG14a) are thus rooted in the activity, and shaped by the participants' recurring practices.

(13)   [Olga, 2;4: *Child's use framed by the activity*]
((Olga and her mother are playing with a picture lotto game.))
OLG11: [sekwa ?] *c'est quoi ?*
        what is this?
MOT13: *ça c'est un cerf-volant*
        this is a kite

```
OLG12:  [sekwa ?] c'est quoi ?
        what is this?
MER14:  un soleil
        a sun
OLG13a: [ɛ̃ solɛj] un soleil
        a sun
OLG13b: [sekwa ?] c'est quoi ?
        what is this?
MER15:  des pommes
        apples
OLG14a: [de pom] des pommes
        apples
OLG14b: [sekwa ?] c'est quoi ?
        what is this?
MER16:  un parapluie
        an umbrella
```

More generally, the child's use could be framed by the shared knowledge of the situation. In Example 14, Iris and her father were playing with a train wagon. Both participants knew that the wagon had just rolled under the chair, giving the NP produced in IRI100, as well as the two NPs produced by the father in FAT87, a referential value. Unlike the apples and the umbrellas in Example 13, these NPs correspond to representations of the chair, which is a concrete object under which the toy has just fallen.

(14) [Iris, 1;11: *Child's use framed by the shared knowledge*]
      ((Iris and her father are playing with a train wagon. The wagon has just rolled under the chair.))
```
IRI100: [ba! ʃɛz] bah! chaise
        chair
IRI101: [a!] ah!
FAT87:  dessous la chaise dessous la chaise
        under the chair under the chair
```

In the second scenario, the child's use was not framed by the context. This corresponds to occurrences appearing in the child's initiating moves, with non-inferable contextual elements (see examples 15 and 16), or in contexts considered as indeterminate, for instance when the adult's productions themselves are indeterminate (as in ADU140 in Example 11).

(15) [Iris, 1;11: *Child's use not framed by the context*]
      ((Iris is playing with various toys. She picks the glasses of M. Potato, and tries to put them on her nose.))
```
IRIS23: [o nenɛt] oh lunettes
        oh glasses
FAT24:  elles sont trop petites pour toi
        they're too small for you
```

In Example 15, Iris was discovering different toys that the observer brought with her. She picked a pair of little glasses. The father was silent at that point of the interaction and her discovery did not constrain any particular type of discourse.

Therefore, *[nenɛt]* can be interpreted either as a labelling move (it could be rephrased as *'these are glasses'*) or as an existential utterance (it could be rephrased as *'there are glasses'*) or, else, she could be just calling the attention of her father on the glasses (which could then be rephrased by *'oh look glasses'*). We can observe that the father replies on the basis of a referential interpretation of the child's utterance (see Section 5).

(16)   [Alice, 1;11: *Child's use not framed by the context*]
       ((Alice lifts the carpet in front of her.))
       ALI 56: [tapi !] *tapis !*
               carpet!
       MOT 53: *ça c'est un tapis*
               this is a carpet

In Example 16, Alice's use of *tapis ('carpet')* is an initiating move, and just as in the previous Example (15), the value of the child's NP is indeterminate (again, no linguistic nor contextual cue allows to favor a referential or nonreferential value). It can be interpreted either as a labelling move (rephrased as *'this is a carpet'*) or as an existential utterance (rephrased as *'there is a carpet'*).

6.   The evolution of the values of NPs in dialogue

In addition to the focus on preceding context, we also considered the values of the NP depending on the subsequent development of dialogue. In examples 15 and 16 discussed in the previous section, the adult's reply selects one of the interpretations, and the child's NP is taken up either in a referential utterance (*see the anaphoric pronoun elles* 'they' in FAT24, Example 15) or a labelling utterance (MOT53 in Example 16), which then shapes the dialogue towards a referential or nonreferential use. However, is this kind of phenomenon specific to the adult's reaction to indeterminate NPs, or can we find cues showing that all kinds of occurrences are processed in the same way? To answer this question, we examined the way the NPs were taken up and developed in dialogue.

We observed that the adult's subsequent contribution could serve four different functions. When the child's utterance was not ambiguous, the adult's utterance confirmed the child's value (see among others FAT152 in Example 12) and when the child's utterance was indeterminate, the adult's contribution could either select a potential value (as in FAT24 in Example 15), or maintain the indeterminacy (see FAT493 in Example 4).

Very often adults do take up the NP produced by children, but in some cases the following dialogue stands on an implicit uptake. In Example 17 below, the child also initiates the sequence with an indeterminate NP (MAD147), but in this case the mother carries on the dialogue on the basis of a referential value of the child's NP. Even if in her reply (MOT148), the mother does not overtly take up the child's item *voiture* ('car'), the referent is inferable from the interaction of the previous context of the story (one of the characters, M. Bump, just missed a bus that would take him to the station) and the use of the predicate *emmener à la gare*, 'take to the station' which corresponds to an action that needs to be accomplished with a car. Therefore the existence of the car is implicitly confirmed together with the explicit reference to its driver (M. Forgetful) which is referred to with the third person pronoun *il* 'he'.

(17) [Madeleine, 1;9]
      ((Madeleine and her mother are reading a Mr Men book. The child turns the page and points at a car. Mr Bump is asking M. Forgetful (in the car) to take him to the train station.))
```
MAD146: [esa mamã !] F ça maman !
        F this mum!
MAD147: [evwaty] F voiture
        F car
MOT148: tu vois il lui dit <est+ce+que vous pouvez m'emmener à la gare> [reported
        speech] ?
        you see he tells him could you take me to the station?
```

Example 18 exhibits a more complex configuration as it shows that adults can follow up a child's indeterminate NP with different values. Alice's first utterance is indeterminate (ALI 31); again it can be interpreted either as a labelling utterance (which could be rephrased as *'it is a button'*) or as an existential utterance (which could be rephrased as *'there is a button'*). The mother (MOT 32) selected the labelling value by giving the child the expected label, *'it's a velcro'*. We can observe in this utterance and in the following one that the demonstrative pronouns *c'* 'it' and *ça* 'this/that' convey the reference to the object under their joint attention.

ALI 32 is a second indeterminate utterance ([*pa butɔ̃*] 'no button'), which again can be interpreted as a labelling utterance (which could be rephrased by *"it is not called button"*) or a non-specific use of the noun (possibly rephrased as *"there is no button here"*). The mother's reply (MOT 33) selected the second value. This example illustrates a very frequent scenario in our data: the values of NPs are continuously fashioned by the ongoing dialogue.

(18) [Alice, 1;11]
      ((Alice is playing with the shoes of a doll.))
```
ALI3:  [butɔ̃] bouton
       button
MOT32: regarde c'est un velcro tu vois hop. comme ça ça tient
       look it's a velcro you see there you go. it sticks this way
ALI32: [nɔ̃ nɔ̃ pa butɔ̃] non! non! pas bouton
       no! no! no button
MOT33: non il n'y a pas de bouton sur cette poupée
       no there's no button on this doll
```

Our last Example (19) shows that indeterminacy can in some cases be maintained over several turns. In Example 19 below, the child (CLE) is playing with her mother and brother (GEO) a card game where they have to match the picture of an animal with the picture of its usual feed.

(19) [Clémence, 2;3]
      ((Clémence is playing a card game with her mother and brother.))
      CLE14:   [ɛ̃ lapɛ̃] *un lapin*
               a rabbit
      MOT29a: *un lapin !*
               a rabbit!
      MOT29b: *le petit lapin*
               the small rabbit
      MOT29c: *qu'est-ce qu'il mange un lapin Clémence ?*
               what does a rabbit eat Clémence?
      MOT29d: *tu sais Geoffroy ?*
               you know Geoffroy?
      GEO14:   *des carottes*
               carrots
      MOT30:   *oui*
               yes
      CLE15:   [imɑ̃ʒ de fit] *i(l) mange des frites*
               it eats fries
      MOT31:   *pas des frites Clémence ! <sourire>*
               not fries Clémence! ((smile))
      GEO15:   *mais mais elle est là la carotte*
               but but the carrot is here
      MOT32a: *regarde Clémence il l'a trouvée Geoffroy la carotte*
               look Clémence, Geoffroy found the carrot
      MOT32b: *tu la mets avec le lapin ?*
               you put it with the rabbit?
      GEO16:   *là à côté*
               here beside

In CLE14, the child first mentions the card of a rabbit by saying *un lapin* (*'a rabbit'*). As other cases presented here (examples 11, 15 or 16), this utterance is typically indeterminate, and can be interpreted either as an existential utterance (which could be rephrased as *"there is a rabbit"*) or as a labelling move (rephrased as *"this is a rabbit"*). The mother's first utterance MOT29a maintains the indeterminacy and could be interpreted in both ways. Even though in her second utterance, MOT29b, the mother switches to a definite NP with the adjective *petit* ('little'), this utterance could still, to a lesser extent, be considered potentially as a new label (since no cue allows here to pinpoint one singular rabbit more than the whole category). In MOT29c, *qu'est-ce qu'il mange un lapin Clémence ?* ('what does a rabbit eat Clémence?'), the use of an indefinite NP in a dislocated construction is usually considered generic in French (de Cat 2007). However, in the context of this card game, the question prompts the children to look for a specific card. The brother's contribution in GEO14 answers the question with an indefinite NP that maintains the generic value (*des carottes* 'carrots') but in GEO15 the brother locates a specific card. The following contributions by the mother (MOT32a and MOT32b) confirm this specific referential value.

This example not only provides a good illustration of both child and adult's indeterminate utterances (which can be observed through multiple turns), but also highlights the co-construction of changing values, within the dynamics of dialogue and within the framework of activities, leading to distinctive discourse genres, and uses of NPs.

7. Discussion

In the introductory sections (Sections 1 and 2) we saw that one dividing line between approaches of (non)referentiality is the way the value of the NP is ascribed: is it by its form, by its context and/or by its usage? We saw also that experimental studies tend to consider that young children do not possess the contrast between referential and nonreferential uses of nouns, whereas results of studies on dialogue tend to show evidence of an early pragmatic competence. Our aim in this study was not to assess the existence of early pragmatic skills, but rather to explore the way children experience referential and nonreferential values, both as speakers and as interlocutors. The qualitative analysis of the thematic sequences containing isolated NPs underscored that the values of NPs take shape in the interaction, and are framed both by the situational and linguistic context, for the children as well as for the adults interacting with them.

As seen, the function of adults' contributions is twofold. They have a retroactive effect on the child's utterances by selecting or confirming a potential interpretation of the NP and, at the same time, they set the ground for the subsequent dialogue. These contributions thus show both the adult's involvement within the discursive space, and interactional cues that the child can use to grasp how his/her preceding utterances were interpreted by the interlocutor. By constructing his/her own turns from these interpretations of the child's utterances, the adult contributes to the very progressive process of constructing the child's consciousness of referential and nonreferential values.

Our findings might also shed a new light on the results of experimental studies. Let's return to the contradiction between Karmiloff-Smith (1979, 1985) and Schafer and de Villiers (2000). The former concluded that young children did not possess the multifunctionality of determiners and that they tended to use indefinite determiners only for labelling and non-specific values whereas the latter found uses of indefinite determiners for specific ones. Without claiming that young children possess adult-type skills, our observations suggest that children might take in the adults usage as an example. Moreover, in the everyday interactions we analysed, children do not have the opportunity to observe contrasting uses of NPs for referential and nonreferential values. On the contrary, they experience non-homogeneous uses by adults. This does not imply that adults do not have canonical skills. When talking to children, adults are in a particular position: they fully take part in the activity (for instance, playing with children or feeding them) and, at the same time, they scaffold the children's involvement in the activity and their use of language (Wood, Bruner & Ross 1976). For instance, in the early mother-child dialogues, labelling has a much higher prevalence than in any other type of dialogue, even more so than in adult-adult interactions. In these dialogues children are therefore frequently exposed to back and forth moves from referential uses to labelling uses.

In the same vein, we can make the assumption that the children's and adults' uses of NPs are determined by the activities and speech genres they are involved in. In previous studies we showed that activities and genres impact children's and adults' uses of referring expressions (de Weck *et al.*, 2021; Le Mené *et al.*, 2023; Salazar Orvig *et al.*, 2018; Vinel *et al.*, 2021). Some of the sequences studied here suggest that some playing activities may favor labelling moves (examples 12 or 13) and others foster some level of indeterminacy between generic and specific uses of NPs (examples 11 or 19).

Therefore, the models children are exposed to do not necessarily correspond to the canons experimental studies target. The construction of adult-like uses of referring expressions probably involves a more complex process of language socialization and exposure to a greater diversity of interlocutors, activities and speech genres (de Weck *et al.*, 2019).

Other questions remain. First, do the uses of NPs change along with language development? We did not consider an age variable in our data, because at these ages the individual variability in linguistic development can override the chronological age. So we might ask if the different types of sequences we highlighted here appear at the same time in the course of linguistic and dialogical development of the child. Moreover, we approached the data from a formal starting point, the occurrences of isolated NPs that are particularly distinctive of children's first stage of linguistic development. Even if we showed that mothers' NPs also present some indeterminacy, does the acquisition of grammar and syntax reduce the proportion of indeterminate NPs?

Second, still with regard to the issue of language development, we might wonder whether dyads' uses tend to be progressively more homogeneous, selecting one value all along a thematic sequence, or whether this variability precisely characterises adult-child dialogues at all ages (and to go further, we might even wonder if it does characterise any dialogue). We did not observe age related differences in our corpus, but of course we worked on a narrow range of age. Complementary longitudinal studies should be conducted to answer this question.

8.   Conclusion

This chapter proposed a first exploration of the dynamics between referentiality and nonreferentiality (and all the intermediate values between these two opposite bounds) in adult-child dialogues.

Our analyses showed that, in dialogue, children and adults' NP occurrences have neither predetermined nor stable values. Referentiality or nonreferentiality may be considered as values constructed in the dialogical context rather than features of the NP itself. The values of NPs are co-constructed through the verbal and non-verbal contributions of the participants, both child and adult, within the ongoing activity and on the basis of previous discourse. At the same time the result of this co-construction is not necessarily permanently set. Indeed, the data suggest that the possible interpretations of an NP are the outcome of an unstable balance. Potential values may emerge or re-emerge along with new utterances, and the same NP may support another value in the same topical sequence when participants switch from one perspective to the other.

This variability reflects the multifacetedness of NP uses and thus, sheds some light on the issue of referentiality and nonreferentiality, at least from the acquisitional perspective. Children do not experience a clear-cut contrast between different uses or values. On the contrary they seem to experience (both in the adult discourse and in the way adults react to their utterances) the fact that noun phrases potentially present various facets, which can be successively or simultaneously activated in dialogue. And this experience at the level of the micro-temporality of one single interaction feeds the cumulative experience that constitutes the macro-temporality of the child's development.

References

Abbott, Barbara. 2014. "Reference." In *The Oxford Handbook of Pragmatics*, ed. by Yan Huang, 240–258. Oxford: Oxford University Press.

Allen, Shanley E. M., Mary Hughes, and Barbora Skarabela. 2015. "The role of cognitive accessibility in children's referential choice". In *The acquisition of reference*, ed. by Ludovica Serratrice and Shanley E. M. Allen, 123–153. Amsterdam: John Benjamins.

Bach, Kent. 2008. "On Referring and Not Referring". In *Reference: Interdisciplinary Perspectives*, ed. by Jeanette K. Gundel and Nancy Hedberg, 13–58. Oxford: Oxford University Press.

Bakhtin, Mikhaïl. 1979/1986. *Speech Genres and Other Late Essays*. Austin: University of Texas Press.

Bassano, Dominique, Isabelle Maillochon, Katharina Korecky-Kröll, Marijn van Dijk, Sabine Laaha, Wolfgang U. Dressler and Paul van Geert. 2011. "A Comparative and Dynamic Approach to the Development of Determiner Use in Three Children Acquiring Different Languages." *First Language* 31 (3): 253–279.

Bresson, François. 1974. "Problèmes de psycholinguistique génétique : l'acquisition du système de l'article en français". *Problèmes actuels en psycholinguistique*, 62–72. Paris: Editions du CNRS.

Bruner, Jerome S. 1975. "From Communication to Language: A Psychological Perspective." *Cognition* 3 (3): 255–287.

Bruner, Jerome S. 1983. *Child's Talk: Learning to Use Language*. New York: W.W. Norton & Company.

Chastain, Charles. 1975. "Reference and Context." In *Language, Mind and Knowledge*, ed. by Keith Gunderson, 194–269. Minneapolis: University of Minnesota Press.

Chen, Ping. 2009. "Aspects of Referentiality". *Journal of Pragmatics* 41 (8): 1657–1674.

De Cat, Cécile. 2007. *French Dislocation: Interpretation, Syntax, Acquisition*. Oxford: Oxford University Press.

De Cat, Cécile. 2013. "Egocentric Definiteness Errors and Perspective Evaluation in Preschool Children." *Journal of Pragmatics* 56: 58–69.

de Weck, Geneviève, Rouba Hassan, Julien Heurdier, Janina Klein, and Nathalie Salagnac. 2021. "Activities and Institutional Contexts: Their Role in the Use of Referring Expressions." In *The Acquisition of Referring Expressions: A Dialogic Approach*, ed. by Anne Salazar Orvig, Geneviève de Weck, Rouba Hassan, and Annie Rialland, 261–286. Amsterdam: John Benjamins.

de Weck, Geneviève, Anne Salazar Orvig, Stefano Rezzonico, Élise Vinel, and Mélanie Bernasconi. 2019. "The Impact of the Interactional Setting on the Choice of Referring Expressions in Narratives." *First Language* 39 (3): 298–318.

Du Bois, John W. 1980. "Beyond Definiteness: The Trace of Identity in Discourse." In *The Pear Stories: Cognitive, Cultural, and Linguistic Aspects of Narrative Production*, ed. by Wallace L. Chafe, 203–274. Norwood, NJ.: Ablex.

Ford, Cecilia E., Barbara A. Fox, and Sandra A. Thompson. 2003. "Social Interaction and Grammar." In *The New Psychology of Language, vol. 2*, ed. by Michael Tomasello, 119–143. Malhaw, N.J.: Laurence Erlbaum Associates.

Gundel, Jeanette K., Nancy Hedberg, and Ron Zacharski. 1993. "Cognitive Status and the Form of Referring Expressions in Discourse". *Language* 69(2): 274–307.

Hopper, Paul J. 1998. "Emergent Grammar." In *The New Psychology of Language: Cognitive and Functional Approaches to Language Structure*, ed. by Michael Tomasello, 155–175. Mahwah, N.J.: Lawrence Erlbaum Associates.

Hopper, Paul J. 2015. "An Emergentist Approach to Grammar." In *The Handbook of Language Emergence*, ed. by Brian MacWhinney and William O'Grady, 314–327. Chichester: John Wiley & Sons.

Karmiloff-Smith, Annette. 1979. *A Functional Approach to Child Language: A Study of Determiners and Reference*. Cambridge: Cambridge University Press

Karmiloff-Smith, Annette. 1985. "Language and Cognitive Processes from a Developmental Perspective." *Language and Cognitive Processes* 1(1): 61–85.

Kupisch, Tanja. 2007. "Determiners in Bilingual German-Italian Children: What They Tell Us about the Relation Between Language Influence and Language Dominance". *Bilingualism: Language and Cognition* 10 (1): 57–78.

Laury, Ritva. 2001. "Definiteness and Reflexivity: Indexing Socially Shared Experience." *Pragmatics* 11 (4): 401–420.

Le Mené-Guigourès, Marine. 2017. L'acquisition d'un paradigme: éclairage multidimensionnel sur la mise en place des déterminants chez quatre enfants entre 1;6 et 3;5 (PhD dissertation, Université Sorbonne Nouvelle-Paris 3, Paris, France). Retrieved from https://tel.archives-ouvertes.fr/tel-01719263

Le Mené, Marine, Anne Salazar Orvig, Christine da Silva-Genest, and Haydée Marcos. 2023. "The Choice of Referring Expressions in Adult-Child Dialogues. The influence of formal and functional factors". In *Reference: From conventions to pragmatics* ed. by Laure Gardelle, Laurence Vincent-Durroux, and Hélène Vinckel-Roisin, 323–345. Amsterdam : John Benjamins Publisher.

Maratsos, Michael P. 1974. "Preschool Children's Use of Definite and Indefinite Articles". *Child Development* 45(2): 446–455.

Ochs, Elinor, Emanuel A. Schegloff, and Sandra A. Thompson (eds). 1996. *Interaction and Grammar*. Cambridge: Cambridge University Press.

Peters, Ann M. 2001. "Filler Syllables: What is Their Status in Emerging Grammar?" *Journal of Child Language* 28: 229–242.

Rozendaal, Margot I. and Anne E. Baker. 2008. "A Cross-Linguistic Investigation of the Acquisition of the Pragmatics of Indefinite and Definite Reference in Two-Year-Olds." *Journal of Child Language* 35: 773–808.

Salazar Orvig, Anne, Geneviève de Weck, Rouba Hassan, and Annie Rialland (eds.). 2021. *The Acquisition of Referring Expressions: A Dialogical Approach*. Amsterdam: John Benjamins.

Salazar Orvig, Anne, Haydée Marcos, Stéphanie Caët, Cristina Corlateanu, Christine Da Silva, Rouba Hassan, Julien Heurdier, Marine Le Mené, Jocelyne Leber-Marin, and Aliyah Morgenstern. 2013. "Definite and Indefinite Determiners in French-Speaking Toddlers: Distributional Features and Pragmatic-Discursive factors." *Journal of Pragmatics* 56: 88–112.

Salazar Orvig, Anne, Haydée Marcos, Julien Heurdier, and Christine da Silva. 2018. "Referential Features, Speech Genres and Activity Types." In *Sources of Variation in First Language Acquisition: Languages, Contexts, and Learners*, ed. by Maya Hickmann, Harriet Jisa, and Edy Veneziano, 219–242. Amsterdam: John Benjamins.

Schaeffer, Jeannette and Lisa Matthewson. 2005. "Grammar and Pragmatics in the Acquisition of Article Systems". *Natural Language & Linguistic Theory* 23(1): 53–101.

Schafer, Robin J. and Jill de Villiers. 2000. "Imagining Articles: What 'a' and 'the' Can Tell Us about the Emergence of DP". In *Proceedings of the 24th Annual Boston University Conference on Language Development*. 2, ed. by S. Catherine Howell, Sarah A. Fish, and Thea Keith-Lucas, 609–620. Somerville: Cascadilla Press.

Thompson, Sandra A. 1997. "Discourse Motivations for the Core-Oblique Distinction as a Language Universal." In *Directions in Functional Linguistics*, ed. by Akio Kamio, 59–82. Amsterdam: John Benjamins.

Veneziano, Edy. 2003. "The Emergence of Noun and Verb Categories in the Acquisition of French." *Psychology of Language and Communication* 7: 23–36.

doi   Vinel, Élise, Anne Salazar Orvig, Geneviève de Weck, Salma Nashawati, and Somayeh Rahmati. 2021. "The Impact of Speech Genres on the Use of Referring Expressions." In *The Acquisition of Referring Expressions: A Dialogical Approach*, ed. by Anne Salazar Orvig, Geneviève de Weck, Rouba Hassan, and Annie Rialland, 287–316. Amsterdam: John Benjamins.

Vygotsky, Lev S. 1934/1962. *Thought and Language.* Cambridge, MA: M.I.T. Press.

doi   Wood, David, Jerome S. Bruner, and Gail Ross. 1976. "The Role of Tutoring in Problem Solving." *Journal of Child Psychology and Psychiatry* 17 (2): 89–100.

CHAPTER 6

(Non)referentiality of silent reference in Japanese conversation
How and what are inferred

Yoshiko Matsumoto
Stanford University

Japanese speakers carry out successful conversations in which arguments and adjuncts of predicates are not expressed. I call such unmentioned members of an event or state that can be inferred INFERABLES. Inferables present a range of interpretations from specific to more general and indeterminate. This chapter explores principled explanations for this phenomenon in Japanese, which allows a variety of disparate interpretations. The discussions find that frame semantics, a semantic theory that provides an envisionment of a described event with the attendant roles, can offer an explanation. Hearers and speakers TRUST each other that some plausible entities (inferables) instantiate the unmentioned elements. When clarification is needed, they seek to ENSURE the construal by providing more explicit descriptions

Keywords: Japanese, ellipsis, zero-anaphora, inferables, frame semantics, conversational principle, trust-ensure, (non)referentiality, indeterminacy, pragmatics

1. Introduction

1.1 Background

Japanese speakers carry out successful conversations often without the use of explicit forms that refer to the members of a described event or state, including the main figures such as the actors and undergoers as well as less prominent roles, e.g. the time, the place, and the instrument. This chapter will seek a semantic and pragmatic explanation for this phenomenon, illustrated by natural everyday talk in Japanese.

https://doi.org/10.1075/pbns.344.06mat

The ubiquity of unexpressed syntactic arguments in Japanese has been well-noted in the past linguistic literature especially after the functional syntactic study by Kuno (1973, 1978, 1987). Kuno drew attention to Japanese sentences such as Example (1), in which the subject of *itta* 'went' and the object of *ai* 'see' are not explicitly expressed, contrary to what would be expected from English (or many European languages).

(1) ジョンが来たので、会いに行った。
    John ga kita node, ai ni itta.
    NOM came since see to went
    'Since John came, (I) went to see (him).'   [Kuno 1973, p. 17]

This phenomenon, called "ellipsis" by Kuno and others, was analogized with the use of pronouns in English, as the translation of the example suggests. From this analogy, linguists have often referred to the phenomenon in Japanese as "zero pronominalization", "zero anaphora", or in some versions of generative syntax "pro-drop", implicitly equating the conditions for so-called ellipsis in Japanese with those for pronouns in English. Under that assumption, the unexpressed arguments, like English pronouns, are considered either recoverable from the prior linguistic and/or extra-linguistic context or being arbitrary or generic.

The analogy between unexpressed arguments in Japanese and pronouns in English produced numerous analyses in various areas of linguistics, including syntax, semantics, discourse pragmatics, and natural language processing (e.g. Hinds 1982; Kameyama 1985; Kuroda 1979; Nariyama 2000; Ohso 1976; Shibatani 1990; Walker et al. 1995), yet there remained many difficult unanswered questions, especially when actual discourse data were examined. For instance, Fry (2001) in his corpus study illustrates that existing accounts are not always supported by natural, rather than constructed, discourse and do not successfully explain the resolution and coreference of unexpressed arguments. The analogy has also been disputed by other studies that examined naturally-occurring data (e.g. Eckert & Strube 1999; Matsumoto 1981 a, b, c, 2002; Ono and Thompson 1997; Ono and Suzuki 2020). Together, these suggest that unexpressed reference in Japanese cannot be considered simply equivalent to an invisible or inaudible counterpart of an English pronoun, and we should not rely on the analogy in order to understand the conditions for explicit or silent reference in Japanese.

Departing from the assumption that what is silent is a syntactically missing argument that is represented by a zero pronoun, I will examine the ubiquity of silent reference in Japanese and the possibility that what is not mentioned can be underdetermined or indeterminate. I will also consider the empirical and theoretical implications of the phenomenon, drawing on semantic and pragmatic explanations based on human experience. My analysis here takes as background previous studies of unmentioned potential referents in written and spoken discourse (e.g.

Matsumoto 1981 a, b), previous work questioning the concept of argument structure in conversational data (e.g. Ono and Thompson 1997; Ono and Suzuki 2020), and a proposed frame-semantic alternative to the concept of argument structure (e.g. Matsumoto 1997) as well as the accounts of the discourse functions of referential expressions (e.g. Clancy and Downing 1987).

1.2   The proposal

In Japanese, an utterance such as *tabeta* 'ate' can be a grammatically independent natural utterance even though no arguments are explicitly expressed. Since the verb is in a finite form with no marking of person, gender, or number, it does not provide sufficient grammatical information to retrieve inexplicit referents. Moreover, no non-linguistic clues are available when the potential referents are not present in the speech context. Such potential referents can be indeterminate, as Example 2 and others in the next section illustrate. How, then, can conversations be smoothly conducted in such uncertainty? To account for the question, I will propose the concept of INFERABLES and the principle of TRUST – ENSURE, both of which can be theoretically supported by frame semantics, as developed by Fillmore (e.g. 1977, 1982), in conjunction with Grice's Cooperative Principle.

INFERABLES are members of an event or state in discourse that are not mentioned but that can be inferred at the time of conversation. This concept is intended as an alternative to "referents", reflecting that there is no explicit referring expression and thus nothing that can be called a referent. Non-explicit members of an event or state are inferred, or alluded to (Ewing, this volume), through available linguistic and non-linguistic information rather than being clearly referred to by an explicit expression. The exact identity of an unmentioned entity may not be important depending on the purpose of the ongoing discourse. As will be illustrated by the examples in the following sections, the non-explicitness facilitates a range of interpretations of inferables from specific to more general, or even indeterminate.

The concept of inferables presents a clear contrast to the conventional syntactically based approach to referentiality that assumes that arguments are required to be expressed and that the referents of null-arguments must therefore be fully recoverable from the previous linguistic context. The view presented in this paper finds a theoretical and analytical basis in frame semantics (e.g. Fillmore 1982; Fillmore and Atkins 1992; Matsumoto in print for an overview), a semantic theory that prioritizes language users' human experience rather than the truth-conditional aspect of language and that views the meaning of linguistic materials (e.g. a word) in terms of a network of experiential information. The analysis in this chapter also draws on ideas similar to the notion of the conversational cooperative principle (e.g. Grice 1975), which also closely incorporates cognitive and interactional perspectives of actual language use and users. The frame semantics approach suggests, for example, that a predicate, such as *tabeta* 'ate' in Japanese, evokes participating roles in the event, such as the Eater and the Food (and Time, Place and other general concomitants of the event).[1] Similarly, a noun, such as *hon* 'book,' can evoke associated objects, such as the cover, as well as general activities associated with it, such as reading.[2] This network of understanding reflects the fact that, based on their real world experience and linguistic knowledge, language users can envision that the Eater and the Food[3] are crucially involved in carrying out the action of eating in general. Importantly, these roles in the action can be envisioned even without knowing exactly who or what instantiates such roles. What this means for the participants of a conversation is that they are not left with a complete void of information, even when no explicit mention is made, and they can choose to go along with the flow of the conversation with a limited amount of information, making inferences in the context of the ongoing conversation. If and when more concrete information is communicatively desired, the participants can seek explicit reference to the specific instantiation of the evoked roles.

Relying on general linguistic knowledge supported by human experience, as has been theorized in frame semantics, the hearers can *TRUST* that some plausible specific or nonspecific inferables can instantiate the unmentioned members of the action or the state, and the speakers also trust that the hearers can follow along with the story from the amount of information provided. Thus, the participants of a verbal interaction trust that semantic, pragmatic and other discoursal or real-world information can be relied upon when no explicit reference is made. When the participants of a conversation want to *ensure* the understanding of a specific member – i.e. person, object, location, etc. – involved in the event or state, explicit expressions are sought and used. This can be called a system or principle of *TRUST – ENSURE*.

The idea that information is made explicit when and only when needed is reminiscent of Grice's Cooperative Principle of conversation and, in particular, its attendant Maxim of Quantity, which says "1. Make your contribution as informative as is required (for the current purpose of the exchange), 2. Do not make your contribution more informative than is required," (Grice 1975: 45). Although it is not always apparent what can be considered as a required contribution to

---

1. See e.g. Matsumoto (1997) for a more detailed description of potential participant roles evoked by a predicate.

2. Qualia theory proposed by Pustejovsky (1993) provides further detail.

3. Notations such as "the Eater" and "the Food" in Frame Semantics are used to refer to abstract roles.

a conversation, the Maxim of Quantity plausibly suggests that some referential information can remain unexpressed as long as it is not required for the accepted purpose or direction of the talk exchange. This Maxim is relevant to all instances involving inferables in that it provides a general pragmatic explanation of why inferables can remain unexpressed and indeterminate once the interactional participants have been given sufficient information for the purpose of the ongoing conversation.

As was pointed out earlier, and as we will observe in examples of actual conversations in the next section, there are cases in which no specific member instantiates an inferable and the inferable can thus be said to be indeterminate. In passing, it is worthwhile to note that some philosophers who have addressed referentiality and definite descriptions, such as Quine and Davidson, have questioned the assumption of a clear association of words to reality and have suggested that reference may be indeterminate (e.g., Davdison 1984; Quine 1960, 1992; see also the chapters in this volume by Ewing, Helasvuo & Suomalainen, and Tao). Although the philosophers' concerns are about reference of explicit words rather than inference about something not explicitly expressed, and although they did not consider natural examples, it is of interest that the question of indeterminacy is a recognized issue in the philosophy of language.

In the next section, we will examine conversational excerpts to consider how interlocutors carry out conversations successfully without explicit mention of referents. In the section following these observations, I will summarize the findings and discuss their implications to our understanding of referentiality and grammar.

2.   Referentiality and inferentiality: A Variety of inferables

Based on examinations of free-flowing everyday conversations in Japanese, I will illustrate that potential referents that are inferred in context, or inferables, generally remain unexpressed and indeterminate unless the participants in the interaction require that the specific identities be made explicit for the purpose of the ongoing conversation. The frame semantic understanding of an envisioned event or a state provides the theoretical grounding for understanding this phenomenon. The observations in this study will be found consistent with the findings of Ono and Suzuki (2020) that so-called zero-anaphora in Japanese does not involve the deletion/ellipsis of arguments of the predicate that are tracked in discourse. While Ono and Suzuki's study focuses on instances in fixed expressions in their everyday talk data, where zero-anaphora is predominantly found, the study in this chapter investigates a variety of examples that are found in the more general environment of productive uses.

The examples below come from my collection of spontaneous conversations among friends and relatives of varied age groups – younger (20s–30s), middle aged (40s–60s) and older (70s),[4] except for one short excerpt (Example 4), which was taken from a video clip on YouTube.

2.1   Fluid and flexible indeterminate inferables

Example 2 illustrates a situation in which there is neither apparent antecedent in the prior conversation nor persons/items that are present in the context that can be indexed by nonexplicit elements, i.e. inferables. It demonstrates that having indeterminate and flexible inferables causes no problem for continuing the thread of conversation. The inferables here are not simply generic, but different categories of people over the course of the conversation. Frame semantics can provide a principled explanation and a theoretical background to understanding this phenomenon, unlike a conventional analysis in terms of ellipted referents.

Example 2 below is an excerpt from a casual conversation between two young friends (20s–30s), an instructor of the Japanese language at a university in the U.S. (A) and his friend (B), a graduate student originally from Japan. The instructor, A, just started offering his thoughts about what seems needed in the current state of language instruction and of textbooks available in the U.S. In translations of this and other excerpts, the notation *(words)* indicates words that are not said in Japanese but are supplied for intelligibility, while the notation (( )) indicates positions that typically require referential expressions in English but no expressions are used in Japanese. As will become clear in the discussions to follow, inferablity and indeterminacy form a cline, but for ease of presenting the examples, these conventions are used in the translations.

(2)   Conversation about Japanese language instruction between an instructor and his friend
    1　B: 今、中級教えてるの?
         ima, chuukyuu oshieteru no?
         Are (you) teaching the intermediate level now?
    2　A: そう
         soo
         right
    3　B: 中級というか.. 二年目の
         chuukuu toyuu ka .. ninenme no
         the intermediate level .. or the second-year level
    4　A: 二年生三年生っていうところが.. 教材ってのが
         ninensei sannensei tteiu tokoro ga .. kyoozai tte no ga
         at the levels of the second year and third year, .. teaching materials

---

4.   The data was collected with the consent of participants. The names that appear in the paper are all pseudonyms.

5   ..あまりないのよね
     ..ammari nai no yo ne
     (there) aren't many, y'know'
6 A: でぇ.. 日本へ行ったらさ..
     de: .. nihon e ittara sa ..
     and   Japan to go:COND PP
     and if (( )) go to Japan..[5]
7 B: うん
     un
     uh-huh
8 A: 原文主義でさ
     genbun-shugi   de   sa
     original.text-principle COP:TE PP
     (( )) is/has the principle of reading the originals
9 B: うん
     un
     uh-huh
10 A: どんどんどんどんさ
     dondon dondon sa
     at a   great speed
11   .. ほんとに..生のもので読んでいくっていう感じん.. なるでしょう?
     .. hontoni .. namano mono de yondeiku tteyuu kanji n naru   desho:?
       really   raw   thing INS read.go QT   feel DAT become COP:EVD
     .. really .. seems like (( )) keep reading with the real thing, right?
12 B: うん
     un
     uh-huh
13 A: ま..日本だったらそういうのできると思うけども
     ma.. nihon dattara sooyuu   no dekiru to omoo kedomo..
     well Japan COP:COND like.that NMLZ be.able COMP think though
     Well..if (it were) Japan, (( )) think something like that is doable but..
14 B: うん
     un
     uh-huh

In the first five lines of the excerpt, A conveys that there are not enough teaching materials for the second- and the third-year Japanese courses. In line 6, he says *de: .. nihon e ittara sa* 'and.. if (( )) go to Japan,' followed by line 8, *genbun-shugi de sa* '(( )) is/has the principle of reading the originals.' The identity of who goes to Japan in line 6 is not singularly determinable in this context.[6] It can be speaker A, but it could be *gakusei* 'student.' Beyond the specific linguistic context, from the general topic of the conversation, it could also be Japanese language learners or

---

5. Interlinear morpheme-to-morpheme glosses are given only for examples in which translations include (( )).

6. In the segment that precedes Example 2, explicit noun phrases referred to items related to textbooks such as *tango* 'vocabulary,' *jisho* 'dictionary' as well as *kyookasho* textbook' appeared most frequently. Two senior educators in Japan and *gakusei* 'student' were mentioned once. Concepts such as *nihongo kyooiku* 'Japanese language education' and *gogaku* 'language study' had one mention each. None seem to be a possible referent of the unmentioned element.

instructors who are overseas, or even non-specific people in general. Nothing in the context specifically points the hearer to a definitive interpretation. Importantly, however, the predicate (in the conditional form) *ittara* 'go:COND' evokes the role of the Goer, and the conversation participants can at least envision a situation of someone (without knowing the specific identity) going somewhere (in this case, Japan). Similarly in line 8, from the semantic and pragmatic content of the utterance, 'the principle of reading the originals' (= reading materials in the unedited Japanese) can be inferred to be a principle of an abstract entity, such as *nihongo kyooiku* 'Japanese language education,' or of some professional organizations, or groups of Japanese teachers in Japan. Any of the possibilities mentioned above (and conceivably others) would make sense as an inferable – that is, the entity that A claims to follow the 'principle of reading the originals.' In other words, the inferable is indeterminate, yet the utterance is understandable at the time of the conversation because the hearers trust that at least there is an entity that follows that principle, consistent with frame semantics. If the conversation had been conducted in English, A might have said *'if you go to Japan, they follow the principle of reading the originals/there is the principle of reading the originals,'* since such underlined positions are syntactically required to be expressed. It should be emphasized that not only could there be any number of entities or subgroups, 'they' could also be interpreted as either the same or different entities or subgroups.

A similar point is illustrated by the inferable in line 11. The specific identity of the inferable is unclear but the hearer can trust the existence of someone who can instantiate the role of the Reader; it can be anyone or any (sub)groups relevant to the activity expressed by the predicate *yondeiku* 'continue to read, keep reading' in the context of Japanese instruction (e.g. students or students and teachers). As evidenced in B's responses *un* 'uh-huh' in lines 7, 9, and 12, which accept A's utterances without inquiring about the identities of the nonexplicit referents, the ambiguity or indeterminacy of an inferable at each stage in the conversation, including whether or not there is continuity of a reference, does not hinder communication or comprehension. In fact, when I asked speaker A to specify the identity of who was unsaid, he could not do so. If such identities were important to continuing the conversation, B would likely request clarification, as speakers in other examples we will consider (e.g. Yuki in line 14 of Example 6).

While the inferables that we discussed above suggest a range of possible groups of people and entities that are nonspecific indeterminates, they are all related to the field of Japanese language education. What we observe here suggests that conversation participants can use their experience and knowledge to infer a variety of nonspecific indeterminate persons or objects relevant to the general topic of the ongoing conversation that may instantiate participants of the events or states described in the utterances. The participants may choose one or more plausible interpretations at the time of an utterance, but that is not required for conducting a conversation. Indeterminacy is tolerated or even potentially effective in letting a conversation flow smoothly. The flexibility and fluidity of inferables are also likely to be an advantage rather than a problem in everyday talk.

2.2   Indeterminate inferables and non-explicit switch reference

The following excerpt is from a conversation among four female cousins in their seventies. There are at least two points of interest: (i) switch reference without explicit expressions (lines 13–19), and (ii) non-specific inferables alluded to in the utterances are not simply generic entities but are more restricted (lines 2, 4, 5, 8, 9, 16 and 17) or more tightly delineated than the instances in Example 2 in the last section.

In this excerpt, Saya, who is an advanced practitioner of the Way of Tea (or 'tea ceremony'), has started talking about a fellow tea practitioner, who is the oldest among the group of Saya's fellow practitioners and who took care of business matters as the representative of the group. However, as this oldest member had not been good at it, Saya was given the role of money management for the last few years.

(3)   Excerpt from a conversation among cousins in their seventies [S=Saya, H=Hide, M=Mayu, Y=Yuki]

```
1    S: そいでね、その人がね一番いわゆるお茶では古いし、
        soide ne, sono shito ga ne ichiban iwayuru o-cha de wa furui shi,
        and, that person is the oldest in the so-called tea (circle),
2       やっぱり立てないと[まずい の。
        yappari    tatenaito       [mazui no.
        after.all keep.face:NEG COND bad    PP
        (( )) have to pay due respect (( )).
3    H:                             [ああ
                                    [aa
                                     ah
4    S: そいでお中元お歳暮の時期は、先生にあげきゃなんないの。
        soide ochuugen     oseebo    no jiki   wa, sensei ni age-nakyanaranai no.
        and   summer.gift winter.gift LK season TOP teacher DAT give-have.to    PP
        and in the seasons of summer gifts and winter gifts, (( )) have to give (( ))
        to the teacher
5       そいで、今、まではその人にやらしてたんだけどね。
        soide, ima, made wa sono shito ni yarashiteta-   n-da    kedo ne.
        and    now until TOP that person DAT do:CAUS:IPFV:PST- NMLZ-COP but  PP
        and until now (( )) had that person do (( )), but
6       当日になってもねえ、お金ちゃんと作ってこないのよ。=
        toojitsu ni nattemo     nee, okane chanto   tsukutte konai  no yo.=
        that.day DAT become:TE:CNSV PP   money properly make:TE come:NEG PP PP
        even on the very day, (( )) isn't ready with the money
7    M: =あら
        = ara
        oh
```

8   H: [ああ 今日 あげましょうつうことに　　[なっても
       [a: kyoo agemashoo tsuu koto ni   [nattemo
       ah today give.shall QT thing DAT   become:TE:CNSV
       ah, even when (( )) decide to give (( )) (( )) today

9   S: [そいで困っちゃって、　[なっててても
       [soide komatchatte,   [nattetemo
       so   in_trouble:COMPL:TE become:TE:IPFV:CNSV
       so (( )) didn't know what to do, even when

10   Y: あ[らあ
       a[ra:
       ooh

11   S: [そいでねえ、結局あたしが次に歳だもんだから、
       [soide nee, kekkyoku atashi ga tsugini toshi da monda kara,
       and, in the end, because I am the next oldest,

12   あたしの方におはちが回ってきて、ここ 二三年は
       atashi no hoo ni ohachi ga mawattekite, koko ni-san nen wa
       (it) became my turn, in these two-three years

13   [あたしがやってんだけども、書いて、
       atashi ga yattenda   kedomo, kaite   kichinto shite,
       I   NOM do:TE-NMLZ-COP although write:TE properly do:TE
       I have been doing (( )), writing (( )), properly doing (( )), but,

14   Y: [ああやって###
       [a:: yatte #####
       ah do:TE
       ah (( )) doing (( )) ######

15   S: それでないとね、でその場でもって当日になってからね、
       soredenai to ne, de sono ba demotte toojitsu ni natte kara ne,
       if that's not the case, then right there and then on the very day,

16   お金集めたりするとね、
       okane atsumetari suru-to ne,
       money collect.or do-COND PP
       if (( )) collect money,

17   間違っちゃうのよ[ね、[うーん。[それだもんで、
       machigatchau   no yo[ne,[u::n. [sore da monde,
       mistake:TE:COMPL PP PP PP yes   that COP because
       (( )) make mistakes, ye::s because of that

18   Y: [そうよね [ちゃんと [やってないと、
                [soo yone:,[chanto [yattenai-to
                so PP PP properly do:TE:IPFV:NEG- COND
                right, if (( )) don't do (it) properly,

19   S: 信用 なくなっちゃって、[この頃あたしが
       shinyoo nakunatchatte,   [konogoro atashi ga,
       trust   lost.become:TE:COMPL:TE recently I   NOM
       (( )) lost trust and, these days I,

20   Y: [@ @ @ @,
                        [@ @ @ @,
                        (laughter),

21   S: や-やること(.) になって、
       ya-yaruko(.)to ninatte,
       d-do.things   become:TE
       wa (.)s (asked) to do (( ))

22   であたしは、そすとあたしもお金集めるのが
       de atashi wa, sosuto atashi mo okane atsumeru no ga

23   下手くそだから
       hetakuso dakara,
       and I, then I am also bad at collecting money,

Switch reference is illustrated in lines 13–19, in which the inferables are ambiguous and not constant across the lines, without any indication of switching. The Do-er and the Writer in line 13 most likely point specifically to the speaker, who was just explicitly brought into the discourse in lines 11–13. However, in the subsequent lines, the one who might collect money (line 16), make mistakes (line 17), and not do something properly (line 18) is not made explicit, potentially suggesting Saya herself, or the older fellow tea practitioner (referenced as *sono shito* "that person" in lines 1 and 5), or some relevant but nonspecific people (such as the inferable in line 16, which could be translated into English as the "generic" *you*). Yuki's laughter in line 20 seems to have prompted Saya to use the explicit reference to herself repeatedly in the subsequent utterance to make a contrast to ensure that she is *not* the one who lost the trust, made mistakes, and so forth in her earlier utterances. What these lines illustrate is that the interpretations of inferables is presumed to be shared, or at least not questioned, until the need of clarification arises.

The second point of interest in Example 3 is the varied scope of an inferable when it is nonspecific and indeterminate. Some examples are seen in lines 2, 4, 5, 8, 9, 16 and 17. In line 2, Saya conveys that due respect has to be paid to the older fellow tea practitioner. It is said not in the passive but the active form with nonexplicit subject. The members who should pay respect to elders might be expressed as *we* in English, pointing to the rest of the fellow practitioners in the same tea circle. The human inferable in line 4 (who should give gifts to the teacher) is similar, but it could include the older practitioner. In the paragraph above, I said that the inferable in line 16 could be translated to generic *you* in English, but it suggests a restricted group such as some of the people in the tea circle who were in the position of collecting money (see also Suomalainen and Varjo 2020, Helasvuo and Suomalainen this volume). The interpretation is more restricted than those discussed in the last section.

The fact that both cases of switched and indeterminate inferables discussed above apparently cause no problem in conversational interaction suggests that the participants rely on the frame semantic information – i.e. the fact that there are relevant roles in the frame evoked by each predicate – and the participant trust that some entity instantiates the relevant role even when the specific identity of the entity is not given.

2.3 Latent resolution of inferables

We have observed in the last sections the flexibility and fluidity of what or who can be inferred to instantiate a role in an evoked frame of an event or state. In this section, Example 4 illustrates what we may call the latent (or after-the-fact) resolution of inferables. Such latent resolution leans heavily on frame semantic information, as we will also observe later in Example 5.

The example below is an excerpt from a natural conversation posted on YouTube, which was recorded by a Japanese language instructor for the purpose of providing her online learners an example of authentic casual conversations among friends.[7] Three young Japanese women (probably in their late twenties to thirties), who were close friends in college, were chatting in a cafe. They all seem to have majored in foreign languages and were reminiscing about the classes they took. In the excerpted segment, Speaker Y tried to recall who was taking German. Speaker X said in response that all in their group took Korean. This reminded Speaker Y that a male professor taught the Korean class. Confirming this, Speaker X continued and pointed out in lines 10–11 and 13–14 that there were many students present although it was a language class and that only grammar explanations were given without any conversation practice. The point of interest is line 10 in which Speaker X says *hirokute* '(is/was) spacious' without specifying what object or entity is/was spacious.

(4)   Conversation among three close friends from college days

```
 1  Y: 誰かドイツ語取ってなかった?
        dareka doitsugo tottenakatta?
        Didn't someone take German?
 2  X: うちらの中ではいなか(.)った[と思う。
        uchira no naka de wa inaka(.)tta [to om(oo).
        we     LK. among LOC TOP exist:NEG:PST COMP think
        (( )) think (there) wasn't (one) among us.
 3  Y:                              [そだっけ-
                                     [sodakke-
                                     Was (that) right-
 4  X: みんな韓国語だったのよ=
        minna kankokugo datta no yo=
        (It was) Korean (for) everyone (i.e we all took Korean)
 5  Y: = 男の先生のやつかぁ
        = otoko no sensei  no yatsu ka:
          male  LK teacher LK one   Q
        the one with a male professor, I guess
 6  X: . あそう男の [先生のやつ
        . a soo otokono[sensei no yatsu
        (.) ah right the one with a male professor
 7  Y:             [ああ [ああそうだそうだ
                    [a::: [a: sooda sooda
                    ah::: ah: (that's) right (that's) right
 8  X:                 [そうそそそうそう
                       [soo so so soosoo
                       right ri- ri- right right
```

7. In the segment that precedes Example 2, explicit noun phrases referred to items related to textbooks such as *tango* 'vocabulary,' *jisho* 'dictionary' as well as *kyookasho* textbook' appeared most frequently. Two senior educators in Japan and *gakusei* 'student' were mentioned once. Concepts such as *nihongo kyooiku* 'Japanese language education' and *gogaku* 'language study' had one mention each. None seem to be a possible referent of the unmentioned element.

9 Z: だったっけ?
 datta kke?
 was (it)?
10 X: 結構広くて、結構なんか語学の、授業なのに、⁸
 kekkoo hirokute, kekkoo nanka gogaku no, jugyoo nanoni,
 quite spacious:TE quite somehow language.study LK class although
 (( )) (is) quite spacious, quite um although (it is) a language class
11 結構 [人数が、いるから
 kekkoo [ninzuu ga, iru kara
 quite headcount NOM exist because
 quite many people are there
12 Y: [うんうんうん
 [un un un
 yeah yeah yeah
13 X: そう会話練習とか一切なかったよね?
 soo kaiwa-renshuu toka issai nakatta yone?
 right (there) was nothing like a conversation practice at all, right?
14 [ひらすら文法なんか説明されて、わかんないみたいな、
 [hitasura bunpoo nanka setsumeisarete, wakannai mitaina,
 single.mindedly grammar something explain:PASS:TE understand:NEG like
 singly-mindedly (( )) were given grammar explanations, and (we were) like "((
 )) don't get it"
15 Y: [うんうんうん
 [un un un
 yeah yeah yeah

After confirming Y's statement that the Korean class they took was taught by a male professor, Speaker X in line 10, seemingly all of a sudden, comments that '(( )) (is/was) quite spacious.' What is/was spacious was neither explicit nor clear from the prior conversation. A frame semantic analysis suggests that the suspended resolution does not jeopardize the conversation since the predicate *hirokute* (the TE-form of *hiroi* 'is/was spacious') evokes the 'being spacious' frame, which allows the hearers to envision the role of the thing (the 'Space') that is spacious and to trust that there is some entity (specific or not) that instantiates the 'Space.' Speaker X continues and says *kekkoo nanka gogaku no, jugyoo nanoni, kekkoo ninzuu ga iru kara* 'quite um although ((it))(is) a language class, quite many people are there.' The mention of *jugyoo* 'class' can evoke the Location in the frame of class (as an activity), which can readily be associated with (or instantiated by) a classroom as a class is normally held at a location, such as a classroom, which entails space. This interpretation can retrospectively invite the construal that the classroom instantiates the Space which was described in line 10 as spacious. In addition, the predicate *iru* 'exist, (there) are' evokes the Location in the frame of existing, and further supporting the retrospective construal that the classroom must be what instantiates the space that was spacious. This is so regard-

---

8. https://www.youtube.com/watch?v=shacAPbsc4U. I thank Alan Cheng for pointing this website to me.

less of the fact that Speaker X never explicitly mentioned *kyooshitsu* 'classroom' anywhere in the conversation.

This example suggests that the process by which hearers construe nonexplicit elements may not be as straightforward as simple reference tracking of the arguments of a predicate.

2.4   Ambiguous inferables

The flexibility and fluidity inherent in interpretations of inferables can be a source of ambiguity, as we observed in Section 2.2, because a role in a frame evoked by a predicate can be instantiated by a variety of entities if they are semantically, pragmatically and interactionally plausible. Example 5 presents an instance in which the speaker's selection of lexical items that index sociocultural information disambiguates the interpretation of the inferable.

The excerpt in Example 5 is from a casual conversation among middle-aged long-time female friends (Yuri, Emi, Aki and Mie) who belong to an amateur singing group. It was recorded just after their concert, and most of the utterances were compliments directed toward Mie, who sang solo. As part of the compliments, Yuri reported that she said to Mie's children, who were at the concert, "((Your)) mother was fabulous, wasn't ((she))?" Emi enters in the conversation and says in line 2 *soo itteta yo* '(( )) said so'. The identity of the inferable in line 2 is potentially ambiguous between Yuri and Mie's children.

(5)   Excerpt from post-concert conversations among amateur singers

```
1 Yuri: お母さま素敵だったでしょうって言ったら、あのう
         okaasama  suteki    datta deshoo tte ittara, anoo
         mother.HON fabulous COP:PST COP.EVD QT  say:COND umm
         When ((I)) said, '(( )) mother was fabulous, wasn't ((she))?', umm
2 Emi:  そう言ってたよ
         soo itteta        yo
         so  say:TE:IPFV:PST PP
         (( )) said so.
3 Yuri: そう言ってましたよ、[そう言っていらしたわええ。
         soo ittemashita  yo, [soo itteirashita  wa ee.
         so  say:IPFV:PST.PH PP  SO   say:IPFV:PST.RH PP yes
         (( )) said so, (( )) said so, yes.
4       素敵だったってねえ。
         sutekidatta      tte nee.
         fabulous.COP:PST QT  PP
         ((they)) (said that) (( )) was/were fabulous, right?
5 Aki:                     [ああそう。
                           [aa soo.
                           ah, (is that) so.
```

The two predicates in line 3, *ittemashita* 'said.PH' and *itteirashita* 'said.RH', carry the same semantic content as *itteta* 'said' in line 2, but are so-called honorific forms: the Performative Honorific form (PH) and the Referent Honorific form (RH), respectively and index different sociocultural information. These honorific forms give a more formal tone and a stance of regard toward the subject referent of the predicate. In light of the general practice of not using honorifics to describe oneself or one's own act, Yuri's utterances in lines 3 disambiguate retrospectively the inferable in line 2 and the referent who 'said so' is clarified as the solo singer Mie's children and not Yuri. What is notable here is that the potential ambiguity is resolved not by the explicit use of a noun phrase with definite reference but by pragmatic and interactional information indicated by elements of the predicate clauses, in this case honorifics.

2.5   Ensuring specific inferable when needed

Example 6 below illustrates a case in which a participant (Yuki) of a multimember conversation interjects to ensure the identity of the inferable after a chain of utterances with no explicit expressions of the core member of the described events or states, i.e., the core member (or role) of the frames evoked by the predicates. It is revealed that Yuki's guess was wrong, but she apparently followed the storyline. We can reasonably conjecture that she trusted the existence of an entity (in this case, a person) that instantiates the role and that this was enough for her purpose of conversation until she felt the need of clarification.

In this extract, the same four female cousins in their seventies as in Example 3 are talking about injuries. Hide and Saya are twins whose mother is a sister of Yuki and Mayu's father. At the beginning of the excerpt, Hide shifts the topic of the conversation to the health condition of their (Hide and Saya's) mother from Yuki's recovery from an injury. The story is that their mother often recovered from an injury surprisingly quickly despite her advanced age.

(6)   Excerpt from a conversation among cousins in their seventies [H=Hide, M=Mayu, S=Saya, Y=Yuki]
```
1 H: ゆきちゃんはでもね、そういう風にね、割合と傷してもね、
     Yuki-chan wa demo ne, soyufuni ne, wariaito  kizushitemo  ne,
     (name)-DIM TOP but  PP   that.like PP  relatively injury.do:CNSV PP
     Yuki will, but, even though (( )) got wounded like that,
2    早く治ると思う。
     hayaku naoru to  omoo.
     soon   heal COMP think
     (( )) get better soon, (( )) think.
3    うちのお母さんが案外そうだったのね
     uchi no okaasan ga angai soodatta no ne
     our mother was surprisingly like that
4 M: ああそうな[の? うん。ああ
     aa soona [no? un. aa:
     ah is (that) so? mm. right.
```

5 H: [うん.
          [un.
          yeah

6   あの、なんか怪我したりしてもね=
      ano, nanka kegashitari-shite mo   ne,=
      Well somehow injury.do:or-do:TE even PP
      well, even when (( )) was somehow injured

7 S: = そう
     = so
     yup

8 H: 割合とね、すぐよく[治っちゃう。[あらあたしはね、 ⁹
     wariaito ne, sugu yoku, [naottyau. [ara atashi wa ne,
     relatively PP soon well heal:COMPL oh I   TOP PP
     relatively, (( )) gets better.   oh I,

9 S: [肉 があるの [歳の割には
                           [niku ga aru no [toshi no warini   wa
                           flesh NOM exist PP age   LK relatively for
                           (( ))'s well-padded for (( )) age

10 H: 寝ちゃ-もう 寝込んでる時に[さ、お風呂かなんか入ってね
      necha-, moo, nekonderu   toki ni [sa, ofuro ka nanka   haitte ne
      lie-, INJ lie.down:IPFV when DAT PP   bath or something enter:TE PP
      lie-, y'know, when (( )) was bedridden, (( )) took bath

11 S: [そうね
                            [soo ne
                            (that's) right

12 M: 滑っ[たの?
      subet[ta no?
      slip:PST PP
      did (( )) slip?

13 H: [うん、このしざのとこね、ひどく怪我してさ、それで
       [un, kono shiza no toko ne, hidoku   kegashite sa, sorede
       yes this knee LK place PP terribly injury.do:TE PP then
       yup, around this knee, (( )) injured terribly, and then

14 Y: おばあちゃん?
      obaachan?
      grandma?

15 H: [ううん
      [uu:n,
      no:

16 S: [ううんうちのお母さん。
      [uun uchi no okaasan.
      uh-uh, our mother

The new topic, *uchi no okaasan* 'my/our mother' is introduced in line 3 with the nominative *ga*. In the absence of any newly introduced topic, it remains the topic in the stretch of discourse carried out mainly by Hide and Saya and as the unexpressed element of the predicates, as marked by double parentheses, in lines 6–14. The inferable specifically points to the mother of the twin sisters. When Mayu asks in line 12, whether she (the mother of the twins) slipped, Yuki interjects in line 14 the word *obaachan* 'grandma?' with a question contour. Yuki meets a quick

---

9. In lines 10–11, the predicates are used in the non-past form. The translation retains that choice.

negation and the correction by the twins, *uu::n, uchi no okaasan* 'no:, my/our mother'. This suggests that Yuki was going along with the story without knowing clearly who the unmentioned member of the described events was. Perhaps, she was not paying attention to Hide's utterance at the beginning. She sought to clarify in line 14 by offering her speculation. That is, Yuki seemed to follow the turn of events without knowing the definite identity of the main character, until she expressed the need for the specific information. The difference between this example and a conventionally discussed case of ellipsis in which the inferable is easily trackable after an explicit prior mention is that it is unclear whether or not the recipients of this story had in mind a specific instantiation of a role in the evoked frame.

It should also be pointed out that, while the translation of Saya's utterance in line 9 *niku ga aru no* is given as '(( ))'s well-padded', no argument is missing in the original Japanese sentence since *niku* '(lit. flesh) is the subject of the predicate *aru* 'exists, there is'. What is not expressed is where the flesh exists or belongs to (the Location), and that is the most relevant element in this story. An advantageous feature of frame semantics is that the frame evoked by the predicate *aru* 'exists, there is' includes the role Location, in contrast to the conventional notion of argument structure, which excludes such role as an adjunct.

3. Conclusion and implications

The examples we considered suggest that conversational storytelling can be more concerned with depictions of actions and states than with the exact or specific identity of the entities (e.g. people and items) that are involved in the depicted actions or states. Reference to such entities can often be silent, and such unmentioned members of depicted events are called INFERABLES in this present study. There can be different reasons for reference to be silent. We observed in the examples that in some stories the exact identity of inferables was not crucial, and the identity could be indeterminate in a variety of ways (as in Examples 2 and 3). In other stories, the speakers seem to have considered that the identity of the inferables was clear from prior mentions or the speech context and did not require explicit reference (as in Examples 4, 5, and 6). This was found to be the case even when the relevant inferables changed from one clause or sentence to another. The participants in conversations have a variety of contextual resources at their disposal to assess and access the inferables in the stories as they encounter them, e.g. prior mention, world knowledge, pragmatic use of honorifics, or perhaps the speaker's gaze if the relevant inferable is present at the speech context. But there is a question of how the conversation participants can manage disparate types of fluid and flexible inferables from indeterminate to specific. This chapter sought an explanation that can account for the question in a principled way and proposed that frame semantics in conjunction with Grice's conversational principles are at work.

The advantage of frame semantics is that it is grounded in human experience; not simply based on grammatical relations or logic. As the theory is based on an envisionment of the scene with associated roles evoked by linguistic materials (e.g. a word), the conversational participants can at least envision the basic events described in the story without the details about the event members. The participants (as both speakers and hearers) judge how much information (e.g. the exact identity of an event member) is necessary for the purpose of the conversation at a specific moment. Hearers TRUST that some plausible entities ("inferables") can instantiate the unmentioned elements, and speakers trust that the hearers can follow along with the story from the amount of information they provided. When either the speaker or the hearer, or both, need to clarify at a point in a conversation, they ENSURE the construal by providing explicit expressions or by other means. The investigation of how silent reference works in Japanese provides us with the important insight that mechanisms of language and their uses should be examined from the point of view of human action and experience.

Acknowledgements

I would like to express my sincere gratitude to the editors of this volume, Michael Ewing and Ritva Laury, who kindly offered valuable comments, as to well as Sandra A. Thompson, for their intellectual open-mindedness and generosity. My thanks also go to Andrew P. Nelson and Ryo Nomura for their assistance in providing glosses to the examples.

Abbreviations

CAUS	causative	LK	linker
CNSV	concessive	LOC	locative
COMP	complementizer	NEG	negative
COMPL	completive	NMLZ	nominalizer
COND	conditional	NOM	nominative
COP	copula	PASS	passive
DAT	dative	PP	pragmatic particle
DIM	diminutive	PST	past
EVD	evidential	QT	quotative
HON	honorific form	RH	reference honorific form
INS	instrumental	TE	the gerund form −*te*
IPFV	imperfective	TOP	topic

References

Clancy, Patricia M. and Pamela Downing. 1987. "The Use of *wa* as a Cohesion Marker in Japanese Oral Narratives." In *Perspectives on Topicalization: The Case of Japanese wa*, ed. by John Hinds, Senko Maynard, and Shoichi Iwasaki, 3–56. Amsterdam: John Benjamins.

Davidson, D. 1984. *Inquiries into Truth and Interpretation*, Oxford: Clarendon Press.

Eckert, Miriam and Michael Strube. 1999. "Resolving Discourse Deictic Anaphora in Dialogues." In *Proceedings of EACL-99*. Bergen, Norway.

Fillmore, Charles J. 1977. "The Case for Case Reopened." In *Syntax and Semantics. Vol. 8: Grammatical Relations*, ed. by Peter Cole and Jerrold Sadock, 59–82. New York: Academic Press.

Fillmore, Charles J. 1982. "Frame Semantics." In *Linguistics in the Morning Calm*, ed. by Linguistic Society of Korea. Seoul: Hanshin Publishing. 111–138.

Fillmore, Charles J. and Beryl T. Atkins. 1992. "Toward a Frame-Based Lexicon: The Semantics of RISK and its Neighbors." In *Frames, Fields, and Contrasts*, ed. by Adrienne Lehrer and Eva Feder Kittay, 75–102. Hillsdale, NJ: Lawrence Erlbaum Assoc.

Fry, John S. 2001. Ellipsis and Wa-Marking in Japanese Conversation. Unpublished Ph.D. Dissertation. Stanford University.

Grice, H. Paul. 1975. "Logic and Conversation." In *Syntax and Semantics*, ed. by Peter Cole and Jerry L. Morgan, 41–58. New York: Academic Press.

Hinds, John. 1982. *Ellipsis in Japanese*. Alberta: Linguistic Research.

Kameyama, Megumi. 1985. Zero Anaphora: The Case of Japanese. Unpublished Ph.D. Dissertation. Stanford University.

Kuno, Susumu. 1973. *The Structure of the Japanese Language*. Cambridge: MIT Press.

Kuno, Susumu. 1978. Danwa no Bunpoo [*Grammar of discourse*]. Tokyo: Taishukan.

Kuno, Susumu. 1987. *Functional Syntax: Anaphora, Discourse and Empathy*. Chicago: University of Chicago Press.

Kuroda, Shige-Yuki. 1979. *Generative Grammatical Studies in the Japanese Language*. New York: Garland.

Matsumoto, Yoshiko. 1981a. "Written and Spoken Language in Japanese: From the Aspect of Ellipsis." Unpublished manuscript, University of California, Berkeley.

Matsumoto, Yoshiko. 1981b. "Noun Phrase Ellipsis in Japanese Discourse." Unpublished manuscript, University of California, Berkeley.

Matsumoto, Yoshiko. 1981c. "How do People Refer to Things?" Unpublished manuscript, University of California, Berkeley.

Matsumoto, Yoshiko. 1997. *Noun-Modifying Constructions in Japanese: A Frame-Semantic approach*. Amsterdam: John Benjamins.

Matsumoto, Yoshiko. In press. "Frame Semantics." *The Cambridge Handbook of Construction Grammar*, ed. by Mirjam Fried and Kiki Nikiforidou. Cambridge: Cambridge University Press.

Matsumoto, Yoshiko. 2002. "Silent reference in Japanese discourse," a paper presented in a panel "Toward a Cognitive and Interactional Understanding of Person Reference in Japanese: A Usage-Based Approach" at the 45th Annual Meeting of the Association for Asian Studies. Washington, D.C. April 4–7, 2002

Nariyama, Shigeko. 2000. Referent identification for ellipted arguments in Japanese. Unpublished Ph.D. Dissertation. The University of Melbourne.

Ohso, Mieko. 1976. A Study of Zero Pronominalization. Ph.D. Dissertation. The Ohio State University.

Ono, Tsuyoshi, and Sandra A. Thompson. 1997. "Deconstructing 'Zero Anaphora' in Japanese." In *Annual Meeting of the Berkeley Linguistics Society* 23 (1): 481–491.

Ono, Tsuyoshi, and Ryoko Suzuki. 2020. "Exploration into a new understanding of 'zero anaphora' in Japanese everyday talk." In *Fixed Expressions. Building language structure and social action*, 41–69. John Benjamins Publishing Company.

Pustejovsky, James. 1993. "Type Coercion and Lexical selection." In *Semantics and the Lexicon*, ed. by James Pustejovsky, 73–94. Dordrecht: Kluwer.

Quine, Willard Van Orman. 1960. *Word and Object*. Cambridge, MA: MIT Press.

Quine, Willard Van Orman. 1992. *Pursuit of Truth*. Cambridge, MA: Harvard University Press.

Shibatani, Masayoshi. 1990. *The Languages of Japan*. Cambridge: Cambridge University Press.

Suomalainen, Karita, and Mikael Varjo. 2020. "When Personal is Interpersonal. Organizing Interaction with Deictically Open Personal Constructions in Finnish Everyday Conversation." *Journal of Pragmatics* 168: 98–118.

Walker, Marilyn, Masayo Iida, and Sharon Cote. 1995. "Japanese Discourse and the Process of Centering." *Computational Linguistics* 20 (2): 193–233.

Transcript conventions

[	beginning of overlapped utterances
=	latched utterances
:	prolongation of the sound
,	non-final intonation contour
.	falling or final intonation contour
?	rising intonation contour
##	inaudible segments
@	laughter
..	pause; longer with more period marks

Symbols in translation

| (words) | words that are not said in Japanese but are supplied for intelligibility |
| (( )) | positions that require referential expressions in English but no expressions are used in Japanese |

CHAPTER 7

The indeterminacy and fluidity of reference in everyday conversation

Tsuyoshi Ono & Sandra A. Thompson

University of Alberta | University of California Santa Barbara

We focus on (a) the indeterminacy of reference, i.e., noun phrases which are described as having a 'given', 'old' or 'definite' referent, where that referent is unspecified; (b) the ways in which speakers shift reference between categorial and specific designations. The data reveal that talk displaying indeterminate and shifting reference is consistently accepted without being challenged. These facts show that reference can only be understood by considering how speakers refer locally, in the unfolding of social action, and that referential common ground is generally established despite the referential indeterminacy and fluidity. We thus promote the view that reference is a deeply social phenomenon, an emergent set of practices that is used and negotiated by people in real time.

Keywords: indeterminacy, fluidity, reference, conversation

1. Background

The question of how we name, refer to, and keep track of categories and specific entities has fascinated researchers for a very long time. In the first half of the twentieth century, proposals concerning naming and referring were mainly made by a group of philosophers pursuing a program known as 'Ordinary Language Philosophy'. Roughly speaking, its goals were to approach traditional philosophical questions by introspectively contemplating the meaning of expressions of everyday "ordinary" language (e.g., Frege 1892; Russell 1905, Moore 1993, Strawson 1950; Kripke 1972; Evans 1982), e.g., the question of whether 'the morning star' and 'the evening star' refer to the same entity. For discourse linguists, their insights have been thought-provoking; unfortunately, however, their contemplations took place without the benefit of empirical data from language as used in its social setting.

https://doi.org/10.1075/pbns.344.070no

More relevant to the study of actual 'ordinary language' use is a substantial body of empirical research on referring to, and keeping track of, specific entities, especially people. Studies in this tradition have centered around anaphora and deixis (e.g., Auer 1984; Chafe 1980, 1994; Cornish 2011; Enfield and Stivers 2007; Ewing 2015; Fox 1987, 1996; Givón 1983; Hanks 1990; Laury 1997; Oh 2005, 2006; Sacks 1987, 1992; Schegloff 1996, 2007).

When it comes to studies of reference in everyday interaction, issues of indeterminate and fluid reference, while not new (see, e.g., the influential analyses in Hanks 1990; Ochs et al. 1996), have not received much attention so far. While much discussion has centered on this phenomenon in Japanese (see especially Matsumoto, this volume) and other languages with 'allusive reference', like Murriny Patha (Blythe 2009) and Indonesian (Ewing 2018), we will argue that English, for all its consistent overt expression of arguments, exhibits a very similar lack of referential specificity. We aim to add to the small body of findings in this area by focusing on two frequent referential practices in conversation that have not been studied in any depth.[1] As we examine reference in everyday interactions, it becomes immediately apparent how consistently indeterminate and fluid speakers' referring practices are. We are specifically interested in the indeterminacy of pronominal forms such as English *it, this,* and *that,* when used without a clear referent in either the preceding or following talk, and in the ways in which reference shifts back and forth between categorial designation and specific designation. In both cases, the data recurrently reveal that talk displaying indeterminate and shifting reference is consistently accepted as satisfactory without being challenged by recipients (Schütz 1967, Garfinkel 1967, Du Bois 1980; Hanks 1990, 1992; Laury 1997; Linell & Lindström 2016; Raymond 2019).[2] We argue that these facts show that reference can only be understood by considering how speakers do referring in the real-time unfolding of a course of social interaction.

Our data come from approximately 10 hours of our personal corpus of American audio- and video-recorded everyday interactions among friends and family. The names of the participants have been anonymized, and the conversations are reproduced here by permission of the participants.

---

1. We thus hope to make a modest contribution to the area of interactional semantics (cf. Deppermann 2005, 2011a, b, 2018; Raymond & White 2017).

2. As Garfinkel (1967:8) puts it, data from everyday talk consistently shows that the level of intersubjectivity that we achieve in interaction is "adequate-for-all-practical-purposes" or "good enough" (Schütz 1953: 8; see also Du Bois 1980: 233 and Karimi and Ferreira 2016: 1014).

2.   Findings

2.1   Indeterminacy

By 'indeterminate' we refer to a noun phrase whose referent, at the moment of its production, is not apparent from the context and cannot be inferred with precision; this will include cataphoric reference, as well as vague or unspecified reference. Consider Extract (1), for example. Here, Alan and two friends Jason and Ellen are sitting in Alan's living room snacking and talking. In this extract, the prior sequence has been closed, and Alan, sitting on the floor, looks down at his dog Tank, lying on the floor beside him:

```
(1)   Some carrots                          [Cool Apt.: 12 06:24 (Video 1)]
      1 ALAN:  Tank you want some carrots? [addressing
      2        dog and picking up a few mini carrots from the tray on the coffee table]
      3        (0.1)
      4        let's break these up. [stands up, steps backwards, and breaks mini carrots
      5        into smaller pieces]
      6        so Tank does this thing,
      7        where if we give him a piece of food too big,
      8        he'll just spit it out and look at us.
      9        (0.5)
     10 ELLEN: oh that's nice
     11 ALAN:  yeah
     12 ELLEN: @@@
               (1.5)
     13 JASON: that's adorable
     14 ELLEN: @[@
     15 ALAN:   [@@
```

In line 1, picking up a few mini carrots and gazing at Tank, Alan asks the dog if he wants *some carrots*. Since Alan's question has opened a sequence visibly addressed to Tank, the two friends do not self-select to take a turn, but wait to see what Tank's 'response' is; indeed, as Alan stands up and takes a few steps backwards, Tank visibly responds by standing up, wagging his tail, and following Alan.

Just off camera, presumably feeding the carrot pieces to Tank, in line 6 Alan informs Jason and Ellen of a family routine involving Tank: Tank will not eat food unless it is broken into small pieces. This informing, containing the referential cataphoric NP *this thing*, serves as a justification for Alan having had to break the carrots into smaller pieces (lines 4–5). As speech-community members, we, the analysts, as well as Jason and Ellen, can understand *this thing* to be an instance of what Wald (1983) calls the 'new this', where *this N* is used prospectively, to introduce a 'new' participant that will figure in the talk to follow.[3] Accordingly, after

---

3.   Also known as 'presentative *this*' (Cutfield 2018: 94), 'prospective indexical' (Goodwin 1996), and 'cataphoric use of the indefinite *this*' (Gernsbacher and Shroyer 1989).

Alan's *this thing*, Ellen and Jason say nothing, and Alan informs them in lines 7–8 what might happen if he doesn't break up the mini carrots into pieces, *if we give him a piece of food too big, he'll just spit it out and look at us*. This extract thus highlights the temporal nature of reference in that the initially indeterminate referent becomes more precise as the interaction proceeds.

Another very common kind of indeterminacy among English speakers, which has also been previously noted, is illustrated in the next extract. Four women are talking about having seen a snake in their rural neighborhood.

(2) Snakes – Farmhouse: 13
```
1 Laura:    Brenda's um cousin Jake's roommate has a python (..) for a pet.
2 Michelle: o-o-h.
3 Laura:    it just freaks me out a little bit.
4 Donna:    do they do studies on people who have snakes for pets?
5 Mom:      I wonder.
6 Laura:    I…
7 Donna:    there's gotta be something.
```

In line 4, Donna introduces a referent new to the interaction with *they, do **they** do studies on people who have snakes for pets*? Known as the 'impersonal *they*' (cf. Siewierska & Papastathi 2011; Kaiser 2015), this pronoun is indeed highly indeterminate in reference, but for speakers of English it conventionally invites the inference that Donna is asking about whether such research is being done, the unspecified agent being whoever might study people with certain characteristics.

The following extracts further illustrate this 'indeterminate' property of reference in interaction. The data show that even noun phrases representing what discourse linguists would designate as 'Given', 'Old' (Chafe 1980, Prince 1981), 'Definite' (Du Bois 1980; Epstein 2002), or 'Indexical' (Kaplan 1989) have no clear referents.

In Extract (3), Tammy, a female shopper in an audio shop in the early 1990s, has just entered the audio shop and is telling salesman Brad what she wants:

(3) Never done this
```
1 TAMMY: … I want a tape deck .. that's gonna sound about,
2         … you know,
3         as good as it ca=n,
4 BRAD:  [okay],
5 TAMMY: [and I] think I want a tape deck with two= --
6         .. places for two tapes,
7         so I can copy,
8 BRAD:  .. [okay].
9 TAMMY: [(H) but] I've never done this before.
10        I <X don't X> know much about tapes.
11        [I mean] I h- --
12 BRAD: [okay].
```

In line 9 we consider what Tammy is doing in conceding that she's never done *this* before. Demonstrative pronouns often occur as anaphors, but is that the case here? And if this *this* is anaphoric, then what is its antecedent? *Is* there even an antecedent? Does Tammy's *this* in line 9 refer back to copying tapes, shopping for a tape deck, talking about tape decks, ...? In fact, there is nothing in what Tammy has said in this entire interaction from the moment that she entered the audio shop that can be clearly identified by Brad or us analysts as the referent for her *this* in line 9. We argue that Tammy's *this* in line 9, rather than *refer* to anything, actually works as an *invitation* to Brad to go along with her less-than-fully specified demonstrative indexical pronoun, and to glean from the context and the talk so far a sense of what it is that she has never done before so that the interaction can proceed.[4]

Brad accepts Tammy's concession with an immediate *okay* in line 12, showing that he is indeed willing to go along with her *this* in line 9, and that he can attribute enough meaning to her multi-unit turn in lines 9–10 to continue being a recipient to her telling what she's looking for. This extract shows how interactants can achieve a shared understanding during a stretch of talk wherein a participant uses an indeterminate indexical linguistic reference form like *this* in line 9. We suggest, then, that, while the traditional-grammar term 'antecedent' may be useful in discussing many instances of anaphora, where there is a 'first mention' and a 'subsequent mention' in the talk, an understanding of Tammy's *this* in (3) is best achieved without the term 'antecedent'.

A similar set of noun phrases formally marked with a definite determiner or demonstrative, which most commonly indexes 'Given/Old Information', with no clear referent can be seen in the next extract. Emma, on the phone with her sister Lottie, is complaining about her husband, who has just walked out on her:

(4) Isn't this ridiculous? NB 024: 1[5]
```
 1 EMM: .hhhh and then when he c-came in w- ah-uh from fishin'
 2      and I said gee lookit I: did a:ll the hhh things with aw-the va:cuum
 3      cleaner I've been all over the(b) f::-
 4      well .hhh (.) he says well how could you do i:t.6
 5      uh: uh did you do a good jo:b, h.hh .hhh
 6      well |that| tee:d me o::ff, hh
 7      (.)
 8 LOT: hkhh huh huh [he:h,
 9 EMM:              [.hh.hh So HE ↑PACKED HIS CLO:THES AND HE WENT,
10      and he says he won't even be down for Thanksgiving.
11      so I think I'll ca:ll Barbara and cancel |the who:le thing|. °°hmhh°°
12      (2.2)
13 EMM: Isn't |this| ri:diculous an- and BILL AND GLADYS WAITIN' OUT THERE to GO
14      to DINNER and I: had to go tell them isn't he ri:diculous?
15      (1.0)
```

---

4. This practice, then, is reminiscent of Ewing's 'allusive reference' (Ewing 2018); he says, "There are a number of discourse and interactional reasons to think that such utterances are produced exactly as they need to be at that point" (354; see also Goffman 1974 and Djenar et al. 2018).

There is much that Lottie might infer here; as is well-known, such inferences draw on years of experience with a shared language in social contexts, shared personal history, earlier talk, and/or cultural knowledge and probabilities (Deppermannn 2018).[7] Of particular interest for our argument are Emma's demonstrative pronouns *that* in line 6 and *this* in line 13. What is Emma asserting here, and what does her use of these forms tell us about reference? Again we see that referents must often be 'created' by recipients upon hearing such demonstratives. In line 6, for example, when Emma says *that teed me off*, her indeterminate *that* could refer to the entire reported interaction between herself and her husband, the beginning of which had been described a few lines prior to this extract, or it could refer to just her husband's challenges in lines 4–5. In the event, Lottie chuckles in line 8, apparently not needing to pin down Emma's exact referent more precisely, and Emma continues with her narrative.

And what about Emma's definite NP *the whole thing* in line 11? We suggest that it can be seen as a fixed expression, here referring just as vaguely to unspecified aspects of the Thanksgiving celebration she had planned with her daughter Barbara.

In line 13, when Emma says *isn't this ridiculous?*, without specifying just what is ridiculous, she is now inviting Lottie to align with her complaints about her husband and allow the sequence to progress. We argue, then, that in this sequence, Emma is recruiting Lottie to draw on much shared experience to empathize with her situation and accept, without requesting further specification, these several indeterminate indexical expressions.

2.2 Fluidity

Having looked at examples which highlight one property of referential practice in interaction, 'indeterminacy', we now turn our attention to interactions which support our finding that participants readily and frequently shift between reference to general types and to specific entities, expecting their interlocutors to be able to continue to engage in the interaction without disruption to progressivity (Schegloff 2007, Stivers and Robinson 2006).

---

5. Capital letters indicate greater volume; *.hh* indicates an inbreath, and *hh* an outbreath.

6. Emma's *how could you do it* does not make sense in this context; we interpret it as to mean something like 'how did you do it', i.e., 'did you do it well?'.

7. For example, when Emma mentions *his clothes* in line 9, she probably does not mean to assert that her husband packed *all* his clothes. Similarly, English speakers have much experience making sense of what others are doing with the *it* of *do it* (line 4).

Extract (5) provides support for reference being fluid, routinely shifting between general and specific uses. Vivian and her boyfriend Shane have fixed dinner for their friends Nancy and Michael. Shane is putting butter on his baked potato and trying to mash the potato with his fork, but he finds that the potato is too hard to mash:

(5)   Ice on it [0:47]
```
 1 SHA: did you cook this all the way through?
 2      (1.0)
 3 VIV: ↑ye:s.
 4      (0.2)
 5 SHA: think there's still ice on it.
              |
            [Fig. 1]
 6      (1.3)
              |
            [Fig. 2]
 7 VIV: i:[ce:?
 8 SHA: [°kheh-heh-heh-h[eh°
              |
            [Fig. 3]
 9 VIV:               [they weren't even [frozen.
10 SHA:                           [.k-h-h-h
11 NAN: Michael zih- the wine's down [there=
                            [pointing]
12 VIV:                           [leave-
13 NAN: =°if you want some,°
```

Here we focus on the three pronouns in boxes in lines 1, 5, and 9. In line 1 Shane asks Vivian if she cooked *this* all the way through. Shane's *this* in line 1 indexes 'his' potato, the one on his plate that he's trying to spread butter on. Upon being answered affirmatively by Vivian in line 3, Shane teasingly complains in line 5 that he thinks that there's still ice on *it* (Figure 1), with *it* again indexing 'his' potato. But now in lines 7 and 9, Vivian pushes back against Shane's complaint, initiating repair with *ice?*, and then asserting that *they* weren't even frozen. We and Vivian can guess that Shane is teasing in line 5 because in line 6, he turns toward her (Figure 2), and chuckles, as we see in line 8 (Figure 3).

What is Vivian doing with *they* in line 9? What group of entities is she referring to? Is her *they* anaphoric? No, not in a strict sense, because it's *plural*, and there are *no candidate plural NPs* anywhere in the previous interaction. In line 9, when Vivian says *they*, we see that she has switched her referent from *Shane's potato on his plate* to *the whole set of potatoes* (Vivian's *they* (line 9)) of which 'his' (Shane's *this* (line 1)) is one. In other words, Shane's mention of the specific potato he is trying to mash allows Vivian to use *they* to refer to some group of unindividuated potatoes of which Shane's potato is a member. A reasonable inference that Vivian's recipients might be drawing is that she is referring to the whole bag of potatoes that we later find out that she and Shane had bought earlier that day.

Nevertheless, we readily acknowledge that we cannot know for sure what inferences any of them might have drawn. Our point is that none of them display any problem with this switch, showing how fluidly speakers can shift referents without any interactional disruption.

Vivian Shane   Nancy Michael

Figure 1. Shane at line 5: *think there's* still ice on *it*[8]

Figure 2. Shane at Vivian's *ice?* in line 7

In the next extract, which is the beginning portion of the interaction in (3), we illustrate a shift in the opposite direction, this time between general categories and specific entities, occurring with a lexical NP (Laury 1997; Schegloff 1988, 1996). Here Tammy has just told Brad that she is pleased with the audio set-up he has recently installed in her home. In line 1, she goes on to describe a new purchase she wants to make:

---

8. The pictures are reproduced with explicit permission of the participants.

Figure 3. Shane chuckling in line 8

(6)   Want a tape deck
```
1 TAMMY: … I want a tape deck .. that's gonna sound about,
2         … you know,
3         as good as it ca=n,
4 BRAD: okay,
```

In line 1, Tammy introduces the generic category *a tape deck*. We and Brad know that what she wants is not the *category* of tape decks, but rather one instance of that category. In lines 1–3, she gradually specifies what she wants. In line 3, she uses the pronoun *it* to further characterize the as-yet-unspecified tape deck she might buy. In uttering the antecedent NP *tape deck* in line 1, Tammy is invoking a *non-specific instance* of the category. With her *it* in line 3, we suggest, she is no longer referring to any instance of the category of tape decks; rather she is referring more specifically to the hypothetical tape deck that she might buy, which she wants to sound good.

Socially, we again see that there is no disruption in the progressivity of the interaction; Brad's response *okay* in line 4 shows he has no trouble with Tammy's *it*, and is prepared to continue discussing her possible purchase. We take this extract to further illustrate the fluidity of reference: giving no clear indicators, everyday users of English frequently shift the specificity of what is being talked about between general categories and specific entities, a phenomenon not observable with the decontextualized imagined sentences on which semanticists and philosophers have based their claims.

Extract (6) illustrated shifting from a non-specific instance of a general category (*a tape deck*) to a more specific referent (*it*). In the next extract, we see a shift in the 'opposite' direction, from a specific existing entity (*this Luxman*) to a general category (*one of the things you'd wanted me to think about*).

Extract (7) shows what Tammy says nine seconds later:

(7) This Luxman
```
1 TAMMY: … (H) so,
2        … I wonder if you would .. suggest that |this .. Luxman| … is the- --
3        … is w- |one of the things you'd wanted me to think about|.
```

Here Tammy is not implying that Brad had had wanted her to think about buying
the very Luxman item on the shelf in front of them. By mentioning the item on
the shelf, she is actually asking Brad if he had suggested that she consider a Luxman model tape deck. The specific item which is physically present provides an
opportunity for her to use it to invoke the category of which it is a member.

We have observed referential shifts from specific to general and general to
specific, a referential practice which speakers regularly engage in, routinely
achieving intersubjective understanding as the talk is produced bit by bit.

2.3   Indeterminacy and fluidity

Our final examples involve both of the two characteristics of reference in conversation which we have highlighted above, indeterminacy and fluidity. In (8), Alan,
Jason, and Ellen are discussing the vegetable platter they're snacking from.

(8) Ugly carrots Cool Apt-01: 14 [7:26]
```
 1 JASON: I think it's funny,[9] 'cause like |these|,
              [picks up and gazes at two mini carrots]
              [Figure 4]
 2 (0.5) |these| are made from ugly carrots, and |they| shave |them| down,
 3        there's no such thing as like a mini carrot apparently?
 4 ALAN: hm.
 5 JASON: so. (0.7) I think that's an interesting nuance like –
 6 ALAN: I mean at lea-- it's resourceful
 7        and |they|'re using you know what |they| actually grew.
 8 JASON: (1.3) well especially because Americans don't want to buy
 9        (0.4) like ugly vegetables –
10 ALAN: [mhm.]
11 ELLEN: [mhm.]
12 ALAN: quote unquote.
13 JASON: you know, it's not even Americans, it's actually
14        (0.8) it's an issue like all over
15        the- you know- first worlds, like-
16        (0.5) or rather I should say first-world countries.
17        cause |they| have so much,
18        (0.6) |they| want to choose the ones that look the best
19        you [know?]
20 ALAN:     [yeah.]
```

How does this extract exemplify both indeterminacy and fluidity? To begin, we
note that in line 1, Jason uses the pronoun, *these*, gazing at two mini carrots he has

---

9. On the referentiality of this cataphoric *it*, see Couper-Kuhlen and Thompson (2008) on
apparent 'extraposition'.

just taken from the platter (Figure 4); the prosody of the phrase *'cause like these* is strongly projective, and in line 2, he again uses *these* (and later a co-referential *them*). Here Jason's recipients are unlikely to infer that he is claiming that *these are made from ugly carrots* refers only to these two mini carrots, but is he now referring to the category of mini carrots in general or the mini carrots on the platter? We suggest in fact that it could be either, and that his recipients do not need him to be more specific for the interaction to continue smoothly. We argue that with *these* in line 2 (***these** are made from ugly carrots*), Jason has shifted his referent from the two mini carrots he is still holding to a more generic and indeterminate referent. Evidence in favor of this analysis is his use of present tense in line 2, which invites the inference that he is now referring to mini carrots in general. Once again, this referential switch is apparently no problem for Alan and Ellen, and Jason continues with his telling.

Figure 4. Jason holding up two mini carrots at line 1[10]

We also see that this ordinary, everyday extract reveals several instances of indeterminacy. Consider Jason's first *they* in line 2, ***they** shave them down*. To maintain subject continuity, the most likely antecedent would be *these*, referring to mini carrots, in Jason's previous clause. But that won't do, since 'shave' is a verb requiring an animate subject. Again, as English speakers, these participants all conventionally understand this to be the 'impersonal *they*' (as we saw in (2) earlier), designating simply 'the relevant people or organization', in this case probably the vegetable processing companies who produce mini carrots.

In line 6, with *it's resourceful*, Alan now responds to Jason's informing by assessing the retail practice of cutting up 'ugly' carrots to make 'mini carrots'. Alan supports his positive evaluation with the assertion that ***they're** using you know*

---

10. The picture is reproduced with explicit permission of the participants.

what they actually grew in line 7, with two occurrences of an 'impersonal *they*'. What is curious about the clause in line 7 is that, without a detailed knowledge of the route from field to market taken by mini carrots in general, these two *theys* are referentially quite indeterminate. The carrot growers and processors may be part of one operation, or it may be that each *they* requires inferring two *different* agents: the farmers, who have done the *growing*, and the food processorss, who *are using* what is grown. In any case, once again, since neither Jason nor Ellen, nor Alan himself, initiates repair, and the interaction continues smoothly, our analysis must again recognize this indeterminacy and leave it unresolved as well.

As for fluidity, an equally curious instance of two *theys* in the same turn, which seems to invite two different referential inferences, can be seen in lines 17–18, where Jason claims that *they have so much they want to choose the ones that look the best*. Here Jason's first *they*, who 'have so much', is indeterminate between 'first-world countries' in line 16, the previous full noun phrase, and, by metonymic inference, 'people living in first-world countries'. But when he says *they want to choose the ones that look the best*, he now appears to be more clearly referring to 'people living in first-world countries'.

We see, then, that speakers using pronouns such as *they* can shift referents even within the same clause. With this example we also see that a referent is again left *indeterminate* (both Alan and Jason keep using *they*), but no trouble is registered in the interaction; the indeterminate reference is good enough for them to understand each other. At the same time, interestingly, we can see that the those involved in these activities *keep shifting* (e.g., first-world countries and people in first-world countries).

Consider another extract exhibiting both indeterminate reference and shifting reference, Extract (9), where Stan is asking his sister Joyce on the phone for advice about buying a hat:

(9)   A variety of things Joyce & Stan: 4

```
1 S: ˙hhhh well where can I find something like that. Joyce. I mean a
2    good hat. y'know I don't care paying ten dolla:rs or so ˚or even
3    more˚.
4 J: [(pt)
5 S: [y'know a good ha:t, [something that would look- something=
6 J:                      [((sigh))
7 S: =that I'd- uh:[I'd have a variety of things to loo:k at[:,
8 J:               [why don't-
                                                           [why
9    don't you: go into Westwoo:d, (0.4) and go to Bullocks.
10   (1.2)
11 S: Bullocks? you mean that one right u:m (1.1) tch! (.) right by
12    the: u:m (.) what's it the Plaza Theatre::=
13 J: =uh huh,
14   (0.4)
15 S: ˚(memf::)
```

```
16 J: °yeah,
17 S: why that Bullocks. Is there something about itw
18 J: they have some pretty nice things. and you could probably
19    f[ind one you like(d) there,
20 S:  [(˙hh ˙hh)
```

When Stan finishes the clause *you know a good hat* in line 5, Joyce sighs (line 6), arguably because Stan has been carrying on for several seconds. Overlapping with her sigh, in line 5, Stan begins to suggest a new characterization of the kind of hat he wants, with *something that would look-* and then breaks off. As he continues, he becomes disfluent. Joyce, hearing his hesitations and disfluencies in lines 5 and 7, starts to respond in overlap with the advice-giving format *why don't you* in line 8, but then cuts off to let him finish his turn, resuming her *why don't you* at the end of line 8 in the clear.[11] Stan is presumably trying to say that he wants Joyce to recommend a store with a variety of hat choices, picking up on the request he had already made in lines 1–3.

Upon the completion of Stan's turn, despite its troubled production in line 7, Joyce apparently gets enough of his meaning to maintain progressivity; she continues with her advice in lines 8–9: he should go to Bullock's in nearby Westwood, a department store, where she presumably thinks he will find a large variety of hats.

Focusing on Stan's two instances of *something* in line 5, we observe both referential indeterminacy and fluidity: whereas a referent for his first *something* is probably 'hat', a referent for his second *something*, with its non-normative relative clause, is unclear. Still Joyce can apparently glean an idea of what Stan is trying to formulate. Thus, in spite of Stan's problems in articulating his considerations for a new hat in lines 5 and 7, and his shift of referent from the hypothetical hat he wants to buy to some space in which he would have a variety of things to look at, Joyce doesn't initiate repair or give any other indication of a problem. Instead she proceeds with advice relevant to her best guess as to a referent, something like 'store' (*go to Bullock's*, line 9), and Stan initiates repair in line 11, seeking confirmation and displaying that its relevance is acceptable to him.

3.   Summary and discussion

What have we learned about reference from studying everyday conversation? Rather than take a top-down approach, attempting to define notions such as 'referentiality', 'specificity', and 'generic' as semantic abstractions, we have opted for a bottom-up approach; together with the other chapters in this volume, we thus

---

11. On *why don't you X* as an advice-giving response, see Couper-Kuhlen and Thompson frthc. and Thompson and Couper-Kuhlen 2020.

consider how participants interacting with each other use the referential resources of their language, such as indeterminate and fluid reference, to create alignment between interactants, to arrive at intersubjectivity, that is, to achieve a satisfactory sharing of experience (Linell 2017).

Our data strongly suggest that participants readily and frequently make referential shifts, as we just saw with Extract (9), and including those between reference to general types and specific entities, as we have seen with Extracts (5)–(8). Furthermore, participants routinely use noun phrases that discourse linguists have designated as 'Given' or 'Definite', or 'Indexical', for which no exact referent can be determined, as seen with Extracts (1)–(4), and (8). It is clear that participants, relying on convention and on deeply shared cultural knowledge, expect their interlocutors to be able to continue to engage in the ongoing interaction without clear marking of these shifts and without precise referential formulations. Our analysis thus confirms earlier research showing that reference is jointly accomplished in the course of an interaction (Enfield & Stivers 2007; Ford & Fox 1996; Schegloff 1982).

Finally, we address the question of whether these findings are specific to English, or whether similar processes are at work in languages in general. Evidence so far, including many of the studies in this volume, strongly indicates that analogous processes are used by speakers around the world, though the morphosyntactic resources are of course very different from one language to another. For example, a refreshing body of research has now appeared dealing with referential practices with respect to so-called "unexpressed referents" in everyday interaction, which many languages are famous for, e.g., Tao (1996), Ono and Thompson (1997), Ewing (2005, 2018, 2019), and Ono and Suzuki (2020), and there is reason to expect that further studies on indeterminacy and fluidity of reference are forthcoming as well.

We intend our findings, in clear opposition to discussions of reference in philosophical and semantic traditions, to contribute to a deeper understanding of the work participants routinely do to achieve intersubjectivity through referential practice in real time (Hanks 1990), and to provide further support for much research showing that reference, indeed language itself, is a profoundly social phenomenon – entirely context-dependent, temporal, non-discrete, constantly negotiated, and continually emergent.

Acknowledgements

We appreciate the feedback we have received on the ideas in this paper from the editors of this volume and Satomi Kuroshima. We alone are responsible for the way we have incorporated their input.

References

Auer, Peter. 1984. "Referential Problems in Conversation." *Journal of Pragmatics* 8: 627–648.

Blythe, Joe. 2009. Doing Referring in Murriny Patha Conversation. Ph.D. thesis, University of Sydney.

Chafe, Wallace. 1994. *Discourse, Consciousness, and Time: The Flow and Displacement of Conscious Experience in Speaking and Writing.* Chicago: University of Chicago Press.

Chafe, Wallace (ed). 1980. *The Pear Stories: Cognitive, Cultural, and Linguistic Aspects of Narrative Production.* Norwood, New Jersey: Ablex.

Cornish, Francis. 2011. "'Strict' Anadeixis, Discourse Deixis and Text Structuring." *Language Sciences* 33 (5): 753–767.

Couper-Kuhlen, Elizabeth and Sandra A. Thompson. 2008. "On Assessing Situations and Events in Conversation: Extraposition and Its Relatives." *Discourse Studies* 10 (4): 443–467.

Couper-Kuhlen, Elizabeth and Sandra A. Thompson. Forthcoming. "Action Ascription in Everyday Advice-giving Sequences." In *Action Ascription: Interaction in Context*, ed. by Arnulf Deppermann and Michael Haugh. Cambridge: Cambridge University Press.

Cutfield, Sarah. 2018. "Dalabon Exophoric Uses of Demonstratives." In *Demonstratives in Cross-Linguistic Perspective*, ed. by Stephen C. Levinson, Sarah Cutfield, Michael Dunn, N.J. Enfield, and Sérgio Meira, 90–115. Cambridge: Cambridge University Press.

Deppermann, Arnulf. 2005. "Conversational Interpretation of Lexical Items and Conversational Contrasting." In *Syntax and lexis in conversation*, ed. by Auli Hakulinen and Margret Selting, 289–317. Amsterdam: Benjamins.

Deppermann, Arnulf. 2011a. "The Study of Formulations as a Key to an Interactional Semantics." *Human Studies* 34: 115–128.

Deppermann, Arnulf. 2011b. "Notionalization: The Transformation of Descriptions into Categorizations." *Human Studies* 34: 155–181.

Deppermann, Arnulf. 2018. "Inferential Practices in Social Interaction: A Conversation-Analytic Account." *Open Linguistics* 4: 35–55.

Djenar, Dwi Noverini, Michael C. Ewing and Howard Manns. 2018. *Style and Intersubjectivity in Youth Interaction.* Berlin: De Gruyter Mouton.

Du Bois, John W. 1980. "Beyond Definiteness: The Trace of Identity in Discourse." In *The Pear Stories*, ed. by Wallace Chafe, 9–50. Norwood, NJ: Ablex.

Enfield, N.J. and Tanya Stivers (eds). 2007. *Person Reference in Interaction: Linguistic, Cultural and Social Perspectives.* Cambridge: Cambridge University Press.

Epstein, Richard. 2002. "The Definite Article, Accessibility, and the Construction of Discourse Referents." *Cognitive Linguistics* 12 (4): 333–378.

Evans, Gareth. 1982. *The Varieties of Reference*, edited by John McDowell, Oxford: Oxford University Press.

Ewing, Michael C. 2005. *Grammar and Inference in Conversation: Identifying Clause Structure in Spoken Javanese.* Amsterdam: Benjamins.

Ewing, Michael C. 2015. "Localising Person Reference among Indonesian Youth." In *Margins, Hubs, and Peripheries in a Decentralizing Indonesia*, ed. by Zane Goebel, Deborah Cole, and Howard Manns. Tilburg Papers in Culture Studies Special Issue 162: 26–41.

Ewing, Michael C. 2018. "Investigating Indonesian Conversation: Approach and Rationale." *Wacana* 19 (2): 342–374.

Ewing, Michael C. 2019. "The Predicate as a Locus of Grammar and Interaction in Colloquial Indonesian." In *Special Issue "Usage-based and Typological Approaches to Linguistic Units"* ed. by Ritva Laury Tsuyoshi Ono and Ryoko Suzuki. *Studies in Language* 43 (2): 402–443.

Ford, Cecilia E. and Barbara A. Fox. 1996. "Interactional Motivations for Reference Formulation: *He* had. *This* guy had, a beautiful, thirty-two O:lds." In *Studies in Anaphora*, ed. by Barbara A. Fox, 145–168. Amsterdam: John Benjamins.

Fox, Barbara. 1987. *Discourse Structure and Anaphora*. Cambridge: Cambridge University Press.

Fox, Barbara A. (ed.) 1996. *Studies in anaphora*. Amsterdam: Benjamins.

Frege, Gottlieb. 1892. Über Sinn und Bedeutung. Zeitschrift für Philosophie und Philosophische Kritik 100 (1892): 25–50. In *Collected Papers on Mathematics, Logic and Philosophy*, 157–177, translated by M. Black, V. Dudman, P. Geach, H. Kaal, E.-H. W. Kluge, B. McGuinness and R. H. Stoothoff. New York: Basil Blackwell, 1984.

Garfinkel, H. (1967). *Studies in Ethnomethodology*. Englewood Cliffs, NJ: Prentice-Hall.

Gernsbacher, Morton A., and Suzanne Shroyer. 1989. "The Cataphoric Use of the Indefinite *this* in Spoken Narratives." *Memory and Cognition* 17: 536–540.

Givon, T. (ed) 1983. *Topic Continuity in Discourse: A quantitative cross-language study*. Amsterdam: John Benjamins.

Goffman, Erving. 1974. *Frame Analysis: An Essay on the Organization of Experience*. Boston: Northeastern University Press.

Goodwin, Charles. 1996. "Transparent Vision." In *Interaction and Grammar*. ed. by Elinor Ochs, Emanuel A. Schegloff and Sandra Thompson, 370–404. Cambridge: Cambridge University Press.

Hanks, William. 1990. *Referential Practice: Language and Lived Space among the Maya*. Chicago: The University of Chicago Press.

Hanks, William. 1992. "The Indexical Ground of Deictic Reference." In *Rethinking Context*, ed. by Alessandro Duranti and Charles Goodwin 43–77. Cambridge: Cambridge University Press.

Kaiser, Elsi. 2015. "Impersonal and Generic Reference: A Cross-linguistic Look at Finnish and English Narratives." *Eesti ja soome-ugri keeleteaduse ajakiri. Journal of Estonian and Finno-Ugric Linguistics*, 6 (2): 9–42.

Kaplan, David. 1989. "Afterthoughts." In *Themes from Kaplan*, ed. by Joseph Almog, John Perry, and Howard Wettstein, eds., *565–614*. Oxford: Oxford University Press

Karimi, Hossein, and Fernanda Ferreira.. 2016. Good-enough linguistic representations and online cognitive equilibrium in language processing. *The Quarterly Journal of Experimental Psychology* (69:5):1013–1040

Kripke, Saul. 1972. "Naming and Necessity." In *Semantics of Natural Language*, ed. by Donald Davidson and Gilbert Harman, 253–355. Boston: Reidel. (Published on its own as a book in 1980, Cambridge: Harvard University Press.)

Laury, Ritva. 1997. *Demonstratives in Interaction*. Amsterdam: John Benjamins.

Linell, Per. 2017. "Intersubjectivity in Dialogue." In *The Routledge Handbook of Language and Dialogue*, ed. by Edda Weigand, 109–126. New York: Routledge.

Linell, Per and Jan Lindström. 2016. "Partial Intersubjectivity and Sufficient Understandings for Current Practical Purposes: On a Specialized Practice in Swedish Conversation." *Nordic Journal of Linguistics* 39 (2): 113–133.

Moore, Adrian W. (ed). 1993. *Meaning and Reference*. Oxford: Oxford University Press.

Ochs, Elinor, Patrick Gonzales, and Sally Jacoby. 1996. "When I come Down I'm in the Domain State." In *Interaction and Grammar*, ed. by Elinor Ochs, Emanuel A. Schegloff, and Sandra A. Thompson, 328–369. Cambridge: Cambridge University Press.

Oh, Sun-Young. 2005. "English Zero Anaphora as an Interactional Resource." *Research on Language and Social Interaction* 38 (3): 267–302.

Oh, Sun-Young. 2006. "English Zero Anaphora as an Interactional Resource II." *Discourse Studies* 86: 817–846.

Ono, Tsuyoshi and Sandra Thompson. 1997. Deconstructing "Zero Anaphora" in Japanese. Proceedings of the Twenty-Third Annual Meeting of the Berkeley Linguistics Society: General Session and Parasession on Pragmatics and Grammatical Structure.

Ono, Tsuyoshi and Ryoko Suzuki. 2020. "Exploration into a New Understanding of 'Zero Anaphora' in Japanese Everyday Talk." In *Fixed expressions: Building Language Structure and Action*, ed. by Ritva Laury and Tsuyoshi Ono, 41–70. Amsterdam: Benjamins.

Prince, Ellen. 1981. "Toward a Typology of Given-New Information." In *Radical Pragmatics*, ed. by Peter Cole, 223–255. New York: Academic Press.

Raymond, Chase W. 2019. "Intersubjectivity, Normativity, and Grammar." *Social Psychology Quarterly* 82 (2): 182–204.

Raymond, Chase Wesley, and Anne Elizabeth Clark White. 2017. "Time Reference in the Service of Social Action." *Social Psychology Quarterly* 80 (2): 109–131.

Russell, Bertrand. 1905. "On Denoting". *Mind* 14 (56): 479–493.

Sacks, Harvey. 1987. "You Want to Find out if Anybody Really Does Care". In *Talk and Social Organisation*, ed. by Graham Button and John R. E. Lee, eds., 217–225. Philadelphia: Multilingual Matters.

Sacks, Harvey. 1992. *Lectures on Conversation I*: 349–350. Oxford: Blackwell.

Schegloff, Emanuel A. 1982. "Discourse as an Interactional Achievement: Some Uses of 'uh huh' and Other Things that Come between Sentences." In *Analyzing Discourse: Text and Talk*, ed. by Deborah Tannen, 71–93. Georgetown: Georgetown University Press.

Schegloff, Emanuel A. 1988. "Description in the Social Sciences I: Talk-in-Interaction." *IPrA Papers in Pragmatics* 2 (1): 1–24.

Schegloff, Emanuel A. 1996. "Some Practices for Referring to Persons in Talk-in-Interaction." In *Typological Studies in Language* 33: 437–486.

Schegloff, Emanuel A. 2007. *Sequence Organization*. Cambridge: Cambridge University Press.

Schütz, Alfred. 1953. "Common-sense and Scientific Interpretation of Human Action." *Philosophy and Phenomenological Research* 14:1–38.

Schütz, Alfred. 1967. *The Phenomenology of the Social World*. Evanston, IL: Northwestern University Press.

Siewierska, Anna and M. Papastathi. 2011. "Third Person Plurals in the Languages of Europe: Typological and Methodological Issues". *Linguistics* 43 (2): 575–610.

Stivers, Tanya and Jeffrey D. Robinson. 2006. A preference for progressivity in interaction. *Language in Society* 35.3:367–392.

Strawson, Peter F. 1950. "On Referring." *Mind* 59: 320–344.

Tao, Hongyin. 1996. *Units in Mandarin Conversation: Prosody, Discourse and Grammar.* Amsterdam: Benjamins.

Thompson, Sandra A. and Elizabeth Couper-Kuhlen. 2020. "English *why don't you X* as a Formulaic Expression." In *Fixed Expressions: Building Social Action from :anguage Structure*, ed. by Ritva Laury and Tsuyoshi Ono, 99–132. Amsterdam: Benjamins.

Wald, Benji. 1983. "Referents and Topic within and across Discourse Units: Observations from Current Vernacular English." In *Discourse Perspectives on Syntax*, ed. by Flora Klein-Andreu, 91–116. New York: Academic Press.

CHAPTER 8

Manipulating referentiality and creating phaticness

Repeated use of novel ad hoc NPs in Japanese conversation

Ryoko Suzuki
Keio University

The focus of this study is the creation of novel ad hoc expressions from the perspective of referentiality. Through the close analysis of three cases from video-recorded conversations in Japanese, we find that speakers create novel NPs by manipulating referentiality and embodiment, and achieve social bonding by humorously and intensely repeating those expressions. Even an onomatopoeic adverbial can be turned into a novel ad hoc NP. After creating and reinforcing those novel NPs with exaggerated delivery, speakers drop the exaggerated delivery, pronouncing the novel NPs as if they are regular NPs.

Keywords: novel expression, onomatopoeia, (de-)embodiment, NP, bonding, phaticness

1. Introduction

New words are created and spread through media, day to day, to refer to various new ideas and entities, for example, *COVID-19* or *SDGs* to mention just a few. However, such word creation happens in the public domain. Do ordinary speakers similarly create expressions in spontaneous everyday talk? At least in Japanese conversation, the answer is positive: speakers do create ad hoc expressions and enjoy repeating them.

In an earlier study of newly-created ad hoc expressions (Suzuki 2020), I identified 45 expressions in 15 video- and audio-recorded conversations as being novel due to, for example, their morpho-prosodic shape or unfamiliar meaning. Most of those ad hoc novel expressions were nominals (37/45 expressions) of various origins and length, and most of those novel NPs could be regarded as part(s) of

https://doi.org/10.1075/pbns.344.08suz

predicates (34 out of 37 instances). Those ad hoc novel predicate NPs were basically non-tracking and hence not "discourse-referential" (Du Bois and Thompson 1991). Out of the 34 NPs, 19 instances occur in predicates of characterizing and categorizing, and 12 occur in predicates of assessments. In other words, I found that in conversation, speakers use ad hoc novel NPs as predicate nominals in talking about entities and situations, i.e., to characterize them or assess them in distinctive ways. The study also showed that among the morphological strategies employed to create novel expressions, suffixation is by far the most frequent (23/45 cases). Other strategies, found much less frequently, include compounding (6 cases), abbreviations (8 cases), and conversion of parts of speech (8 cases) among others (Suzuki 2020:188).

Another important characteristic of newly-created ad hoc expressions in conversation is that they are created interactively. They can arise out of the playfulness of communication whereby speakers collaboratively create enjoyable ways of expressing thoughts relative to the moment (Takanashi 2004, 2020, 2022). Those ad hoc expressions do not appear out of the blue. Rather, speakers create them using linguistic resources produced right before in discourse or referring to a prior text shared in the community such as an experience and knowledge shared between speakers (Takanashi 2020), or popular proverbs (Suzuki 2020).

Word creation in Japanese has been studied based on the internal structure of words (e.g. Kubozono 2002) and sociocultural backgrounds associated with them (e.g. Yonekawa 2002), but research focusing on how speakers in natural conversation create novel expressions on the spot is still underexplored. We still need to accumulate more case studies using video-recorded instances of the moment-by-moment word creation process, referring not only to linguistic features but to other features including prosody, gestures, and others.

Therefore, in this paper, we will look at three instances of novel NPs in video-recorded conversations. Inspired by the line of research on interactional linguistics (e.g., Fox 1999; Couper-Kuhlen and Selting 2018) and the multimodal approach to grammar in social interaction (e.g., Keevallik 2020 on NPs, Tao 2022 on conversational resonance), I will show that the manipulation of referentiality, i.e., treating a non-referential NP as if it is a referential one, is a powerful resource for Japanese speakers to create and enjoy ad hoc NPs. Speakers use various resources, including linguistic structures, prosody, and gestures, to manipulate referentiality in unexpected or unusual ways for the purposes of phatic communion (Malinowski 1949) or social bonding, i.e., "establishing and maintaining a friendly and harmonious atmosphere in interpersonal relations (Senft 2014:107)." In Section 2, I will introduce the data and method for the study. Section 3 describes the three instances of the novel NPs in detail. Section 4 discusses and summarizes the findings.

2.   Data and method

The instances come from video-recorded conversations in the Corpus of Everyday Japanese Conversation (CEJC), collected with speakers' consent, transcribed, annotated, and managed by the National Institute for Japanese Language and Linguistics (NINJAL) (Koiso et al. 2020).[1] In Suzuki (2020), forty-five instances of novel expressions were manually searched and discussed with reference to their internal structures and discourse context. For the current paper, qualitative analysis of three instances of ad hoc NPs of unusual shape from the same corpus (of which two instances were found after the publication of Suzuki 2020) will be performed. Unlike in the earlier paper, I discuss three longer excerpts to study the creation and use of ad-hoc NPs in real time.

3.   The process of creating ad hoc NPs involving referentiality

3.1   Turning an onomatopoeia into a topic NP referring to a concrete object: *Baki*

Example (1) is an instance where participants use the same onomatopoeic word repeatedly,[2] and a referential status shift occurs. Five women are sitting around a table, having a meeting at a community center to decide the theme of the next community gathering (Figure 1). One candidate theme is children's heavy use of mobile phones. Speaker A says it is quite a challenge for parents to enforce in-house rules

---

1. The CEJC transcripts are all anonymized by NINJAL. This paper follows the CEJC Publication Guidelines and uses illustrations instead of captured images of the recordings.
    Overlaps and other paralinguistic information have been added and some corrections have been made to the original CEJC transcripts, by the author wherever relevant. The lines were separated by intonation units, following the notations in Du Bois et al. (1993), but put together in some places for the sake of saving space.

2. Onomatopoeias "permeate Japanese life" (Shibatani 1990:157) and with more than 1,000 entries in dictionaries, "play extremely important roles in Japanese grammar" (Iwasaki 2002:46). They depict the external world such as natural sounds, states and manners of something, as well as our psychological state (Shibatani 1990:154, Iwasaki 2002:46).
    Syntactically, onomatopoeic expressions typically function as adverbs expressing on-going actions followed by the quotative particles *tte* or *to* (or its variant *tto*) as in *poki tto eda o otta* '(I) broke a (small) branch with a snap' (Iwasaki 2002:49). Some expressions have reduplicated forms that can occur as a nominal in a predicate with the copula *da*, generally expressing "qualities rather than actions" (Hamano 1988:136), as in *kono heya wa gucha-gucha da* 'This room is messy' (Kita 1997:389, emphasis added) and *unagi wa nuru-nuru da* 'An eel is slippery' (Shibatani 1990:154).

of use on elementary school children. Then B says she broke her child's flip phone as a punishment because the child kept ignoring the rules of use.

Figure 1. Five women in the room

We notice that an omatopoeic word *baki* is used repeatedly across speakers. *Baki* is a sound mimicry representing the snapping sound of a slender and hard object, for example, the noise of a tree branch breaking. *Baki* typically occurs by itself with an exclamation mark in manga, such as *Baki!* 'Whack!' 'Crack!' or with a glottal stop in conversation. It also occurs in the sound-introducing manner adverbial phrase with a quotative *to* or *tte* as in *eda ga baki tto oreta* 'the branch broke, making a cracking noise "*baki*".' In Example (1), the word is used in repetition across speakers. The pencil-sketched snapshots of another camera (360-degree camera placed on the table) are inserted in relevant places and marked with a pound sign to show the moment in the utterance(s):

(1) "broken flip phone"   [CEJC T004-013]
```
01 B: うちの場合はあのー…切っちゃったからね。
      uchi no baai wa ano: … kitchatta   kara ne.
      home GEN case TOP FIL    cut:PERF:PST PCL  PCL
      In the case of my family, (we) cut (it).
      {left hand: open palm, moving downward}
02 :  あのー…使えなくしちゃって、
      [1 ano: …tsukaenaku shichatte],
      FIL       disable    do:PERF:CONT
      (I/we) disabled (the cellphone),
      {identical gesture as 01}
03 D: ん: 言ってたね。
      [1 n: itteta      ne].
      yeah say:STAT:PST PCL
      Right, (you) mentioned (it before).
```

04 B: ..壊したから。
    … kowa#[2shi#ta <X kara X>].
      break:PST   PCL
    (I/we) broke (it).
      {B's dividing gesture}
      #fig 2 #fig 3

fig 2: A (left) – B (center) – C (right)

fig 3: B's dividing gesture

05 A: バキだからね。
    [2 ba-] baki# da kara [3ne.
      FS   baki COP PCL PCL
    (What you did) is "baki."
    {A uses the word baki as she sees B}
      #fig 4

fig 4: A looks at B as she says baki

06 C: バキだからね。
    [3 ba] [4 ki da kara] [5 ne].
      baki   COP PCL   PCL
    (What you did) is baki.

07 B: バキよ。
    [4 baki yo].
      baki PCL
    Yeah (it's) baki.

08 A: うん。
    [5 un].
    Yeah.

09 E: バキね。
      [5 *baki ne*].
      baki   PCL
      Right (it is) *baki*.
10 B: うん、バキはねー、
      [5 *un*, #*baki wa*] *ne*:,   → topic NP
      yeah   baki TOP PCL
      Yeah, as for *baki*,
      {dividing gesture with both hands smaller than 04}
            #fig 5

fig 5: B's *un*, #*baki wa ne*:,

fig 6: B's *ano mamma tsukatteta.*#
11 B: あのまんま使ってた。
      ano mamma tsukatteta.#
      that state use:STAT:PST
      (my child) kept using (it) in that (broken) state.
                        #fig 6
      {stretch her right arm forward with a holding gesture}
12 A: [6 @]##
      {starts to smile overlapping with B's line 13 to the end of 14}
            #fig 7 #fig 8

fig 7: A's smile and B's *baki* ...*wa*##

fig 8: A's smile and B's *madamada*‡

13 B: バキはまだまだ使えるんだっていう。
   [6 *baki*] …*wa*‡ *madamada*‡ *tsukaeru nda*   [7 *tte iu*].
   baki   TOP   still   usable   NMZ:COP QUO   say
   Baki still works (I'd) say.   → tracked
   {dividing gesture with both hands smaller than fig 3, stretching her right arm
   forward with a holding gesture like fig 6, then to home}
          #fig 7   #fig 8

14 E: バキでも使えるんだ。
   [7 *ba* [8*ki demo*7] *tsukae* [9 *ru nda* 8]9].
   baki   even   usable   NMZ:COP
   So even *baki* works (you mean)/
   So though (it is) *baki*, (it) still works (you mean).   → tracked
      {E gazes at B at -*ru nda*}

15 C: うーん。
   [8 *u:n*].
   yeah.

16 B: 使えるん。 … 使える。
   [9 *tsuka*‡][10*erun*].‡ …[11 *tsukaeru*].
   usable   usable
   (It) works. (It) works.
          #fig 9   #fig 10
   {B looks at E with a light smile, shows the dividing gesture (fig 9) with both
   hands smaller than figs 3, 5, 7, then brings her right hand with a holding
   gesture close to her right ear/forehead (fig 10), and to the desk.}

fig 9 B's line 16: *tsuka*‡*erun*.

fig 10 B's line 16: *tsukaerun*.‡

17 A: バキ。ドラマみたいですね。
　　　　[10 <WH baki WH>]. [12 [11 dorama] mitai desu ne.]
　　　　　　{smiles to B}
　　　　　　baki   drama like COP PCL
　　　　　　"Baki." (It) is like a drama, isn't it.
18 E: おーー。
　　　　[12 o::::::].
　　　　Yeah.

What is striking about this excerpt is that almost all participants utter the word *baki* in rapid succession and intense overlaps. In line 4, as Speaker B pronounces the word *kowashita* 'broke,' she brings her hands close together and shows a gesture of dividing one object into two pieces (see Figure 2 and Figure 3). Gazing at her hand gesture, Speaker A overlaps with B and says *baki da kara ne* '(What you did) is *baki*' in line 5 (see Figure 4).[3]

Baki, usually pronounced with a final glottal stop, is originally an adverb symbolizing a breaking sound. In line 5, speaker A brings this term into discourse without a glottal stop as she paraphrases B's recounting of breaking her child's flip phone. I do not analyze *baki* in lines 5 (*ba- baki da kara ne* by A), 6 (*baki da kara ne* by C), 7 (*baki yo* by B) and 9 (*baki ne* by E) as a genuine sound mimicry "*baki!*" but as a form further transformed from the original use, since none of those speakers pronounce *baki* with a final glottal stop. Furthermore, structurally, *baki* in those lines functions as a predicate nominal followed by utterance-final elements (i.e., the copula *da* and utterance-final pragmatic particles). Since *baki* is not a reduplicated form, it is not expected to occur as a predicate nominal with the ending forms (see footnote 1). So *baki* in those utterances is different from sound mimicry: it stands out due to its pronunciation without a glottal stop, and the unusual combination with predicate ending forms.[4]

---

3. When a causal conjunctive particle *kara* 'because' occurs in the utterance-final position, it can be regarded as a pragmatic particle with much less sense of causality. *Kara* here can be at best understood as hinting at the connection between the situation described in the current utterance with what happened earlier, and it would be appropriate not to add any causal nuance in the translation (see Ono, Thompson, and Sasaki 2012).

4. One reviewer and I think that the participants may have a common understanding of *baki* associated with the phone-breaking incident (so *baki* may not be a "novel" NP for them but still an ad hoc NP). For instance, Speaker D says in line 03 to B that she heard about B's story on breaking the phone before (*nn itteta ne* 'Right, (you) mentioned (it before)'). In addition, speaker A in line 5 is the one who first uses *baki* in this conversation and not B who actually broke the phone. Hence, the participants are likely knowing recipients (Goodwin 1979) and are already familiar with the word *baki* and what it refers to. The reviewer also mentions that B's epistemic status is differentiated from the rest of the participants: B is the only one who uses the final particle *yo*, a marker of epistemic primacy (Hayano 2011) in line 7 as in *baki yo* 'Yeah (it's) *baki*,' and only B uses gestures throughout the excerpt.

Then we see the further change of the grammatical and semantic status of *baki* in line 10 (*un, baki wa ne:* 'yeah, as for *baki*') where Speaker B makes *baki* a topic of her utterance (as shown in the translation) by adding the topic particle *wa*. *Wa* works anaphorically to turn *baki* into an NP. Then B adds a comment in line 11 that *ano mamma tsukatteta* 'my child kept using *baki* in that (broken) state.' In other words, in her utterance in lines 10 to 11, B treats *baki*, not as a predicate nominal indicating the act of breaking the phone, but as a topic NP referring to the child's broken flip phone itself. She continues to use *baki* as a topic NP in line 13 (*baki wa madamada tsukaeru nda tte iu* '*Baki* still works (I'd) say'), and so does speaker E in line 14 (*baki demo tsukaeru nda* 'So though *baki* works (you mean)'. Notice a particle *demo* 'even/also ...' follows an NP, so it works anaphorically to turn *baki* into an NP. The fact that *baki* is being tracked as a topic NP confirms that speakers B and E use *baki* as a referential noun. Furthermore, the use of *baki* to mean the broken phone seems to be treated as humorous by A as she smiles at B (lines 12 and 17), and by B herself as she smiles at E (line 16).

B's hand gestures also change. B first shows the dividing gesture with both hands in line 4 as she utters the verb *kowashita* '(I/we) broke (it)' (see Figures 2 and 3) straightforwardly representing the act of breaking the phone. Then in lines 10 (Figure 5) and 13 (Figure 7), she again shows the same dividing gesture with both hands, though attenuated to some extent, as she says the topic phrase *baki wa* 'as for *baki*.' Then she loosely stretches her right arm to the front as if she is holding an object and showing it as she utters the predicate part *ano mama tsukatteta* '(my child) kept using (it) in that (broken) state' in line 11 and *madamada tsukaeru nda tte iu* '(*baki*) still works (I'd) say' in line 13 (see the pairs of Figures 5/6 and 7/8). In line 16, as B says the predicative utterance *tsukaerun. tsukaeru* '(it) works. (it) works,' she first shows her dividing gesture and then brings her right hand closer to her right ear/forehead as if she is making a phone call (Figure 9 and Figure 10). Thus her right-hand gestures in lines 11, 13, and 16 seem to work "as the predicate," supporting the change in the referential status of *baki*: from a gesture associated with an act of breaking the phone to the gestures of holding and using her child's broken flip phone. We can say that B's repetitive embodiment of *baki* is synchronized with substantiation of the onomatopoeia *baki* as a referential noun (see also Tao 2022 on a matching of linguistic forms, prosody, and the body).

We have seen that speakers take something that would normally never be referential (an onomatopoeic adverbial *baki*) and turn it into a predicate nominal *baki* describing a breaking act (line 5–9), and then into a referential tracking NP (line 10–16) where *baki* refers to the child's broken cellphone. In that process, the participants intensely join in and repeat the keyword *baki* and appreciate the usage as humorous (Takanashi 2020; Tao 2022).

3.2   Turning individual items in a list into a unified topic NP: *Aisu aisu*

Let us examine another example in which people take up an ad hoc, non-referential mention and then turn it into a playful and referential topic of discussion. Four women (H, M, S, Z) are having lunch at a restaurant before they attend a yoga lesson. There are two video cameras diagonally placed on the table, and the images of both cameras are vertically combined in Figure 11. H is featured in both images. In the following description, I will show only one of the images depending on the context.

Figure 11.

In Example (2), M begins to tell a story about the home party she attended recently hosted by *Ai-san* (who is also referred to as *Ai-sensei* indicating that *Ai-san* is an instructor of some kind). M says the host prepared a lot of food including the dessert. By chance as a gift for the host, each guest, including M, brought some ice cream, but from different shops. Since the host made a kind of jello dessert and prepared some chocolate as gifts, everyone ended up eating a huge amount of dessert that day. Notice that in Japanese, a serving of ice cream is called *aisu* (as line 17 shows):

(2) ice cream ice cream   [CEJC K002_018] 5:22:490

01 M: で なんかみんなーやっぱ、
       de nanka minna: yappa,
       and FIL   everyone EMPH
       and everyone (each guest)

02   手ぶらじゃまずいと思って、
       tebura ja   mazui   to omotte,
       no.gift COP:TOP not.good COMP think:CONT
       thinks that having no gift would be bad,

03   持ってくじゃないですかー。
       Motteku   ja   nai desu   ka:.
       Bring:STAT COP:TOP NEG COP:POL PCL
       so brings something (to the host), you know.

04 H: あ:。
       A:.
       {looks at M and nods}

05 M: それがアイス、アイス:、
       sore [ga ai]su,   aisu:,
       that NOM ice.cream ice.cream
       lit. so that was ice cream, ice cream
       -> so (it turned out that each of us brought) ice cream
       {folding fingers as a way of counting and as she says *aisu aisu*}

06 S: さらに？
       [*sarani*]?
       In addition (to the food)?

07   S, Z, H, M: @@@@#
       {all laugh together while M maintains her finger gesture, photo 1}
                    #fig 12

fig 12: M's keeping her listing gesture for *aisu aisu* while everyone laughs

08 M: アイス、アイス、ゼリー、
       aisu,   ai[2su#,   zerii],
       ice.cream, ice.cream, jello
       ice cream, ice cream, jello
       {M restarts the counting gestures}
                    #fig 13

fig 13: M counts again

09 S: それ あいさん全部作ってくれたの？
    [2 *sore aisan*] *zenbu tsukuttekureta   no?*
    That   NAME   all   prepare:CONT:BEN:PST PCL
    Did Ai-san prepare all of those?

10 M: お料理とかは作ってくれてー。
    Oryoori toka   wa tsukut[3tekurete:].
    Dishes or.something TOP cook:CONT:BEN:CONT
    (she) did all the cooking,

11 S: えー。
    [3 *e:*].
    Wow.

12 Z: ふーん。
    [3 *fu:n*].
    (I) see.

13 H: んー。
    [3 *n:*].
    (I) see.

14 M: そうそう。
    [4 *soo soo*].
    Yeah.
    {looks at S and nods}

15 S: アイス アイス アイス なの？
    [4 @*aisu aisu*]#   *aisu   na* [5 *no*]?
    Ice.cream ice.cream ice.cream COP PCL
    lit. (it was/you guys brought) "ice cream, ice cream, ice cream"?
    {S looks at M smiling and starts the counting hand gesture as she says the
    second and third *aisu*}
                  #fig 14

fig 14: S's counting gesture

16 M: アイスはそう、
    [5 *ai*]*su   wa so,*
      ice.cream TOP yes
    As for the ice cream, yes,

17 :   サーティーワンのアイスを友達が買ってきて、
        saatiiwan no aisu   o   tomodachi ga kattekite,
        31   GEN ice.cream ACC friend   NOM buy:come:CONT
        my friend bought some ice cream from Baskin Robbins,

18 :   あたしがあのー、
        atashi ga ano:,
        I   NOM FIL
        (and) I uh,

19 :   何でした ハーゲンダッツ買ってー、
        nandeshita Haagen Dattsu katte [6 *tte:,*
        what.was.it Haagen-Dazs   bought:go:CONT
        whatchamacallit, Haagen-Dazs ice cream, (I) bought

20 S: [6 @@]

21 M: で あい先生がなんかゼリーみたいなの用意しててー、
        de ai]sensei   ga nanka zerii mitai nano   yooishitete:,
        and NAME.teacher NOM FIL   jello like COP:NMZ prepare:CONT
        and Ai-sensei (Teacher Ai) prepared something like jello,

22   Z, H: @@

23 M: で おみやげでチョコレート貰ってー
        de omiyage de chokoreeto moratte: [7 @@@]
        and gift   as chocolate receive:CONT
        and we got some chocolate as the gift (from Ai-san),

24 H: [7 a: @@@]

25 S: で それみんな食べんのアイス、アイス アイス食べたの？
        De sore minna taben no aisu, aisu ai#su tabe[8ta no]?
        so it   all   eat   PCL ice.cream   eat:PST PCT
        so do you eat them all, as for the *ice cream ice cream ice cream*, did you eat
        them all?
        {S again starts the counting gesture as she says the second and third *aisu*}

#fig 15

fig 15: S counts again

26 M: アイスアイスは食べました。
        [8 *ai]su   aisu   wa tabemashita.*
          Ice.cream ice.cream TOP eat:POL:PST
        As for *ice cream ice cream*, (we) ate (it).
        {M looks at S, lightly smiling. N hand gesture for *aisu aisu*. M is occupied
        with mixing the salad dressing}

27   S, Z, H: @@@@
        {M kept smiling as they laugh.}
        ((18 seconds later))

28 S: そのアイスアイスはすごいなー。
        Sono aisu   aisu#   wa sugoi   naa.
        That ice.cream ice.cream TOP amazing PCL
        the *ice cream ice cream* is amazing.
        {S shifts her gaze away from M and looks down. N hand gesture. M smiles as she
        continues to work on her salad.}

fig 16 S (top, left) and M (bottom, right)
29 Z: un.
        Yeah.

The novel NP we focus on is *aisu aisu* (or *aisu aisu aisu*). In the middle of her narrative about the party at Ai-san's place in line 5 (*sore ga aisu aisu:* 'lit. so that was ice cream, ice cream'), M says that each guest brought ice cream as a gift to the host. M's *aisu, aisu* here is delivered as a list (Tao 2019): each *aisu* has the high pitch on the initial vowel [a], hence is pronounced as a separate word. In addition, M moves her hands up and down as she folds her fingers and says *aisu*. Her delivery as a list accompanied by the gesture suggests multiple boxes of ice cream, and other participants appreciate both the delivery and the gesture with laughter (see line 7 Figure 12). M holds the hand gesture until line 8, where she upgrades her list with an additional item, *aisu, aisu, zerii* 'ice cream, ice cream, jello.' She also upgrades the gestures, moving her left hand up and down more clearly, with head nods (see Figure 13).

In line 9, S asks M whether Ai-san made everything, and M replies in line 10 that Ai-san did all the cooking. Then, *aisu, aisu* as separate items on a list becomes transformed into a unitary noun in line 15 when S looks at M and says *aisu aisu aisu na no?* '(Is it) ice cream, ice cream, ice cream?' with light laughter and the rising intonation for a confirmation question. *Na no*, the copula and a final particle, is a predicate-ending form. So structurally, S's *aisu aisu aisu* functions as a predicate nominal as a whole, and is more integrated into the clause than M's earlier *aisu, aisu, (zerii)* delivered as a list. S's *aisu aisu aisu* is less stressed than M's list version, accompanied by a smaller counting gesture (Figure 14) without any vertical motion of hands or head nods, suggesting that it is a more unified expression than three distinct items.

In replying to S's confirmation question in line 15, M provides the details of *aisu* from line 16 through 23, which include the guests' bringing Baskin Robbins (line 17) and Haagen-Dazs (lines 18–19) ice cream, Ai-san's preparing jello (line 21) and the gift chocolate (line 23). Then in line 25, *aisu aisu aisu* changes its grammatical status in the clause when S asks another question, *de sore minna taben no, aisu aisu aisu tabeta no?* 'So, that, do you eat (them) all? As for *ice cream ice cream ice cream* did you eat (them) all?' S's *aisu aisu aisu* is no longer a predicate nominal but can be taken as a topic NP (i.e., the topic marker *wa* could be used according to native judgement after *aisu aisu aisu*). In line 25, S produces two juxtaposed clauses with a parallel structure, as indicated in the translation. The *aisu aisu aisu* is associated with the semantic 'wholeness' of *sore minna* '(lit.) that, all' projected in the first clause.[5] Therefore, *aisu aisu aisu* functions as a topic NP, representing the unified concept of lots of desserts potentially including jello and chocolate.

In comparison with M's original *aisu, aisu* as a list, S's *aisu aisu aisu* in line 25 shows a 'departure' in terms of referentiality, from a concrete list of individual items to a unified NP underscoring the amount (and even variety) of desserts in its entirety. The departure is made possible by an integration of *aisu aisu aisu* into a copula clause in S's line 15 as the predicate nominal, and the structural parallelism (Du Bois 2014) of the two adjacent clauses in S's line 25. Since S produces *aisu aisu aisu* with initial accents on [a] and brings up her hand again to show a quick counting gesture (Figure 15 in line 25), we can see that *aisu aisu aisu*, while functioning as one unified topic NP in a clause, still weakly retains the list qualities as well.

In line 26, *aisu aisu* is further transformed: M replies to S *aisu aisu wa tabemashita* 'As for *aisu aisu*, (we) ate them,' with an explicit topic particle *wa*, which works anaphorically to turn *aisu aisu* into a unified topic NP integrated into a clause. M pronounces the phrase as if it is an ordinary noun, using a single intonation contour without any distinct initial accent on *aisu*; M does not use any counting gesture, so *aisu aisu* is de-embodied.

---

5. In this paper, *sore* 'that' and *minna* 'all' are treated together as a phrase indicating 'all of them' referring to the desserts. Another possible interpretation of *minna* would be 'everyone' referring to people at the party, so the clause could mean 'did everyone have that?' Even if we take the latter view, we still see the affinity between *sore* 'that' with *aisu aisu aisu* in the parallel clause structure.

Then 18 seconds later in line 28, S brings up *aisu aisu* as a topic NP again and makes an assessment by saying *sono aisu aisu wa sugoi naa* 'The *ice cream ice cream* is amazing.' The distal demonstrative *sono* projects an NP, making *aisu aisu* sound like a unified NP. This time, she says *aisu aisu* twice (not three times) with the topic particle *wa*, just like M did in line 26, in a single coherent intonation contour without stress on [a] and without using the counting gesture (Figure 16). So S's *aisu aisu* is also de-embodied and delivered as if it is an ordinary NP.

In this excerpt, we see the change in the functional status of *aisu aisu (aisu)* from separate list items (lines 5 and 8) to a predicate nominal (line 15), a topic NP with a stress on [a] and a gesture (line 25), and finally, an ordinary-looking topic NP without any distinct delivery.

This example also shows that speakers resonate (Tao 2022) with each other and enjoy producing an ad hoc NP not only verbally but also through embodiment and even de-embodiment. The speakers enhance the phatic humor by smiling and laughing as they utter, embody, or hear the phrase *aisu aisu (aisu)*.

3.3   Creating a novel NP through reanalysis: *Den*

The final example involves a phrasal reanalysis of an onomatopoeic expression into an NP. Five women are having a potluck party at Y's place (Figure 17).

Figure 17. Five women

Prior to the conversation shown in the excerpt, Y, M, A and N complain about *nidankai choori* 'two-step cooking' that requires two pans, e.g., steaming ingredients in one pan, and stir-frying them in a different pan. They express their rather negative stance that the two-step cooking consumes enormous energy and time. Yet they admit that the outcome is excellent in quality. Then they praise H's dish and comment that it seems to involve the two-step cooking process.

A rough summary of the excerpt is as follows: In Line 4, H begins presenting her counter-stance by saying *demo* 'but', meaning that her dish is actually very easy to cook. She points to her dish and says that instead of deep-frying the chicken and vegetables, she just pan-fried the meat (line 6) and vegetables (line 9) and quickly poured *amazu* 'sweetened vinegar' in the same pan (line 10). She uses the onomatopoeia *Den!* 'Boom!' to reenact the scene of pouring *amazu* into a pan all at once in a large motion.[6] Then in the remaining part of the excerpt, the others humorously question this explanation. Because *amazu* is usually prepared separately by boiling rice vinegar with sugar, they say she must have used a different pan, which means this involved the very two-step cooking process that they complain about. For example, in line 12, speaker A directly points out that H's cooking involves two-step cooking. The other women point to the same fact, but do so in a playful manner by turning the onomatopoeia *den* into a noun, creating a novel nonsense NP *amazu no den* 'lit. sweetened vinegar's *boom*' and repeating it in intense overlap and laughter:

(3) Amazu no *den* 'Sweetened vinegar *den*'   T003021
    1. Y: そ、何かしてから、さらに何かするってゆう、その二段階。
        so, nanika   shite kara,   sarani   nanika   suru [1 *tteyuu,*
        yeah, something   do   after.that additionally something do   QUO:say
        sono] [2 *nidankai*].
        the   two.steps
        yeah, (you) do something and do an additional thing, and that's the two steps.
    2. N: そうそうそう、そう。
        [1 *soo soo   soo*], [2 *soo*].
        right right right right
        Exactly right.
    3. M: そうだよね。
        [2 *soo da yo ne*].
        right COP PCL PCL
        That's right.
    4. H: でも、でもさー、
        [2 *demo, demo*] [3 *sa:*],#
        but   but   PCL
        but, but,
        {points to her dish, holding chopsticks}
                  #fig 18

---

6. The onomatopoeia *den* is not a sound mimicry like *baki* discussed above. *Den* is associated with the heaviness of a substance or the solid and/or imposing attitude of a person, but is not considered a referential noun. It occurs in a fixed expression as *den to kamaeru* '(for someone) to take the stout and unswerving attitude' where *den to* works as an adverbial phrase of manner.

fig 18: H points to her dish
5. N: うん。
    [3 *un*].
    uh-huh.
6. H: 肉焼いてー、
    [4 *niku yaite:*],
    meat   stir-fry
    (you) stir-fry meat,
7. A: 何かしてうん
    [4 @ *nanka shite un* @]
      something do   yeah
    (you) do something, yeah.
8. N: うんうん、おいし。
    un. un, [5 *oishi*].
    yeah yeah tasty
    yeah. Tastes good.
9. H: 野菜炒めて、そこに、
    [5 *yasai*] *itamete,   soko ni:#,*
    vegetables stir-fry.and there in
    after we stir-fry some vegetables, then in there (i.e., in the pan),
    {shifting from pointing to the preparatory gesture for "den"}
                              #fig 19

fig 19 preparatory gesture for "den" in line 9
10   甘酢の..でーん！
    amazu   no# .. <EMPH % de#:n!# % EMPH>
    sweetened vinegar NMZ   ONOMA
                    #fig 20   #fig 21 #fig 22
    って入れるだけだからー。
    tte ireru dake da kara:.
    QUO put.in only COP so
    all we need to do is just pour the sweetened vinegar thing like 'boom!'

fig 20 preparatory motion gazing Y

fig 21 moving upward

fig 22 pouring "den!"

11 M: …でも甘酢のでんをさ、

    … *demo amazu*   *no* .. [1 %@*den o*   *sa*@]#,
    but   sweetened vinegar GEN   N   ACC PCL
                                     #fig 23

    But "sweetened vinegar *den*,"
    {M uses hand gesture as she reenacts "*den*" and laughs}

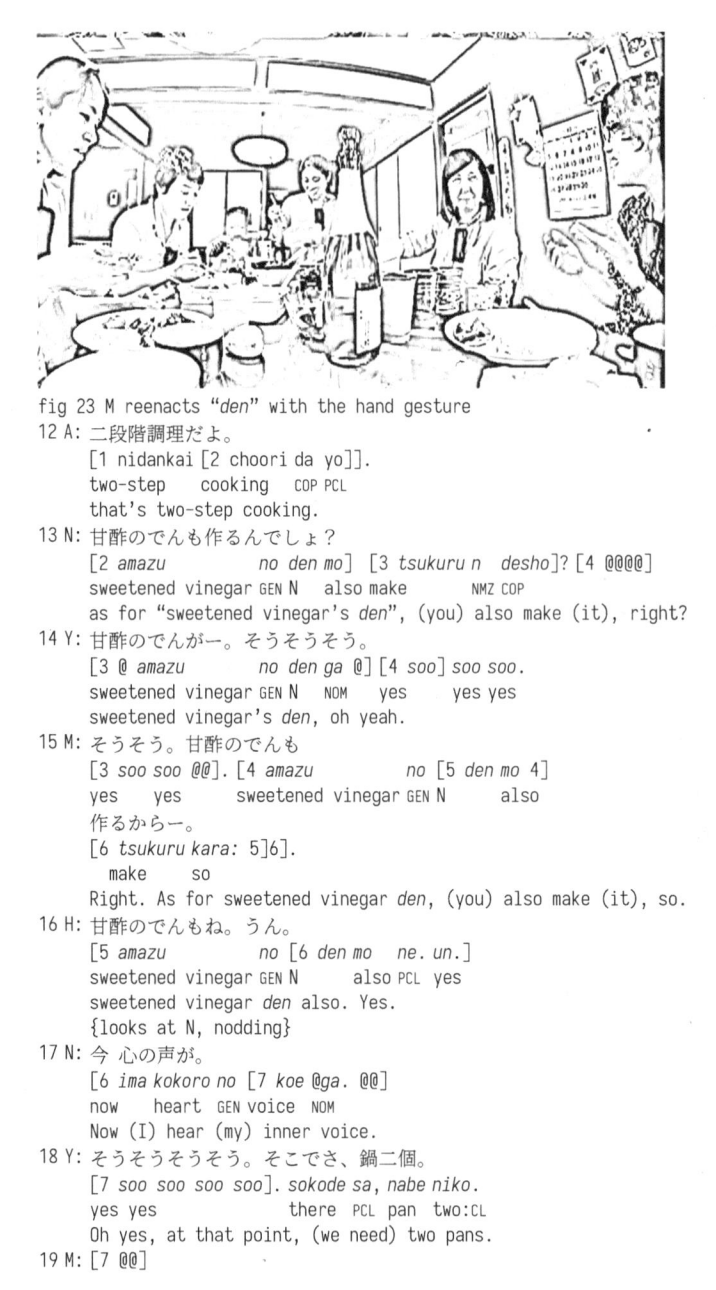

fig 23 M reenacts "den" with the hand gesture

12 A: 二段階調理だよ。
　　　[1 nidankai [2 choori da yo]].
　　　two-step   cooking   COP PCL
　　　that's two-step cooking.

13 N: 甘酢のでんも作るんでしょ？
　　　[2 amazu   no den mo] [3 tsukuru n desho]? [4 @@@@]
　　　sweetened vinegar GEN N   also make   NMZ COP
　　　as for "sweetened vinegar's den", (you) also make (it), right?

14 Y: 甘酢のでんがー。そうそうそう。
　　　[3 @ amazu   no den ga @] [4 soo] soo soo.
　　　sweetened vinegar GEN N   NOM yes   yes yes
　　　sweetened vinegar's den, oh yeah.

15 M: そうそう。甘酢のでんも
　　　[3 soo soo @@]. [4 amazu   no [5 den mo 4]
　　　yes   yes   sweetened vinegar GEN N   also
　　　作るからー。
　　　[6 tsukuru kara: 5]6].
　　　 make   so
　　　Right. As for sweetened vinegar den, (you) also make (it), so.

16 H: 甘酢のでんもね。うん。
　　　[5 amazu   no [6 den mo   ne. un.]
　　　sweetened vinegar GEN N   also PCL yes
　　　sweetened vinegar den also. Yes.
　　　{looks at N, nodding}

17 N: 今 心の声が。
　　　[6 ima kokoro no [7 koe @ga. @@]
　　　now   heart GEN voice NOM
　　　Now (I) hear (my) inner voice.

18 Y: そうそうそうそう。そこでさ、鍋二個。
　　　[7 soo soo soo soo]. sokode sa, nabe niko.
　　　yes yes   there PCL pan two:CL
　　　Oh yes, at that point, (we need) two pans.

19 M: [7 @@]

The key string in this excerpt is *amazu no den* from lines 11 through 16. *Den* is used as an onomatopoeia in line 10. However, speakers M, N, Y and H repeat *amazu no den*, as if *den* is an ordinary noun that has some referential meaning, which makes the entire exchanges humorous as we see in the speakers' intense repetition and laughter. The expression is an instantly-made mock NP which could be translated as 'sweetened vinegar's "*boom*".

How does the NP *amazu no den* emerge in the interaction? To answer the question, we should pay attention to the way H enacts the string in line 9. H starts the preparatory gesture of holding an imaginary container (e.g. a bowl, a pan) with both hands (Figure 19). In Line 10, as H says *amazu no* 'the sweetened vinegar,' she maintains the same hand gesture and gazes at Y (Figure 20). In this utterance, *no* in *amazu no* is a nominalizer: the phrase can be translated as "the sweetened vinegar one." Then she straightens her back (Figure 21) and after a brief pause, says "*den!*" pronounced with glottal constriction, lengthening, higher pitch, and louder volume in an exaggerated intonation. She also moves her arms quickly to gesture "dumping something from a container into a pan" (Figure 21–22). We can see that H's line 10, especially *den*, is planned (prepared) and performed.

H's distinct delivery seems to trigger M's creation of a novel NP in line 11. M reenacts *amazu no den*, the same string H used in line 10. It is marked as 'reen-actment' due to her distinct delivery of *den* that shares the characteristics of H's original *den*: a slight pause before *den*, and a stress and higher pitch on the vowel. Furthermore, imitating H, M also uses both hands as she pronounces *den* though her gesture is smaller. Then M does something different: she continues to add an accusative case particle *o* and final particle *sa*, and looks at H, N and Y with a smile (Figure 23). M's addition of the particles immediately and anaphorically completes the process of turning the entire string into a unitary novel NP with a funny-sounding nonsense head noun *den*, and her smile shows that she is aware of the humorous effect this creation brings about.

Notice that in Japanese, the nominalizer *no* and the genitive particle have an identical shape, so the homophony affords the possibility of the reanalysis of the string *amazu no den* as represented in the change of bracketing in (4).[7] Therefore, *amazu no den* is actually a grammatical pun (Michael Ewing, p.c.) contributing to the humorous mood:

(4) Creation of a novel nonsense expression through reanalysis (simplified)
```
H's Line 10: [amazu          no]NP [[den tte]MAN ireru]VP
             sweetened vinegar NMZ  ONOMA QUO   put.in
             'to dump sweetened vinegar thing (into a pan)'
```

---

7. In line 10 (*amazu no den! tte ireru* 'to dump sweetened vinegar one'), H pronounces *no*, which can be considered a nominalizer 'one.' Some may say that H meant to say *amazu no o* (NOM and ACC) or *amazu o* (ACC) instead but mispronounced it. Indeed, with the accusative marker *o*, the utterance would be grammatically correct. However, in spoken Japanese, the non-occurrence of *o* is considered the unmarked option (Fujii and Ono 2000: 1; see also Ono 2006). Therefore, we will not treat *no* in line 10 as a speech error.

M's Line 11: [[*amazu*   *no den*]$_{NP}$ *o*]$_{PP}$
            sweetened vinegar GEN N   ACC
            'sweetened vinegar "*boom*"' ((no predicate expressed))

As mentioned earlier, not only M in line 11, but other participants (N in line 13, Y in line 14, M in line 15 and H herself in line 16) pick up and repeat the newly created phrase overlapping and laughing intensely. Remarkably, each of them adds a particle (*mo* 'also', *ga* 'NOM') to *amazu no den*, which quickly and intensely endorses M's treatment of *amazu no den* as a unitary NP. Furthermore, in line 13 and the following lines, the speakers remove all distinct prosodic and bodily features deployed by H and M in lines 10 and 11, including a pause, exaggerated voice quality, and noticeable hand gestures. Instead, they pronounce *amazu no den* quickly and smoothly as if it is an ordinary NP. In addition, they make the expression a topic in their utterances, as shown in line 13 when N asks *amazu no den mo tsukuru n deshoo?* 'as for sweetened vinegar *den*", (you) also make (it), right?'. In other words, *amazu no den* is transformed into a unified topic NP interactively by the speakers, which creates an additional layer of phaticness (Malinowski 1949) to the playful mood already created by M in line 11.

4.   Discussion

We have seen how novel ad hoc NPs (*baki, aisu aisu, amazu no den*) are created and tracked in interaction. In all three cases, there are the base expressions in the preceding discourse that lead to the creation of the novel NPs; in other words, the novel expressions do not appear out of the blue (Suzuki 2020). The source expressions have impactful shape and/or exaggerated prosodic and gestural delivery that may contribute to the creation and repetition of novel NPs in a humorous manner. Then speakers (including other speakers) constitute and reinforce referentiality in ad hoc novel expressions through intense repetition, laughter (Glenn 2003), and embodiment (Examples 1, 2, 3) and also de-embodiment (in Examples (2) and (3)). In this section, I will point out two major characteristics of referentiality: as an interactive process and as a source of playfulness.

First, referentiality is an interactive process. Speakers take something that would normally never be referential (e.g., the onomatopoeic adverbial *baki*) and turn it into a referential, tracking NP (e.g., *baki* meaning the child's flip phone) which creates phatic humor through repetition, i.e., the novel NP acquires an added layer of referentiality. Structurally, after the source expression is introduced in the predicative position as a non-referential NP, the novel NP is taken up and marked as the topic in an utterance and gets repeated as the semantically substantial tracking NP. The examples discussed above show a parallel shift from an expression of non-single-noun origin (onomatopoeias or list items) into a single referential topic NP via the predicate-nominal stage.

In addition to verbal repetition, prosodic and gestural repetition plays an important part in the process of constituting the referentiality of the novel NPs. In Example (1), speaker B's hand gestures evolve from the act of breaking the phone to mean the child's phone itself, and A smiles. In (2), speaker M's listing gesture is repeated by S who starts to treat it as a unified NP with laughter. In (3), speaker H's hand gesture of "*den!*" is repeated by M who creates a nonsense NP *amazu no den* 'sweetened vinegar *boom*' and starts the playful mode by laughing. As pointed out by Glenn (2003:153), speakers' laughter also seems to help the participants maintain the relationship with each other even if there is a stance difference (e.g., regarding two-step cooking between H and others):

Next, referentiality is an interactional resource for playfulness. The examples discussed in this paper show that people take up a sort of temporal, non-referential mention and then turn it into a playful topic of discussion. In that process, we see the radical change of the parts of speech of the source: even ono-matopoeias, which are normally treated as adverbs, can be reformulated as refer-ential nouns. Furthermore, the speakers create novel ad hoc NPs by adding topic particles *wa, mo* 'also', *demo* 'also' (as in all excerpts) or case particles *ga* 'NOM', *o* 'ACC' as in (3) after the key expressions.[8] Those particles anaphorically turn the expressions into NPs. Such a backward creation of NPs (cf. Keevalik (2000)'s discussion of articles/demonstratives/adjectives as "projective" devices) based on unusual forms stands out and instantly becomes the source of playfulness. In addition, the distinct prosody and embodiment of the source expressions, and their removal (i.e., the plain prosody and de-embodiment) contribute to make an expression sound as if it is a referential and ordinary NP that the all participants enjoy using.

Thus, various types of manipulation of referentiality are found to work in the spontaneous creation of a novel expression in interaction, which can also function as a resource for playfulness (Takanashi 2004, 2020, 2022; Tao 2022). A novel ad hoc NP can be tracked in terms of referentiality and also in terms of social bonding and shared feelings or values, that is, phatic communion (Malinowski 1949:316).

---

8. Ono and Thompson (2020) point out that NPs in Japanese conversation tend not to be "embellished," i.e., they are often not accompanied by 'case', 'semantic', or 'topic' particles, con-trary to the common assumption. They also state that embellished nouns "are infrequent and tend to be used in pragmatically marked situations (2020:326)." The present study supports their observation. By adding a particle to an unusual source expression, speakers in this study seem to reinforce 'nounhood' of the expression, and such creation of a novel NP is a sheer pragmatically-marked situation.

The cases discussed in this paper were found as the result of closely examining the video conversations one by one. Those newly created ad hoc NPs do not fall into the major pattern of novel NPs reported in Suzuki (2020), where it was shown that most of those NPs are predicate nominals created by suffixation. Nevertheless, we now know that speakers make use of referentiality, an abstract notion of discourse profile (Du Bois and Thompson 1991), to spontaneously make ad-hoc and/or nonsense expressions sound substantial and humorous at the same time.

Acknowledgements

My deepest gratitude to the editors of this volume, Mike Ewing and Ritva Laury for their insightful comments, strong support, and patience throughout the process of writing. I also thank the two anonymous reviewers, Tsuyoshi Ono, Hiroko Takanashi, Hongyin Tao, Sandy Thompson, the participants of the Alberta Conference 2019, and the members of Yurui Kenkyukai for their encouragements, and Ruth Fallon for her careful proofreading and helpful comments. I am solely responsible for any shortcomings of this paper.

Abbreviations

BEN	benefactive	POL	polite
CL	classifier	PST	past
COP	copula	QUO	quotative
CONT	continuative -*te*	STAT	stative
FIL	filler	TOP	topic marker
FS	false start	<WH WH>	whispering
GEN	genitive	@	(one pulse of) laughter
MAN	manner	[ ]	overlapping utterances identically numbered
NMZ	nominalizer		identically numbered
PCL	particle	:	(a colon) lengthening
PERF	perfective		

References

Couper-Kuhlen, Elizabeth, and Margaret Selting. 2018. *Interactional linguistics: Studying Language in Social Interaction*. Cambridge: Cambridge University Press.

Du Bois, John W. 2014. "Towards a Dialogic Syntax: Dialogic Resonance: Activating Affinities across Utterances." *Cognitive Linguistics* 25 (3): 359–410.

Du Bois, John W., and Sandra A. Thompson. 1991. "Dimensions of a Theory of Information Flow." Unpublished manuscript, University of California, Santa Barbara.

Du Bois, John W., Stephan Schuetze-Coburn, Susanna Cumming, and Danae Paolino. 1993. "Outline of Discourse Transcription." In *Talking Data: Transcription and Coding in Discourse Research*, ed. by Jane A. Edwards and Martin D. Lampert, 45–89. New York: Psychology Press.

Fox, Barbara. 1999. "Directions in Research: Language and the Body." *Research on Language and Social Interaction*, 32 (1–2): 51–59.

Fujii, Noriko and Tsuyoshi Ono. 2000. "The Occurrence and Non-occurrence of the Japanese Direct Object Marker *o* in Conversation." *Studies in Language* 24 (1): 1–39.

Glenn, Philip. 2003. *Laughter in Interaction*. Cambridge: Cambridge University Press.

Goodwin, Charles. 1979. "The Interactive Construction of a Sentence in Natural Conversation." In *Everyday Language: Studies in Ethnomethodology*, ed. by George Psathas, 97–121. New York, Irvington Publishers.

Hayano, Kaoru. 2011. "Claiming Epistemic Primacy: *Yo*-marked Assessments in Japanese." In *The Morality of Knowledge in Conversation*, ed. by Tanya Stivers, Lorenza Mondada, and Jakob Steensig, 58–81. Cambridge University Press.

Iwasaki, Shoichi. 2002. *Japanese*. Amsterdam: John Benjamins.

Keevallik, Leelo. 2020. "Multimodal Noun Phrases." In *The 'Noun Phrase' Across Languages: An Emergent Unit in Interaction*, ed. by Tsuyoshi Ono and Sandra A. Thompson, 153–177. Amsterdam: John Benjamins.

Kita, Sotaro. 1997. "Two-Dimensional Semantic Analysis of Japanese Mimetics." *Linguistics* 35 (2): 379–416.

Koiso, Hanae, Haruka Amatani, Yuriko Iseki, Yasuyuki Usuda, Wakako Kashino, Yoshiko Kawabata, Yayoi Tanaka, Yasuharu Den and Ken'ya Nishikawa. 2020. "Nihongo nichijyoukaiwa koopasu" monitaaban no sekkei, hyooka, yobiteki bunseki [Design, Evaluation, and Preliminary Analysis of the Monitor Version of the Corpus of Everyday Japanese Conversation]" Kokuritsu Kokugo Kenkyujo Ronshu [*NINJAL Research Papers*] 18, 17–33.

Kubozono, Haruo. 2002. Shingo wa kooshite tsukurareru [*Strategies of Word Creation*]. Tokyo: Iwanami Shoten.

Malinowski, Bronislaw. 1949. "The Problem of Meaning in Primitive Languages." Supplement to *The Meaning of Meaning, Tenth Edition*, ed. by Charles Kay Ogden, and Ivor Armstrong Richards, 146–52. London: Routledge and Kegan Paul.

Ono, Tsuyoshi. 2006. "The Actual Status of So-called Particle Ellipsis in Japanese: Evidence from Conversation," In *Acquisition, Diachrony, and Contact: Empirical and Experimental Methods in Cognitive/Functional Research*, ed. by Sally Rice and John Newman. CSLI Publications, 1–12.

Ono, Tsuyoshi, and Sandra A. Thompson. 2020. "What Can Japanese Conversation Tell Us about 'NP'?" In *The "Noun Phrase" Across Languages*, ed. by Tsuyoshi Ono and Sandra A. Thompson, 315–327. Amsterdam: John Benjamins.

Ono, Tsuyoshi, Sandra A. Thompson, and Yumi Sasaki. 2012. "Japanese Negotiation Through Emerging Final Particles in Everyday Talk." *Discourse Processes* 49 (3–4): 243–72.

Senft, Gunter. 2014. *Understanding Pragmatics*. Oxfordshire: Taylor and Francis.

Shibatani, Masayoshi. 1990. *The Languages of Japan*. Cambridge: Cambridge University Press.

Suzuki, Ryoko. 2020. "Shin hyougen no soohatsu: atarashiku nai naka ni meccha atarashisa mieteru apiiru [The Emergence of Novel Expressions: 'The Appeal that We See Novelty in Non-novel Expressions']." In Ninchi gengogaku to danwakinoo gengogaku no yuukiteki setten [*Toward Dynamic Interaction between Cognitive Linguistcs and Discourse-functional Linguistics: New Frontiers in the Usage-based Approach to Grammar*], ed. by Toshihide Nakayama and Naoki Otani, 183–208. Tokyo: Hituzi Shobo.

Takanashi, Hiroko. 2004. The Interactional Co-construction of Play in Japanese Conversation. Ph.D. dissertation. Linguistics Department, University of California, Santa Barbara.

Takanashi, Hiroko. 2020. "Playful Naming in Playful Framing: The Intertextual Emergence of Neologism." In *Bonding through Context: Language and Interactional Alignment in Japanese Situated Discourse*, ed. by Risako Ide and Kaori Hata, 239–264. Amsterdam: John Benjamins.

Takanashi, Hiroko. 2022. "Language Reproduction and Coordinated Agency through Resonant Play." *East Asian Pragmatics* 7 (3): 395–423.

Tao, Hongyin. 2019. "List Gestures in Mandarin Conversation and their Implications for Understanding Multimodal Interaction." In *Multimodality in Chinese Interaction (Applications of Cognitive Linguistics)*, ed. by Xiaoting Li and Tsuyoshi Ono, 65–98. Berlin: De Gruyter Mouton.

Tao, Hongyin. 2022. "Multimodal Amusement Resonance as a Conversation Interactional Device: Evidence from Mandarin Chinese and English." *East Asian Pragmatics* 7 (3): 333–363.

Yonekawa, Akihiko. 2002. "Gendai nihongo no isoo [Variations in Modern Japanese]." In Gendai Nihongo Kooza 4 Goi [*Modern Japanese vol. 4: Vocabulary*], ed. by Yoshifumi Hida and Takeyoshi Sato, 46–70. Tokyo: Meiji Shoin.

CHAPTER 9

An interactional approach to generic second person expressions in Mandarin conversation

Hongyin Tao
University of California Los Angeles

This chapter tackles the hitherto under-explored question of when and why conversationalists deploy second person generic expressions that feature a general and vague referential scope. I show that the conversational contexts in which they appear are usually characterized most prominently by their relatively complex and/or controversial subject matters, participants' incongruent stances, and/or opposing positions to be contested. These contexts and their associated interactional demands are argued to give rise to the patterning of clustering (multiplicity of instances in adjacent units), limited generality (as good-enough-yet-not-too-broad general statements), and primary (or attempted primary) speakership. In general, second person generic statements can be seen as a special and powerful rhetorical device designed for marked interactional occasions.

Keywords: second person singular pronoun, generic expression, reference, indefinite, impersonal, truism, informing, persuasion, argumentation, Mandarin conversation

1. Introduction

Referential forms such as personal pronouns, names, and so forth are of great interest to researchers in a wide range of language related fields – from linguistics, conversation analysis to philosophy and anthropology, etc. – due to the multiple roles they play, e.g. communicating ideas, constructing identity, negotiating social relationships between speakers, among others (Wales 1996; Xiang 2019; Stirling & Manderson 2011; Dahmen & Blythe 2022). As a special referential form, generic expressions for persons (e.g. a generic second person or a reference to anyone/ everyone rather than literally just the addressee) are typically investigated from the point of view of semantic properties (see Berry 2009 for a review of such

https://doi.org/10.1075/pbns.344.09tao
© 2024 John Benjamins Publishing Company

works on English 'you'). Thus many influential studies have discussed the differences between such categories as the referential domain (i.e. the specificity of the reference, e.g. 'addressee alone' vs. 'addressee plus others', Sacks 1965/1992, 1966/1992) and the kinds of meanings a reference helps convey (e.g. formulations of morals or truisms, life-drama, and situational insertion (Kitagawa & Lehrer 1990, referencing Laberge & Sankoff 1979)). Others have made the distinction between metaphoricity (whether or not the addressee is included in the reference domain) and normativity (whether or not the addressee approves or identifies with the proposition) with regard to these expressions (Rubba 1996; Bolinger 1979a). Conversation analysts have explored issues such as what sequential features may help determine the meaning of pronouns such as 'you' in English (Sacks 1965/1992), and how to delineate the target of 'you' for turn-taking in multi-party conversations (Lerner 1996). What is conspicuously missing, however, is inquiry into the question of when and why speakers deploy these generic expressions to begin with – in the words of Bolinger (1979b: 290), "why use a pronoun?", or "why repeat the pronoun?". From the standpoint of conversational interaction, a perspective I take here, this means an additional number of questions to be asked regarding the interactional motivations and functions of generic expressions: When do conversationalists evoke or switch to the non-literal use use of second person pronouns and what social actions are accomplished with such uses (Dahmen & Blythe 2022; Helasvuo & Suomalainen, this volume)?

In the field of Chinese linguistics, in addition to descriptions of standard and extended uses (typically termed *fanzhi* 'generalized reference' and *xuzhi* 'non-specific reference', see e.g. Lü 1985: Section 1.2; Xiang 2019), research on the Chinese second person singular pronoun *ni* has yielded notable insights in the area of discourse and grammar. Biq (1991) is one of the earliest that have looked into the function of *ni* in Mandarin conversation. She notes that in addition to the canonical deictic use in reference to the addressee, the second person singular pronoun in Mandarin can have three other functions, depending on the fluid referential scope. These she terms (1) the impersonal (i.e. where the second person pronoun functions as an indefinite pronoun and can be taken to mean anyone and everyone), (2) the dramatic (i.e. the speaker assuming a role in the described situation, acting out the scene, and changing the frame of reference), and (3) the metalinguistic (i.e. non-propositional, vocative, and attention calling) – all of which, according to Biq, "share the characteristic of being devices for reinforcing the addressee's involvement in what s/he is being told" (p. 320). This point echoes the characterization by Siewierska (2004) and Berry (2009) of the generic use of the English second pronoun *you* and that of Laberge & Sankoff (1979) on French indefinite pronouns in terms of their extended uses beyond the literal referential scope. Hsiao (2011) focuses on the apparently free interchange between the first (*wǒ*) and second person (*nǐ*) pronouns in reported speech, illustrating the role that these pronouns play in manipulating participant perspectives and ultimately in the service of achieving intersubjectivity. Finally, Kuo (2002), a study on televised debates by three mayoral candidates in Taiwan, shows an interesting tendency of shifting from the more generic (impersonal) to more referential (personal) as the debates moved from *solidarity* focusing (bonding with the audience/voters) to *confrontational* (directly attacking the opponent in the debate).

As can be seen from this brief overview, while previous studies on the Mandarin second person singular pronoun have revealed interesting patterns of use in discourse, including the non-specific or generic reference use, other than Kuo's work on political speeches, few have explicitly addressed the question of when and why ordinary speakers choose to use the different types of second person pronominal forms in everyday interactive contexts. Against this backdrop, this study looks into everyday Mandarin talk-in-interaction and focuses on the contexts, including conversational sequences, in which the generic second person singular pronoun is deployed. I will especially be concerned with the types of social activities that generic second person expressions help construct. The overall approach is that of interactional linguistic (Couper-Kuhlen & Selting 2018), where grammar is viewed both as part of a larger set of resources that speakers mobilize to conduct or implement social interaction and simultaneously as being shaped by language use. After data analysis in Sections 3 and 4, I will explore the implications of the interaction-based findings and suggest that what has been treated ostensibly as a semantically peculiar second person referential issue needs a social interactional perspective in order to arrive at a fuller account of its natural patterns and their underlying working principles.

2. Materials and methodology

Data for this study come from a variety of audio/video-recorded Mandarin everyday conversations in face-to-face and telephone call situations. The face-to-face conversations were collected over the past two decades by the author and collaborators, while the telephone conversations come from the CallFriend corpus developed by the LDC (Canavan & Zipperlen 1996). A sample collection of the data, consisting of seven conversations from different sub-corpora (six face-to-face and one telephone), with the recording time of about six hours, was used for detailed coding. All the conversations used for this study received participant consent, and anonymization of human subjects was exercised throughout.

A total of 158 instances of second person pronoun use were identified as non-literal generic cases. The identified cases are generally limited to the first two categories defined by Biq (1991), which she calls the impersonal (roughly 'indefinite' i.e. the second person pronoun can be taken to mean anyone and everyone;)[1] and the dramatic ("speaker assigned as an actor in the discourse scene; shift of reference frameworks"), while her third type, the metalinguistic (i.e. attention getting, vocative) are generally excluded.[2] In Biq's taxonomy, the metalinguistic type contains mostly formulas such as *ni shou* 'you say; don't you think', *ni kan* 'you see, look', *ni xiang* '(you) think about it', *ni zhidao* 'you know', etc., which are of a very different type and are thus excluded.

In this chapter, I will refer both of the 'impersonal' and 'dramatic' categories defined by Biq (1991) with the more widely used terms: generic, general, indefinite, or extended, as opposed to literal, deictic, specific, or propositional, unless it is necessary, as is the case on a few occasions, to pinpoint some of the terminological differences. The main goal, as stated earlier, is to investigate the social interactional functions associated with the use of the generic expressions in conversation rather than potential semantic subcategories.

While generic uses can be theoretically distinguished from literal uses, in naturalistic data, very often the identification of specific tokens requires a careful inspection of the local interactional contexts in which they appear. Example (1) provides some useful cases as an illustration.

(1)   Y recounts an experience of losing his wallet on a bus and retrieving it with the help of the police in Hong Kong.

```
1.  Y:    Uh.[3]
           Umm
           Okay.[4]
2.        …结果他说,
           …Jiéguǒ tā shuō,
           so      3SG say
           So he said,
3.        …那么好。
           …Nàme hǎo.
           then good
           Okay then,
4.   →    ..你跟我们一起走。
           ..Nǐ gēn wǒmen yīqǐ    zǒu.
           2SG with 1PL   together go
           you need to come with us.
```

---

1. In Biq's original statement, she defines the impersonal use in terms of "substitution for an indefinite pronoun in casual speech" (Biq 1991: 309).

2. In some rare cases, especially when the second person pronoun is used in a cluster, such as in Extract (3), line 8, where the boundary between the metalinguistic and geneic use is fuzzy, they may also be included.

5. …(1.4)那么就去追那辆巴士[去]了。

 …(1.4) *Nàme jiù qù zhuī nà liàng bāshì [qù] le.*

  then just go chase that CLF bus go PRT

  Then we start chasing that bus.

6. T: [@@]

7. OV: …(.6)他这个是--

  …(.6) *Tā zhège shì--*

   3SG this COP

   This is--

8. …什么目的呢。

 …*Shénme mùdì ne.*

  what purpose PRT.

  What's the purpose (of doing this)?

9. Y: …目的就是[说],

 …*Mùdì jiù shì [shuō],*

  purpose just COP say

  The purpose of this is to say,

10. OV: →   [怕你],

     [*Pà nǐ*],

     afraid.of 2SG

     (Them being) afraid of you,

11. …骗了他。

 …*piàn le tā.*

  lie PRF 3SG

  lying to them.

12. Y: → …不是怕你骗他。

  …*Bùshì pà nǐ piàn tā.*

  NEG afraid.of 2SG lie.to 3SG

  (They are) not afraid of you lying to them.

13. → …他帮你解决问题啊。

  …*Tā bāng nǐ jiějué wèntí a.*

  3SG help 2SG solve problem PRT

  They are trying to help you to solve the problem.

14. T: → 你钱包丢了嘛。

  Nǐ qiánbāo diào le ma.

  2SG wallet loss PRF PRT

  (Since) you lost a wallet,

15. → 不给你把那个钱包[弄回来]?

  Bù gěi nǐ bǎ nà gè qiánbāo [nòng huílái]?

  NEG give 2SG BA that CLF wallet get back

  won't you want (the police) to get it back for you?

16. Y: [钱包]就是什么都--

      [*Qiánbāo*] *jiùshì shénme dōu--*

      wallet just anything all

      The wallet has just--

---

3. Transcription system used here follows Du Bois et al. (1993) and Du Bois (2006). Each punctuation line roughly indicates an intonation unit as defined in Chafe (1987, 1994; Du Bois et al. 1993; Du Bois 2006; Tao 1996). Line numbering generally corresponds to intonation units; to save space, however, some IUs are lumped together under one line number. For a complete list of transcription symbols, see Appendix A.

4. Glossing conventions can be found in Appendix B.

17.   没--
       Méi--
       NEG.have
       There was nothing left.

In this example, Y, the primary speaker, is telling T, Y's campus officemate, and OV, an overseas visitor, about a past incident involving him losing his wallet on a bus in Hong Kong and how he has sought the help of the police to get it back. In line 4, the second person singular pronoun *ni* is used in a reported speech of police addressing Y, the narrator and the protagonist of the recounted story, and in line 10, the token *ni* is used by OV to address the same narrator/protagonist Y. Thus these instances are clearly identifiable as standard deictic uses. However, the other instances – in lines 12 and 13 ('not afraid of you lying to them' and 'help you to solve the problem') and lines 14 and 15 ('(since) you lost a wallet' and 'get the wallet back for you') – can be indeterminate between generic and literal uses if considered out of context, as the lexico-grammatical features in these utterances do not help differentiate their status. To ascertain these cases, we need to look at the participation roles and the relationship between the participants of the conversation. From these perspectives, all of these instances can be identified as general rather than literal for the fact that they are all addressed to OV, the visitor who is not involved in the narrated story and who could not have had knowledge of the incident prior to the conversation. Furthermore, considering the fact that these utterances are produced by Y, the narrator/protagonist (lines 12–13) and T (lines 14–15), the officemate who has demonstrated his access to the information about the incident as a local party throughout the conversation, we can be confident in claiming that none of the second person pronouns in these instances should be taken literally (to refer to the visitor OV), and thus must be understood as generic (or impersonal in the sense of Biq (1991)).

Having described the relevant categories and some of the factors that need to be taken into account in identifying these categories, I now report some initial general observations from the data.

3.   General broad patterns in conversation

Some of the prominent patterns we can notice immediately when conversation data is considered include the following: (1) clustering; (2) locally conditional generalities; and (3) primary speaker roles. I describe these patterns in detail below.

3.1 Clustering

A common pattern throughout the data is that the generic uses of the second person singular pronoun do not tend to appear in isolation but are more likely to occur in multiple instances adjacently. If we take intonation units (Chafe 1987, 1994; Du Bois et al. 1993; Tao 1996) or turn constructional units by the same speaker as the basis for counting, and define clustering as two or more tokens used adjacently in a span of five or fewer consecutive intonation units, we can see that there are more generic uses in clusters than in isolation. Thus in Example (1) just discussed, we can see that there are four tokens (in lines 12–13 and 14–15) forming two clusters. Example (2) below shows a cluster of six tokens in the span of 5 IUs (lines 1, 3, 5, 6, and 7) by the same speaker.

(2) Two officemates at a research institute work in front of a computer chatting about computer screensaver uses and options.

```
1. M: → 这屏幕保护就是说[你--]
        Zhè  píngmù bǎohù    jiùshì shuō [nǐ--]
        This screen protection just   say  2SG
        Screen protection means that [you--]
2. W:                     [也--]
                          [Yě--]
                          Also
3. M: → 你--
        Nǐ--
        2SG
        You--
4. W:   也没人去^换它.
        yě   méi    rén    qù ^huàn tā.
        also NEG.have person go change 3SG
        No one needs to change it.
5. M: → 只要你过一会儿就这个,
        Zhǐyào  nǐ guò yīhuǐ'r jiù zhège,
        just.need 2SG pass a.while then this
        As long as you wait a while,
6.    → ..你到那儿你以为机器是^关着的呢,
        ..nǐ dào nàr  nǐ yǐwéi jīqì   shì ^guānzhe de ne,
        2SG  go there 2SG think machine COP turn-off PRT PRT
        when you get there, you think the machine is off,
7.    → ..然后结果你一^碰就,
        ...ránhòu jiéguǒ nǐ yī  ^pèng jiù,
        afterward then   2SG once touch then
        and if you just touch it,
8.    …<@=>
9.    <@实际, 机器是开着的.@>
        <@shíjì,    jīqì   shì kāizhe de.@>
        actually, machine COP on   PRT
        (you'll see that) actually, the machine stays on.
```

Table 1 provides an overview of the data in this respect.

Table 1. Clustering of general second person uses

	Clusters	Tokens in clusters	Tokens in isolation	Total
HK	10	23	3	26
GEO	10	22	24	46
CALPER-K3	12	33	13	46
OfficeChat	7	17	8	25
JIAOYU	0	0	1	1
DinnerParty	2	4	1	5
LDC-11	2	4	5	9
Total	43	103/65%	55/35%	158/100%

From Table 1, we can see that the majority (103 out of 158 or 65%) of the tokens are in clusters, and 35% of the tokens do not co-occur with others in the defined span of adjacent units.

3.2 Locally conditioned generalities

The second prominent feature in the data is that while the referential target may be elusive, the generality expressed in the utterances is typically locally conditioned and does not involve strictly universally applicable formulations of morals and truisms (following the terminologies of Laberge & Sankoff (1979) and Kitagawa & Lehrer (1990)). By locally conditioned, I mean, first of all, there is no obvious emphasis on the applicability of the statement to every possible human being and at all times – some of the defining traits of a true universal statement; and secondly, the propositions expressed in the utterances are instead tied closely to the topics under discussion in the current conversational sequence. In other words, they are general enough but not truly universal statements. Following Sacks (1975), the statements seen in conversations may best be deemed more "limited statements". Thus in Example (1), lines 14–15, we see that Speaker T indicates that *nǐ qiánbāo diàole ma, bù gěi nǐ bǎ nàgè qiánbāo nòng huílái?* 'Since you lost a wallet, doesn't it makes sense (for the police) to get it back to you?'. This pair of utterances clearly contains some common sense logic (the naturalness of retrieving an important lost personal item and doing so through the help of law enforcement authorities) with a wide scope of applicability (e.g. its applicability to other items and on similar occasions, etc.). However, the universality can be argued to be constrained in many dimensions, of which we just need to list a few as quick illustrations: it is about getting back a lost wallet and not, for example, about the utility or quality of wallets in general; it is also about getting back a wallet and not about, e.g., purchasing a wallet, etc. – and the list can go on. Likewise, in the case of Example (2), while the second person expressions touch on the workings of computer screensavers, it is not about, say, screensaver design principles or energy cost/saving possibilities associated with screensavers, and so on and so forth. The point is that, although the generic statements are made to convey some kind of generality, they lack an emphasis on, e.g. the entire humanity or timelessness and are limited in various other ways in their predication of the subject involved, as there are potentially unlimited ways to make general statements about the relevant entities in question (Sacks 1975). As we will show later, this kind of limited generality constructed through the use of the second person pronoun is not incidental, but rather context driven, designed as a way to illustrate a point, and serves to address contingencies at a particular moment in the ongoing course of conversational interaction.

In this connection, it is useful to revisit some of the earlier literature on the types and scopes of reference that may be delineated from indefinite second person expressions, Laberge and Sankoff (1979), while discussing French indefinite pronouns (*on* 'one', *tu/vous* 'you', etc.), make a distinction between 'situational insertion', which, according to the authors, refers to elevation of a personal experience to a situation where anyone can participate through the insertion of an indefinite agent, and 'formulations of morals and truisms', which are said to be reflections of conventional wisdom (p. 430) and which are deemed more general and forceful in discourse. In a similar vein, Kitagawa and Lehrer (1990) differentiate the notions of impersonal (universal, covering the entire humanity) and vague (limited to some subsets of people) uses of *you* in English. Following the distinctions made in this literature, my survey of the data shows that nearly all of the Mandarin conversational cases can be more precisely characterized as 'situational insertions' or 'vague' uses rather than the broader 'formulations of morals and truisms' or the (more strictly defined, universally applicable) "impersonal" uses. This is additionally illustrated by Example (3) given next.

(3) An academic visitor from the US (M) discussing recent history of China with a local Beijing resident (F).

```
1 F:   要不然= ,
       Yào bùrán=,
       if  NEG
       If not=,
2      ..如果中= ,
       ..Rúguǒ Zhōng=,
       if    Chin(a)
       if    Chin=,
3      ..^政府不投资的话,
       ..^zhèngfǔ bù tóuzī dehuà,
       government NEG invest if
       (the Chinese) government doesn't invest,
```

4   ..那么一家一户的农民谁也做不了。
      ..nàme yījiāyīhù   de nóngmín shéi yě zuò bù liǎo.
      then individual.family ASSO farmer anyone also make NEG PRT
      the individual farmers can't do it.

5 M: ..是啊。
      ..Shì a.
      COP   PRT
      That's right.

6 F: → 可你^政府过去也^政府也穷,
      Kě nǐ ^zhèngfǔ guòqù yě ^zhèngfǔ yě qióng,
      but 2SG government past also government also poor
      But in the past (you see) the government also was poor,

7   全国都穷。
      Quánguó   dū qióng.
      whole.country all poor
      The whole country was poor.

8   → ^那你说这个,
      ^Nà nǐ shuō zhège,
      so 2SG say this
      So you (may want to) say that this (is),

9   ..(H) ^恶性循环,
      ..(H) ^èxìng xúnhuán,
            vicious cycle
            a vicious cycle,

10 → 你从哪儿开始?
      nǐ cóng nà'er kāishǐ?
      2SG from where start
      And where do you start?

11 M: @
12 F: @

In this example, we can see that the scope of reference expressed in association with the second person pronouns goes from the Chinese government to the whole country. Even though these are admittedly large referential domains, what is described here is far from being timeless and covering the entire humanity, namely truly "impersonal" as defined by Kitagawa and Lehrer (1990). Instead, the reference only covers a specific temporal period (during the Chinese Cultural Revolution) and is restricted to China proper. Moreover, the point of inserting the addressee and/or an indefinite agent into the scene (a la Laberge & Sankoff 1979) is to generalize the experience and illustrate the point that is being made by the current speaker in this stretch of the talk.

3.3   Primary speaker roles

The use of the second person pronoun as a generic expression in natural conversations is observed to be associated with a primary speaker role. Conversation analysts have shown that in everyday talk-in-interaction, as far as turn allocation is concerned, each speaker is generally entitled to conversation turns without prescribed amounts or apriori roles (Sack, Schegloff, & Jefferson 1974). However, in the actualization of the flow of conversation, speakers constantly negotiate speaker status based on a host of factors, including the current topic of the conversation or the subject matter of concern, who has the epistemic authority or responsibility, and who is willing to take on the role of the main speaker, among others. In this regard, we often observe that some speakers may take over the floor and dominate the conversation (or stretches of conversations) as the result of speaker negotiation in interaction. One corollary of this phenomenon is the use of generic expressions: typically the party who is, or who attempts to be, the primary speaker tends to use the generic expression more frequently than those who are (or do) not, even though primary speakership is not necessarily bound to yield generic expressions.

Two pieces of evidence may be culled to support this claim. The first comes from conversations where there is a natural or understood primary speaker throughout the conversation.[5] In the coded dataset, two conversations are deemed to qualify for this category: HK, where the entire conversation centers on one speaker (Y) recounting his experience of losing and then recovering his wallet with the help of the police (see Example (1)); and GEO, where one overseas visiting academic is asking a local contact various questions regarding China's geography and recent history (see Example (3)). The association of generic expressions with these speakers and their counterparts is represented in Table 2.

Table 2. Association of generic expressions with primary speaker roles

Datasets	Primary speaker	Non-primary speaker(s)	Total
HK	17 (65%)	9 (35%)	26 (100%)
GEO	29 (63%)	17 (37%)	46 (100%)
Total	46 (64%)	26 (36%)	72 (100%)

Although the tendency (64% vs. 36%) may not seem as robust as it may otherwise be, we can still see an affinity of these expressions with the identified primary speakers in these contexts. I will explain the non-primary speaker contributions when we discuss the various social activities implemented with this linguistic practice in Section 4.

---

5. By natural and understood primary speaker, I do not intend to mean that speakership and any other kinds of relationships held among participants are always predetermined and fixed. Rather, any actualized status and relationships should be understood as a temporary solution, or an 'achievement', based on the dynamic interaction of the settings and the negotiation between speakers during the actual conduct of conversation.

Our second piece of evidence, which concerns the opposite of the preceding case, comes from the other conversations in the database where the speaker role is more dynamically defined throughout the interaction, namely, there are no clearly dominant speakers as all parties are engaged in free exchange of ideas; and if there is any domination in some parts of the conversation, where any one of the participants can attempt to be a primary speaker, it is usually provisional and in limited sequences, which is typical of most everyday interaction.

Table 3. Distribution of generic expressions in less dominant conversations

Datasets	Speaker A	Speaker B/Others	Total
CALPER-K3	21 (46%)	25 (54%)	46 (100%)
OfficeChat	12 (48%)	13 (52%)	25 (100%)
JIAOYU	1 (100%)	0 (0%)	1 (100%)
DinnerParty	2 (40%)	3 (60%)	5 (100%)
LDC-11	2 (22%)	7 (78%)	9 (100%)
Total	38 (44%)	48 (56%)	86 (100%)

At 44% and 56% (or 47% vs. 53% if we consider only the top two high token frequency talks), the disparity between speakers is much less pronounced than the set profiled in Table 2 where a primary speaker can be naturally identified.

To summarize this section, initial observations have shown three prominent patterns in the Mandarin conversation data: (1) clustering of multiple instances in adjacent units; (2) locally conditioned generalities rather than truly universal statements; and (3) the affinity with a primary speaker role (or lack thereof if primary speakership is more dynamically negotiated).

What accounts for such patterns, then? In the following section, I will show that these patterns are not random but are symptoms of interactional activities to which they are closely associated.

4.   Social activities: When and why speakers deploy second person generic expressions?

The short answer to our main research question is that generic expressions comprising the second person singular pronouns are designed as a special and powerful rhetorical device and are taken advantage of to engage the addressee over some rather unusual, complex, and at times controversial topics. From the perspective of interactional activities, they are deployed to accomplish relatively challenging tasks, including (a) complex informing, (b) persuasion, and/or (c) argumentation. Let's examine these activity patterns in turn.

4.1 Complex informing

Informing typically involves relating information or making statements of facts that may or may not be known to the addressee (Labov & Fanshel 1977; Heritage 1984, 2012; Goodwin 1996). Complex informing takes place when the current topic of the conversation in a particular conversational segment involves a relatively complex state of affairs and is of an A-event (Labov & Fanshel 1977:100), where the speaker who assumes K+ epistemic status does the telling to the other speaker(s) who can be assumed to have K− epistemic status (Heritage 1984, 2012).

In Example (2) we saw earlier, for example, the fact that computer screen-savers work in the way described in the conversation is first of all unknown to speaker W (K−) but is known to M (K+); and secondly, it concerns not just some simple fact but instead sequences of changed states (with display patterns amendable to designs by individual users, with changes from locked screen to on screen after some time lapse, and with user intervention such as touching some areas of the device, etc.).

In Example (3), also discussed earlier, the overseas visitor M asks the local contact who has lived in Beijing all through her life questions about what life was like during the Cultural Revolution. The local contact, who can be assumed to have K+ status, explains in her answers a complex situation involving investments by government and (the lack of investment by) citizens during that time.

Complex informing is engendered of course not only by the need to communicate knowledge in history and technology, but also by the need to communicate likely an unlimited number of other subject matters, among them procedures and products. The following example regarding cooking is a common type of complex informing in everyday interaction.

(4) Two Chinese graduate students at a US college discussing specialty Chinese regional cuisine and cooking procedures.

```
1. F:   你想陕西最有名的凉皮是哪儿的?
        Nǐ xiǎng Shǎnxī zuì yǒumíng de liángpí    shì nǎr  de?
        2SG think Shaanxi most famous ASSO jelly.noodle COP where PRT
        What do you think is the most famous cold jelly noodle in Shaanxi?
2.      你知不知道?
        Nǐ zhī bù zhīdào?
        2SG know NEG know
        do you know?
3. M:   ((One long IU deleted))
4.      [就是拉皮吗,]
        [jiùshì lāpí ma,]
        Just   COP  pulling.skin PRT
        Isn't it the pulling skin (noodles)?
```

5. F: [不一样不一样差得远了,]
        [bù yīyàng bù yīyàng chà   dé yuan le,]
        NEG similar NEG similar different COMP far PRT
        No, no. Quite different, (they are) way different,
6.   ((21 IUs by F on ways to make cold jelly noodle deleted.))
7. F: 面皮儿是这样,
        miànpír   shì zhèyàng,
        steamed.flour.noodle COP this
        The steamed flour noodle is like this,
8. →   ..你把一坨面,
        ..Nǐ bǎ yī tuó miàn,
        2SG BA one CLF dough
        You put a block of dough,
9.   就象和面,
        jiù xiàng huò   miàn,
        just like kneading dough
        it's like kneading dough for,
10.   象包- ..包饺子面一样,
        xiàng bāo- .. bāo jiǎozi miàn yīyàng,
        like make make   dumpling dough same
        like kneading dough for .. for making dumplings,
11. →   ...和完以后你放在水里洗。
        ...hé   wán   yǐhòu nǐ fàng zài shuǐ lǐ   xǐ.
        kneading complete after 2SG put in water inside rinse
        After kneading, you put it in water and rinse it.
12. M: (θ)那不就变成变成面筋了,
        (θ) Nà bù jiù biànchéng biànchéng miànjīn   le,
        then NEG just become   become   dough.gluten PRT
        Wouldn't it become, become dough with gluten then?

In this excerpt, two generic second person pronouns are used (in lines 8 and 11) by F to engage the addressee in describing the process of making a specialty noodle well known in the Shaanxi region. Here, F, by virtue of being from the region and by engaging in the extended telling, can be understood to be the primary speaker who assumes K+ status on this particular subject matter; and the procedures for making such a food product can be deemed relatively complex, especially for the current interlocutor, M, who has demonstrated his lack of familiarity with it.

In short, complex informing, with only a few sample activities discussed here, is one of the common social activities where generic pronouns are put to use by someone who assumes K+ status toward a recipient who has K− status in A-event-centered interaction. Complex informing can take place as long as, in the course of interaction, some epistemic asymmetry is made apparent and an informing action involving a complex subject matter is called for.

However, it needs to be emphasized that complex informing, like any other type of social activity, is never a one-way street. Addressees with K− status can also use second person generic expressions to implement various social actions. One of the common actions taken by non-primary speakers in complex informing activities is to demonstrate co-participant's understanding (Sacks 1969/1992; Heritage 2007). That is, upon receiving the information provided by the primary speaker, the recipient can present alternative and similar cases to serve a range of interactional goals: registering receipt of information, demonstrating understanding of the information, and indexing stance congruence. In the next two cases, we will see two slightly different types of non-primary speaker behaviors with the generic expression in response turns: one relatively simple response, in Example (5), and one with more elaboration, in Example (6).

(5) (Same speakers as in Example (4)) M sharing his reflection of viewing a French movie director personally explaining selected scenes in the movie he directed and how he made the shot angle selections.

```
1. M:    (TSK)反正那个片子吧,
         (TSK)Fǎnzhèng nà  gè piànzi ba,
             anyway   that CLF movie PRT
         (TSK)Anyway, the movie,
2.       就是,
         jiùshì,
         like
         (it's) like,
3.    → …你经他那么一讲,
         …nǐ jīng  tā nàme yījiǎng,
         2SG through 3SG that explain
         you (kind of feel it) after he explains,
4.    → …(.4)[你就--]
         …(.4) [nǐ jiù--]
              2SG then
              you just--
5. F: → [你就]明白了.
         [nǐ jiù míngbái  le.]
         2SG just understand PRT
         You just get it.
6. M: → ..你就觉得有点味道,
         ..Nǐ jiù  juédé yǒu  diǎn  wèidào,
         2SG then feel  exist a.bit taste
         You just feel you can appreciate the nuances so much better.
7. F:    嗯.
         En.
         INT
         Right.
```

Here, after M tells his experience in reviewing the director's expert explanation and before he can make a statement with a truncated generic expression (*nǐ jiù--* 'you just--') in line 4, F comes in and furnishes a candidate understanding, which is also with a generic expression (*nǐ jiù míngbái le* 'you just get it'). This is a quick and brief response from the addressee. By contrast, the next example shows a more elaborate response from the non-primary speaker.

(6) An academic visitor from the US (M) discussing flood control issues in China with a local Beijing resident (F).

```
  1. F:   黄河有的地方=,
          Huánghé yǒu dì   dìfāng=,
          Yellow.River have places
          Some places along the Yellow River,
  2.      就是人家^讲的天河。
          jiùshì rénjiā ^jiǎng de  tiān hé.
          just  others call  ASSO sky  river
          are just like what they call "sky river".
  3.      就是,
          Jiù shì,
          just COP
          that is,
  4.      ..^河在= ,
          ..^Hé zài=,
          river in
          the river is up there,
  5.      ...比这个= .. ^地面要高。
          ...Bǐ    zhège =.. ^dìmiàn yào    gāo.
          compare this      ground  really high
          is higher than the .. the ground.
  6.      ((9 speaker exchanges deleted))
  7. M:   (H).. 嗯%,
          (H).. En%,
                Hmm,
  8.      ...(.4) ^淹死了,
          ...(.4) ^Yān sǐ   le,
                  drown dead PRF
                  (it's) drowned,
  9. F:   .. 很多很多人。
          ..Hěnduō hěnduō rén.
          many    many   people
          many, many people (in the past).
 10. M:   ((9 IUs by M deleted))
 11.      .. 证明这个,
          ..Zhèngmíng zhège,
          proves       this
          (So it) proves that,
 12.      .. 黄河的问题之^大。
          ..Huánghé   de  wèntí   zhī ^dà.
          Yellow.River ASSO problem how big
          How big the problem with the Yellow River is.
 13.  →   ..你这^拔一块堤的话,
          ..Nǐ zhè ^bá yī kuài dī  dehuà,
          2SG this pull one CLF  dike if
          If you break up a dike,
 14.      一死就是呵@,
          yīsǐ jiùshì hē@,
          just death surely PRT
          the death will be in@,
 15.      ..一百万。
          ..Yībǎi wàn.
          one     million
          one million.
```

```
16. F:  <X>
17. M:  了不得的事情。
        liǎobùdé de  shìqíng.
        serious ASSO problem
        A very serious problem.
```

Here the speakers are the same as those in Example (3), where the local resident F is answering various questions posed by the overseas visitor M about issues in Chinese geography and its recent history. In this stretch of the talk, the topic is on flood control, especially in areas along the Yellow River, which due to its special geographical makeup, has historically caused serious flood problems. After F has described various background information of the issues involved and what the Chinese government has done in dealing with them, M demonstrates his understanding of the severity of the issues by depicting, with a generic expression in line 13 (*nǐ zhè bá yī kuài dī dehuà* 'if you break up a dike'), a bad case scenario with a concrete number of casualties ('one million'). By doing so, M can be heard not only registering his receipt of the information from F, his understanding of the severity of the problems involved, but also his affiliative stance with F in evaluating the subject matter at hand (cf. Du Bois' (2007) notion of Stance Triangle).

What cases like (5) and (6) show is that in activities such as complex informing, although the primary speaker is responsible for producing the majority of second person generic statements, the recipient also has the option to use them, albeit for very different kinds of social interactional goals. This is one of the reasons, I submit, that even though there is a strong affinity of second person generic expressions with a primary speakership, such an association is not as exclusive or as absolute, as indicated in the numbers shown in Table 2.

4.2 Persuasion

The second type of activity in which second person generic expressions are commonly found is that of persuasion. This typically takes place when there is a disagreement sequence of some kind where both speakers may attempt to display K+ status, with one speaker attempting to win over the other by projecting a stronger epistemic status (call it K++) than the other party. In the end, however, this other party may indicate tacitly or verbally a willingness to reconcile, resulting in a projected congruent stance shared by all parties. In Example (1) discussed earlier, we saw a sequence where Speaker OV first asks why it is necessary for the police to take along the victim and chase the bus that has left, and then raises the question of whether it is because the police is distrustful of the victim. To rebuke OV's incorrect assumption, both local participants Y and T respond immediately with offers of their explanations containing second person generic expressions, with two tokens in each in their respective turns. Here the last two by Speaker T are reproduced:

Excerpt from Example 1.

14. T: 你钱包丢了嘛。
    Nǐ qiánbāo diào le ma.
    2SG wallet loss PRF PRT
    (Since) you lost a wallet,

15.   不给你把那个钱包弄回来?
    Bù gěi nǐ bǎ nà   gè qiánbāo nòng huílái?
    NEG give 2SG BA that CLF wallet get back
    won't you want (the police) to get it back to you?

After the explanations given by both of the local participants, OV does not continue with any further questioning, implying an acceptance of these explanations and access to their stance.

Example (7) below gives another illustration, where reconciliation is explicitly expressed. In this case, three students who share a college dorm room in Beijing are discussing education programs as related to student career prospects in China. M disagrees with L regarding which is more useful for young people seeking employment in their country: a formal degree or personal connections, and M emphasizes throughout this spate of talk that personal connection is much more beneficial than just a degree. M uses a number of second person generic statements, in lines 2 ('how do you understand it'), 6 ('the knowledge that you've learned doesn't really matter that much'), as well as 15 ('anyone and everyone you pick'). L produces one as well in response in line 9 ('but you do need a degree'). However, in the end, in line 12, L produces tokens of agreement by paraphrasing the gist of M's proposition, *jiùshì rènshí rén* 'so it's more like knowing people (helps)', to which M responds with an affirmation token at line 13 (*duì* 'that's right'), acknowledging L's expressed congruent stance.

(7)   Roommates chat and debate over factors impacting college students' career prospects in China.

1. L: 对,我觉得挺棒的,清华。
    Duì, wǒ juédé tǐng bàng de, Qīnghuá.
    right 1SG feel very robust PRT Qinghua
    Right. I thought Qinghua's (program) is great.

2. M: → 不,不,你怎么说呢,
    Bù, bù, nǐ zěnme shuō ne,
    NEG NEG 2SG how   say PRT
    No no. How do you/one understand this,

3.   其实中国所有的,
    qíshí   Zhōngguó suǒyǒu de,
    actually China   all   POSS
    Actually all of the Chinese,

4.   就是现在世界上MBA都不是说是什么特别好的,
    jiùshì xiànzài shìjiè shàng MBA dōu bùshì shuō shénme tèbié   hǎo de,
    even   now   world up   MBA all NEG COP say what   special good PRT
    even the world's top MBA programs are not of much use.

5.   尤其在中国来讲的话，
       yóuqí   zài Zhōngguó lái jiǎng dehuà,
       especially in China   to talk if
       Especially in China,

6.   → …你可能这个知识上学习根本没有太多的，
       …Nǐ kěnéng zhège zhīshi   shàng xuéxí gēnběn méiyǒu tài duō de
       2SG perhaps this knowledge up   learn really NEG   too much PRT
       the knowledge you've learned doesn't really matter that much.

7.   [用处,最主要--]
       [yòngchù, zuì zhǔyào--]
       use,   most matters
       What matters most--

8. R: [嗯是。]
       [En shì.]
       yeah right
       Yeah, right.

9. L: → [对。但是你要拿文凭。]
       [Duì. Dànshì nǐ yào ná wénpíng.]
       right but   2SG need get degree
       Right, but you do need a degree.

10. M: 不,最主要的是人际关系。
       Bù, zuì zhǔyào de shì rénjì   guānxì.
       NEG most major ASSO COP interpersonal relation
       No, what actually matters is having personal connections.

11. L: …(0.5)哦,
       …(0.5)ó,
               Oh,

12.   [就是认识人。]
       [jiùshì rènshí rén.]
       so   know   people
       so it's more like knowing people (helps).

13. M: [那里头]对,
       [Nà lǐtou] duì,
       that there right
       In there, that's right.

14.   那里头,
       Nà   lǐtou,
       that there
       In there,

15. → …你随便拨出来一个人,
       …Nǐ suíbiàn bō   chūlái yīgè rén,
       2SG randomly pick out   one CLF person
       Anyone and everyone you pick,

16.   …(.3)不是-..不是这里头就是那里头。
       …(.3) Bù shì-.. Bù shì zhè lǐtou jiù shì nà   lǐtou.
         NEG COP-.. NEG COP here inside just COP there inside
       (they all have connections) all over the place.

In persuasion cases, the subject matter may or may not be too complex; however, what figures most prominently in the discussion are divergent stances expressed through, or as, personal opinions, which often come with supporting evidence to convince the opponent. In the end, however, the opponent shows reconciliation either implicitly or explicitly.

4.3   Argumentation

The last type of activity in which second person generic expressions are commonly found in my data is that of argumentation. Argumentation in many ways resembles persuasion, in that both sides attempt to win over the other by projecting a stronger epistemic status (K++) than the other. However, unlike persuasion, where a congruent stance is eventually reached, there is no attested reconciliation at the end in identified argumentation sequences.

A case in point is given in Example (8), where the same two Chinese graduate students at a US college as in Example (4) are engaged in a friendly argument over a non-present third party who allegedly prefers a frugal lifestyle by not being willing to spend money at all on eating out.

(8)   Two graduate students gossiping on lifestyle choices of a non-present third
       party.
```
1. M:   他们, ..那天他俩就是,
        Tāmen, .. nèi tiān tā liǎ jiùshì,
        3PL       that day 3SG two just
        So they, .. the other day they were like,

2.      ..说你到哪吃,
        ..Shuō nǐ dào nǎ   chī,
        ask    2SG go  where eat
        asking me: "Where do you eat?"

3.      我说到 Westwood,
        wǒ shuō dào Westwood,
        1SG say  to  Westwood
        I said "Westwood".

4.      <Q 哎哟多贵啊。Q>
        <Q āiyō duō guì a.    Q>
           INT  how expensive PRT
           "Wow, that's expensive."

5.      …他俩是F2嘛。
        …tā liǎ shì F2 ma.
        3SG two COP F2 PRT
        They are both on F2 visas.

6. F:   哦=, [那就是]两人花,
        Ó=, [nà jiùshì] liǎng rén   huā,
        Oh that COP      two   people expense
        Oh, [that is] two people's expenses,

7. M:       [所以就-]…就肯定不舍得吃了那样的。
        [suǒyǐ jiù-] …jiù kěndìng   bù shědé chī le nàyàng   de.
        So     just  just definitely NEG want eat PRF like.that PRT
        So just-…(they) definitely don't want to eat out like that.

8. F:   (0)对。
        (0)Duì.
        Sure.

9.      …(.3)他们也确实紧张,
        …(.3) Tāmen yě     quèshí jǐnzhāng,
              3PL   indeed really tight
              They are really on a tight budget,
```

10. 　　..你想想。
     　　..Nǐ xiǎng xiǎng.
     　　2SG think think
     　　Think about it.

11. M: → ...(.4)哎你想想也紧张不到哪去。
     　　...(.4) Āi nǐ xiǎng xiǎng yě   jǐnzhāng bù dào nǎ   qù.
     　　　　　INT 2SG think think indeed tight   NEG reach where go
     　　　　　Well, you don't have to be so tight, when you really think about it.

12. F: 　...紧张是紧张,
     　　..Jǐnzhāng shì jǐnzhāng,
     　　tight　　COP tight
     　　Well, (having) a tight budget is one thing,

13. 　　但是..所有的[中国人在这儿]都想存钱。
     　　dànshì.. suǒyǒu de [Zhōngguó rén   zài zhèr] dōu xiǎng cún qián.
     　　but　　all　　ASSO Chinese people in here all want save money
     　　but..(more importantly because) all Chinese students here want to save
     　　money.

14. M: →　　　[你吃能-, 就吃--]
     　　　　　[Nǐ chī néng-, jiù chī--]
     　　　　　2SG eat can   just eat
     　　　　　You can eat-, just eating--

15. 　→ 你吃还能吃多少钱?
     　　Nǐ chī háinéng   chī duōshǎo qián?
     　　2SG eat after.all eat how.much money
     　　But just how much do you need to spend on eating (food)?

16. F: 问题是所有的人都要存钱。
     　　Wèntí shì suǒyǒu de rén   dōu yào cún qián.
     　　Problem COP all   ASSO people all want save money
     　　The real reason is that people want to save money.

17. 　　..都要给自己留后路。
     　　..Dōu yào gěi zìjǐ liú   hòulù.
     　　all   want give self leave leeway
     　　everyone wants to have some leeway for themselves.

18. 　　...[你象--]
     　　...[Nǐ xiàng--]
     　　2SG like
     　　You see--

19. M: [我就--]我就现在就快没后路了。
     　　[Wǒ jiù--] wǒ jiù xiànzài jiù kuài méi hòulù le.
     　　1SG just 1SG just now   just nearly NEG leeway PRT
     　　Well I just-- I'm almost out of leeway now.

20. 　　@@@[@],

21. F: 　　[你=], 你一个人花的还少。
     　　　[Nǐ=], nǐ yī gè rén   huā de hái   shǎo.
     　　　2SG   2SG one CLF person spend NOM still little
     　　　Well you=, you are single so you just don't spend as much.

22. M: 啊=。
     　　A=.
     　　Yeah=.

23. 　　...(.5)不..要不然, 也X--
     　　...(.5) Bù ..yào bùrán, yě   X -
     　　　　　NEG if　　NEG　　just X
     　　　　　But no .. Otherwise, just X--

24. F: (θ)哎李学军怎么吃那么点钱啊?
         (θ) Āi Lǐ Xuéjūn zěnme   chī nàme diǎn   qián a?
               INT NAME NAME ˉ how.come eat so   little money PRT
               By the way, how come Li Xuejun spends so little on food?
25. M: 存也存不--
         Cún yě   cún bù--
         Save actually save NEG
         (I) don't save much either--
26.   他交学费。
         Tā jiāo xuéfèi.
         3SG pay tuition
         He pays tuition.

In this excerpt, the central issue surrounding the dispute is whether or not food cost justifies the target third party's choice of not eating out (at all). While Speaker F thinks that this is justified as they have limited resources and still want to save as everyone else does, Speaker M thinks that this is hard to understand since food cost is not that much as consumption is always limited. By using two generic expressions in lines 14 and 15 ('you can eat-, just eating-- But just how much do you need to spend on eating (food)?'), M tries to engage F in direct ways by using a second person pronoun without literal denotation and convince her of his stance. However, there is no sign that the speakers have come to a consensus on this matter by the end of this particular contested sequence – in fact their opposing views have been displayed throughout the excerpt and from various angles. To wit:

Lines 9–11: F: the parties in question are on a tight budget – M: their budget can't be too tight.
Lines 16–19: F: All Chinese students want to save in order to have some leeway – M: As a Chinese student I'm not saving much and I'm about to run out of leeway.
Lines 21–25: F: Because you are single, you may not spend as much. – M: I'm single but still can't save much.

In the end, while they have put their differences on record without a closure, they move on to talking about something else (mainly regarding tuition costs and their own spending habits).

While we have seen that persuasion and argumentation can be shown as two distinct categories – where the former ends with one party showing a willingness to reconcile by shifting stance toward the other, while the latter does not end this way – there is yet a third possibility found in the data, which seems to occupy a middle ground between those two. That is, the disagreement sequence ends with a concession but short of a complete shared stance. This is illustrated by Example (9).

In Example (9), the same two co-workers as in Example (2) at a research institute in Beijing are engaged in a lively discussion about music, namely important factors that may impact symphony concert conducting. M takes the stance that the conductor's role is important as the person in this position controls the flow by approaching individual music players at different points of conducting the concert, whereas W insists that music scores actually play a major role in dictating what musicians do at different points of the playing. While the disagreement is apparent throughout the sequence, how this sequence ends sets it apart from both the typical cases of persuasion and argumentation presented so far.

(9)   Research institute co-workers argue over important factors in conducting a
      symphony concert.

1. M: 还有一种指挥里边儿有一种信息，
         Hái yǒu   yī zhǒng zhǐhuī   lǐbianr yǒu   yī zhǒng xìnxī,
         also there.be one CLF   conducting inside there.be one CLF   information
         There is also a kind of information in conducting music,

2.   可能是^乐器。
         kěnéng shì ^yuèqì.
         perhaps COP instrument
         It may be something about musical instruments.

3.   …(.5)因为什么呢，
         …(.5) Yīnwèi shénme ne,
             because what   PRT
             Because that,

4.   <@那个=@>，
         <@nàgè =@>,
             that,

5.   …但是现在我想呢，
         …Dànshì xiànzài wǒ xiǎng ne,
         but   now   1SG think PRT
         as I think about it,

6.   就说，
         jiù shuō,
         just say,

7.   交响乐队吧，
         jiāoxiǎng yuèduì   ba,
         symphony orchestra PRT
         a symphony orchestra,

8. →   ..你比如说大提琴在这儿，
         ..Nǐ bǐrú   shuō dàtíqín zài   zhèr,
         2SG for.example say cello be.in here
         For example, here is the cello,

9.   小提琴在这儿，
         xiǎotíqín zài   zhèr,
         violin be.in here
         the violin is here,

10. W: 那是[固定位置。]
         nà   shì [gùdìng wèizhì.]
         that COP fixed   positions
         Actually they have fixed positions.

11. M: [他，他，]
            [Tā, tā,]
            3SG 3SG
            s/he, s/he,

12.   对呀,
         duì   ya,
         right PRT
         Yes,

13. → 所以他冲着你,
         suǒyǐ tā chōngzhe nǐ,
         so   3SG lean   2SG
         So if the conductor leans toward you,

14. → 那肯定是你^奏。
         nà   kěndìng shì nǐ ^zòu.
         then must   COP 2SG play
         then it must mean it's you to play.

15. F: ..[嗯].
         ..*[En]*.
         ..Um.

16. M: [那]他要该大提琴了,
         [Nà] tā yào gāi   dàtíqín le,
         then 3SG want should cello   PRF
         Then if s/he wants the cello,

17. → 他就嗯一点你,
         tā jiù ń yīdiǎn   nǐ,
         3SG just PRT once point.at 2SG
         s/he just signal a little bit at you,

18.   ..然后就怎么着,
         ..*Ránhòu jiù zěnmezhe*,
         then   just what.happen
         then it just happens,

19. W: (0) [不=]。
         (0) *[bù=]*.
             NEG
             No=.

20. M: [但是],
         [Dànshì],
         but,

21. W: → 那你-,
         nà   nǐ-,
         then 2SG
         and you-,

22.   那那个谱=子里边儿,
         nà nà gè pǔ=zi   lǐbianr,
         then that CLF music.score inside
         Actually in the music score=,

23.   就说那个=,
         jiù shuō nàgè=,
         just say that CLF
         just say that,

24.   ...咱们都不懂啊,
         ...*zánmen dōu bù dǒng   a*,
         1PL   all NEG understand PRT
         while neither of us are experts here,

25.   ..<@就说@>, @
         ..<@*Jiù shuō*@>,@
            just say
            Let's just say, @

26.　　　..^哪个地方,
　　　　　..^Nǎge dìfāng,
　　　　　that   place
　　　　　in there,

27.　　　..该谁上,
　　　　　..Gāi shéi shàng,
　　　　　should who go.up
　　　　　(to decide) who should go up (when),

28.　→　..你^不点我,
　　　　　..Nǐ ^bu diǎn   wǒ,
　　　　　2SG NEG signal 1SG
　　　　　(even if) you don't point at me,

29.　　　我也知道该我上了,
　　　　　wǒ yě   zhīdào gāi   wǒ shàng le,
　　　　　1SG actually know   should 1SG go.up PRT
　　　　　I would still know it's time for me (to play),

30.　　　[那块儿]。
　　　　　[nà kuàir].
　　　　　that place
　　　　　over there.

31. M:　 [那倒是]。
　　　　　[Nà dǎoshì].
　　　　　that kind.of.true
　　　　　That's kind of true.

32. F:　 是不是。
　　　　　Shì   bù shì.
　　　　　right NEG right
　　　　　Right?

33. M:　 ..不过那个,
　　　　　..Bùguò nàigè,
　　　　　but   that
　　　　　But then,

• 34.　　对。
　　　　　Duì.
　　　　　Correct.

35.　　　因为^我怎么回事呢,
　　　　　Yīnwèi ^wǒ zěnme huí shì ne,
　　　　　because 1SG something.happen PRT
　　　　　Because what's happened with me (was that),

36.　　　我小时候,
　　　　　wǒ xiǎo   shíhòu,
　　　　　1SG little time
　　　　　when I was young,

37.　　　参加宣传队儿,
　　　　　cānjiā xuānchuán duìr,
　　　　　join   performing troupe
　　　　　I was part of this performing troupe,

In this case, the stance incongruence is made apparent throughout, as in the span of lines 11–18, M, with the use of three generic expressions (e.g. *suǒyǐ tā chōngzhe nǐ, nà kěndìng shì nǐ zǒu* 'so if the conductor directs toward you, that must mean it's you to play'), points out the way in which a conductor controls individual musicians. Starting from line 19, however, W registers her opposing view with an explicit disagreement token *bù* 'no', and then follows it with elaborations added with her own generic expression at line 28 (*nǐ bu diǎn wǒ, wǒ yě zhīdào gāi wǒ shàng le* 'even if you don't point at me, I would still know it's time for me to play').[6] After W's expressed disaffiliation, M shows signs of reconciliation with the use of the fixed expression *nà dǎoshì* 'that's kind of true'. Moreover, after W follows it up with another confirmation checking expression *shì bù shì* 'right?' in line 32, M reinforces his commitment with his own follow-up affirmation token *duì* 'correct' in line 34. If the sequence were to end here, we might argue that this is a typical case of persuasion as M shows explicitly his access to W's stance and does so on two occasions at the end of the sequence. However, during this ending stretch of the talk, we also see that M mixes his affirmation tokens with resistance, and the resistance level appears to be stronger than the concession level expressed.

M's resistance stance is expressed lexically in two places: at line 33, where M registers his resistance with a contrastive marker *bùguò nàigè* 'but that/then', and at line 35, where he follows it up with a causal clause *yīnwèi wǒ zěnme huí shì ne* 'because what's happened with me (was)', which takes place in a post-position typically associated with an account for a dispreferred or highly marked proposition (Ford 1994; Song & Tao 2009), and he goes on to recount a long story about what he has experienced in a youth performance troupe where the director picks on players to perform out of position musical acts – all of this is clearly designed to validate his conviction, and in his continued pursuit to convey to his opponent, that the conductor has the power to impact the music production in important ways.

There are also contrastive prosodic cues showing that M's affiliative stance is weaker than his resistance. The Praat (Boersma & Weenink 2021) generated graph below shows that the contrastive expression *bùguò* (*nàgè*) 'but (that/then)' (in the center box) is produced with higher pitch (shown on the bottom line, 270.1Hz vs. 230.6Hz) and more intensity (middle line, 89.62dB vs. 84.22dB) than the agreement markers *nà dǎoshì* 'that's kind of true'; and in comparison with the second affirmation marker *duì* 'correct', while their pitch level is about the same (270.1Hz vs. 271Hz), the intensity level is again much higher on the contrastive expression *bùguò* (*nàgè*) 'but (that/then)' (89.62dB) as opposed to the affirmation token *duì* 'correct' (84.7dB).

From Example (9), we can see that there are cross-cutting cases where a speaker may show a weak affiliative stance but continues to register some sort of resistance. By extension, the relationship among the three types of interactional activities, complex informing, persuasion, and argumentation, should be viewed

---

6. The sense of genericity here is constructed with both the first (*wǒ*) and second person (*nǐ*) pronouns and is helped with the fact that the interlocutors are not musicians by profession.

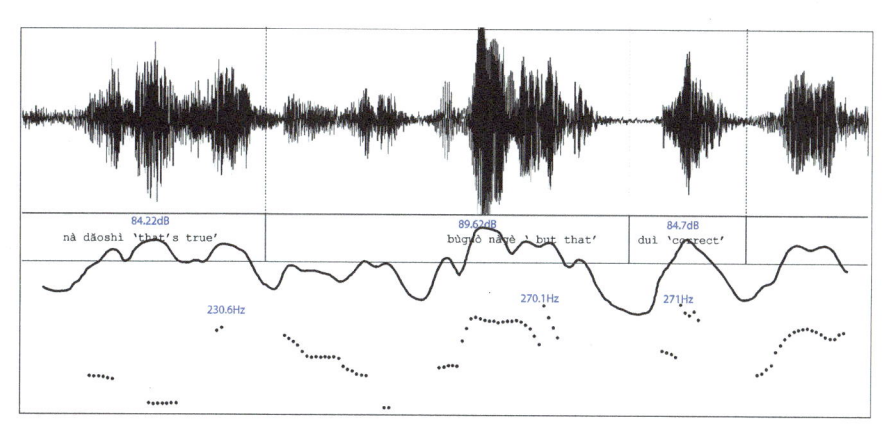

Figure 1. Prosodic cues indexing weaker reconciliation (beginning and ending boxes) and stronger disagreement stances (center box) by M

as closely related rather than discrete categories, for the simple reason that speakers can always alter the nature of the interaction by responding in different ways (agreeing, challenging, reserved reconciliation, etc.), thus changing the interactional dynamics. Moreover, some of the activities can also easily evolve into another type, especially among the adjacent types in the three categories analyzed here, e.g. complex informing can be built into an activity of persuasion, and persuasion can develop into an argumentation.[7] A related issue is that since most of the conversations in my database are between friends and acquaintances, most of the exchanges can be characterized as intimate and/or friendly. There may well be cases where the generic expressions are used in more adversarial and confrontational settings and the function of their use may need to be cast in a much negative light, such as the cases of "attacks", "warnings", and "advices" reported in Sacks (1965/1992: 167) for English. But this should not be considered a counterexample to my overall contention that second person generic expressions are special rhetorical devices designed for rather unusual occasions in interaction in terms of the nature of the topical matter and the way interaction is conducted.

Also, looking at the cases of persuasion and argumentation, plus the cross-cutting cases between persuasion and argumentation, we can see that in these contexts the affinity of the second person generic expressions with speakership shows no strong skewing patterns. This is because there are no natural dominant speakers (so anyone can attempt to be a primary speaker provisionally) and the two sides are taking divergent stances – at least at the beginning. This fact,

---

7. For this and related reasons (e.g. single uses), I have not attempted in this chapter to provide a precise count of the numbers of occurrence for each of these activity categories and focus instead on the qualitative analysis of them.

along with the non-primary speaker's contribution in responses turns in complex informing activities discussed in Section 4.1, contributes to the strong yet non-absolute association of generic expressions across speakers (as captured by the numbers in Tables 2 and 3).

To summarize this section, we have discussed three major categories of conversation interactional activity where second person generic expressions are frequently put to use: complex informing, persuasion, and/or argumentation, which are distinct yet closely intertwined. We have also seen some related secondary patterns, which include the non-primary speaker's use in responses to the primary speaker and intermediate cases traversing multiple categories. Next we discuss some broad issues raised by the Mandarin conversation data before concluding the chapter in Section 6.

5.   Discussion

This chapter starts with three general observations, including: (1) clustering of multiple instances in adjacent units; (2) locally conditioned generalities as opposed to true universal statements; and (3) the association with a primary speaker role (or lack thereof if primary speakership is more dynamically negotiated). Having discussed some of the major interactional uses of the generic expressions in the preceding section, we are now in a position to explain the three observed tendencies initially reported.

5.1   The preference for clusters

We have seen that although isolated uses are not uncommon, it is the multiplicity of instances in adjacent units that constitutes the majority. I believe this is explainable by some of the factors cutting across the three conversation interactional activities just discussed. All three of the functions – complex informing, persuasion, and/or argumentation – can be characterized as somewhat unusual, challenging, and at times contentious, in comparison with mundane exchanges where both the topic and the conduct of conversation are routine affairs in conducting everyday interactional business. To engage the interlocutors in such marked interactive processes – sometimes even with a desire to win over the other party – speakers (especially the natural and provisional primary speakers) need to mobilize effective strategies to accomplish their goal, and multiple uses of the second person generic expression, by way of making reference to the addressee, can help the speaker in this regard in some direct ways.

First, with the second person pronoun, the expression can minimally draw the attention of the addressee (Biq 1991), manipulate the addressee's perspective (or multiple perspectives with multiple saying) for intersubjectivity (Hsiao 2011), and build solidarity with, or opposition to, the addressee (Kuo 2002) in direct ways, no matter how much the literal deictic connotation is to be determined. According to Sacks (1965/1992), for English at least, the second person reference is extensible from the addressee to a broad scope, or as he puts it, *you* may mean 'you alone' and/or 'you and others' (p. 349). Thus, as Sacks (1965/1992: 166) put it, expressions built on the indefinite second person pronoun constitutes a powerful tool for manipulating speaker perspectives (cf. Laberge and Sankoff's (1979: 430) discussion of the forceful nature of true generic statements).

Second, while the single instances of these expressions alone have been recognized as "powerful" and "forceful" in the literature, the multiplication of them serves as 'buildups', to borrow the term of Sacks (1965/1992: 348) on a closely related phenomenon.[8] As our earlier examples have shown, multiple instances in adjacent turn constructional units often demonstrate different angles and different aspects of the complex and/or controversial subject matter under discussion, and as the tokens pile up, multiple applications can only increase the rhetorical effect of telling, persuasion, and argumentation – not to mention the other potentially more adversarial activities/contexts such as verbal attacks and warnings described by Sacks (1965/1992) for English.

5.2   Limited generality

Turning now to the observed feature of locally conditioned generalities rather than broad statements of morals and truisms, earlier we have seen that second person generic statements in the conversation data tend not to emphasize the entire humanity or timelessness and are limited in various ways in their predication of the subject in question. I suggest that a number of principles proposed in the broad Ethnomethodology/CA/anthropological linguistics/pragmatics literature converge to offer an account for this manifestation. First, in conversation analysis, Sacks (1975: 59) has suggested that the truth of what he calls limited statements, as opposed to more broad statements (with subjects such as 'everyone', although a subject term like 'everyone' can be limited in referential scope in some contexts, as pointed out by Sacks in the same paper), which describes the Mandarin data as well, "would be more amenable to demonstration". He further suggests that "the formulation of the population or the choice of a subject term may

---

8. Namely children's use of multiple second person generic expressions in building up complex strings of syntactic structures.

have some important bearing on the acceptability of a statement" (p. 60). From this perspective, the second person singular pronoun is probably among the safest choices of subject terms available on which to build a general statement, as the reference it designates is originally limited (to a singular person).

Second, scholars of anthropological/interactional linguistic research have shown that there are preferences in making references for persons. In addition to Sacks and Schegloff's (1979) proposals of minimalization and recipient design, the preference of association has been suggested by Brown (2007) and Hanks (2007). This preference dictates that (in third person references) "in certain situations speakers work to explicitly associate the referent directly to the current conversation participants' (Stivers, Enfield, & Levinson 2007:14). Thus, expressions such as 'my sister' and 'your friend', which connect with the current interlocutors ('I' and 'you') of the interaction, are common in referring to third parties. Although the association preference is proposed for third person referential categories, it can be taken to be indirectly applicable to the second person generic expressions under discussion, as, by definition, the generic reference is made directly through the second person singular pronoun. Although second person pronouns may have divergent statuses in different languages, and references for second and third persons may exhibit different behaviors, this kind of preference makes sense for our task at hand given the direct association of the second person pronoun with the addressee to whom the speaker tries to engage in these somewhat unusual interactional episodes.

Finally, in Ethnomethodology, Garfinkel (1967) and his coworkers have suggested that in everyday social activities, indexical expressions and indexical actions are primarily built around the satisfaction of the here and now practical social management (p. 6), where members have to make the best of what they have in social encounters in solving the tasks at hand. In pragmatics theorizing, Sperber and Wilson (1995)'s Relevance Theory also attempts to account for some of the constraints on the nature of speaker contributions in verbal communication in terms of current relevance and worthiness of the addressee's attention. Finally, in a somewhat related vein, Du Bois (1980:233) has suggested a *curiosity principle* (again primarily for third person reference), which states that "a reference is counted as identifiable if it identifies an object close enough to satisfy the curiosity of the hearer." Although in our case the second person reference is not made exactly for curiosity reasons or just to attract the addressee's attention but is much more proactive, so to speak, the essences of current relevance and tolerance of vagueness implied in those principles still apply.

Thus, all of those tendencies identified for reference and social interaction in various strands of research on human communication – preferences in subject term choices in general statements, referencing through the current interlocutors, the preoccupation with current concerns and relevancy, the need to make use of available materials, plus the general tolerance of vagueness in online processing – can be brought to bear on conversationalists' recurrent recruitment of the second person singular pronoun, which is a prime example of indexical expressions, for making general-enough-yet-not-too-broad statements often seen in natural conversation. By building utterances with the second person singular pronoun, the speaker both "poses a task and furnishes a resource" (Learner 1995:282) for the interlocutor to engage in intersubjective negotiations of epistemic stances and resolve the most immediate communicative tasks at hand. In other words, statements of limited generality constructed through the use of the second person pronoun are not incidental, but rather context driven and designed as a special and powerful/forceful rhetorical device to address contingencies that speakers face at the moment in the ongoing conversational interaction.

5.3 **The association with a primary speaker role (or lack thereof if primary speakership is more dynamically negotiated)**

Given the interactive utility described in the preceding sections, it is not difficult to understand the close connection of this device with the primary (or attempted primary) speakership. At the same time, as I have shown in the course of describing the social activities underlying the use of such expressions, this observed tendency can be understood as a variable. That is, in contexts where a primary speaker can be naturally established and where the overall environment is less than competitive or contentious, primary speakers have been shown to produce more tokens than non-primary speakers, as they try to mobilize effective linguistic devices in engaging the interlocutors in marked interactive processes (cf. Section 5.1). Also in such contexts, non-primary speakers may respond with this device to demonstrate their receipt and understanding of the informing and display a congruent stance.

In the more competitive and contentious contexts, on the other hand, both sides have the motivation and freedom to take advantage of this powerful device for competitive reasons, and that correlates with the more evenly distributed production patterns in such settings or in spates of talks.

In short, generic statements centered on the second person singular pronoun can be taken as a powerful rhetorical device utilized by conversationalists for rather demanding occasions. The quantitative skewing or lack thereof reflects the diverse fashions in which interlocutors dynamically operate and negotiate with one another.

6.   Conclusions

While research on referentiality is mostly concerned with NPs and the like, this chapter demonstrates some of the complex aspects of second person pronouns in both the referential and, more importantly, the interactional domains. Specifically, this chapter sets out to tackle the hitherto under-explored question of when and why conversationalists deploy second person generic expressions that feature a general and vague referential scope. I show that the conversational contexts in which they appear are rather marked in some ways – characterized most prominently by segments where relatively complex and/or controversial subject matters are involved, incongruent stances are often displayed, and/or opposing positions need to be contested. These contexts and their associated interactional demands give rise to the patterning of clustering (multiplicity of instances in adjacent units), limited generality (as good-enough-yet-not-too-broad general statements), and primary (or attempted primary) speakership. In general, second person generic statements can be seen as a special and powerful rhetorical device designed for, and frequently taken advantage of, marked interactional occasions.

In closing, this chapter shows that what has been considered ostensibly a peculiar kind of semantic referential issue in generic expressions of second persons can be supplemented with a conversational action-centered approach, for it is in conversation interactional contexts where actual discourse patterns and their corresponding social activities can be most directly examined.

Funding

This research is partially funded through a UCLA Senate Faculty Research Grant (2021–22) on patterns of interaction in Mandarin Chinese.

Acknowledgements

I wish to thank the anonymous referee, the co-editors of the volume, Michael Ewing and Ritva Laury, and Sandra A. Thompson for their careful reading and insightful comments and suggestions on a draft version of this paper. I also wish to thank the audiences at the 2019 International Pragmatics Conference at the Hong Kong Polytechnic University, the City University of Hong Kong, Department of Linguistics and Translation, and Stanford University, East Asian Languages and Cultures Department, where I presented the topic. However, none of the people mentioned above should be held responsible for the way I have made use of their feedback.

References

Berry, Roger. 2009. "You Could Say That: The Generic Second-Person Pronoun in Modern English." *English Today* 25 (3): 29–34.

Biq, Yung-O. 1991. "The Multiple Uses of the Second Person Singular Pronoun *Ni* in Conversational Mandarin." *Journal of Pragmatics* 16 (4): 307–321.

Boersma, Paul and David J. M. Weenink. 2021. *Praat: Doing Phonetics by Computer*. https://www.fon.hum.uva.nl/praat/. Last retrieved January 2021.

Bolinger, Dwight. 1979a. "To Catch a Metaphor: *You* as Norm." *American Speech* 54 (3): 194–209.

Bolinger, Dwight. 1979b. "Pronouns in Discourse." In *Discourse and Syntax*, ed. by Talmy Givon, 287–309. New York: Academic Press.

Brown, Penelope. 2007. "Principles of Person Reference in Tzeltal Conversation." In *Person Reference in Interaction: Linguistic, Cultural and Social Perspectives*, ed. by N. J. Enfield and Tanya Stivers, 172–202. Cambridge: Cambridge University Press.

Canavan, Alexandra and George Zipperlen. 1996. *CALLFRIEND Mandarin Chinese-Mainland Dialect*. Linguistic Data Consortium, Philadelphia.

Chafe, Wallace. 1987. "Cognitive Constraints on Information Flow." In *Coherence and Grounding in Discourse*, ed. by Russell Tomlin, 21–51. Amsterdam: John Benjamins.

Chafe, Wallace. 1994. *Discourse, Consciousness, and Time: The Flow and Displacement of Conscious Experience in Speaking and Writing*. Chicago: University of Chicago Press.

Couper-Kuhlen, Elizabeth and Margret Selting. 2018. *Interactional Linguistics: An Introduction to Language in Social Interaction*. Cambridge: Cambridge University Press.

Dahmen, Josua, and Joe Blythe. 2022. "Calibrating Recipiency through Pronominal Reference". *Interactional Linguistics* 2 (2): 190–224.

Du Bois, John W. 1980. "Beyond Definiteness: The Trace of Identity in Discourse." In *The Pear Stories: Cognitive, Cultural, and Linguistic Aspects of Narrative Production*, ed. by Wallace L. Chafe, 203–74. Norwood, NJ: Ablex.

Du Bois, John W. 2006. *Transcription in Action: Resources for the Representation of Linguistic Interaction*. http://transcription.projects.linguistics.ucsb.edu/representing. Last accessed May 22, 2021.

Du Bois, John W. 2007. "The Stance Triangle." In *Stancetaking in Discourse: Subjectivity, Evaluation, Interaction*, ed. by Robert Englebretson, 139–182. Amsterdam: Benjamins.

Du Bois, John W., Stephan Schuetze-Coburn, Susanna Cumming, and Danae Paolino. 1993. "Outline of Discourse Transcription." In *Talking Data*, ed. by Jane Edwards and Martin Lampert, 45–89. Hillsdale, NJ: Lawrence Erbaum Associates.

Ford, Cecilia E. 1994. "Dialogic Aspects of Talk and Writing: *Because* on the Interactive-Edited Continuum." *Text* 14 (4): 531–554.

Garfinkel, Harold. 1967. *Studies in Ethnomethodology*. Englewood Cliffs, N.J.: Prentice-Hall.

Goodwin, M. H. 1996. "Informings and Announcements in Their Environment: Prosody within a Multi-Activity Work Setting." In *Prosody in Conversation: Interactional Studies*, ed. by E. Couper-Kuhlen and M. Selting, 436–461. Cambridge: Cambridge University Press.

Hanks, William. 2007. "Person Reference in Yucatec Maya Conversation." In *Person Reference in Interaction: Linguistic, Cultural and Social Perspectives*, ed. by N. J. Enfield and Tanya Stivers, 149–171. Cambridge: Cambridge University Press.

Heritage, John. 1984. "A Change-of-State Token and Aspects of Its Sequential Placement." In *Structures of Social Action: Studies in Conversation Analysis*, ed. by J. Maxwell Atkinson and John Heritage, 299–345. Cambridge: Cambridge University Press.

Heritage, John. 2007. "Intersubjectivity and Progressivity in Person (and Place) Reference." In *Person Reference in Interaction: Linguistic, Cultural and Social Perspectives*, ed. by N. J. Enfield and Tanya Stivers, 255–280. Cambridge: Cambridge University Press.

Heritage, John. 2012. "Epistemics in Action: Action Formation and Territories of Knowledge." *Research on Language and Social Interaction* 45 (1): 1–29.

Hsiao, Chi-hua. 2011. "Personal Pronoun Interchanges in Mandarin Chinese Conversation." *Language Sciences* 33 (5): 799–821.

Kitagawa, Chisato and Adrienne Lehrer. 1990. "Impersonal Uses of Personal Pronouns." *Journal of Pragmatics* 14 (5): 739–759.

Kuo, Sai-Hua. 2002. "From Solidarity to Antagonism: The Uses of the Second-Person Singular Pronoun in Chinese Political Discourse." *Text* 22 (1): 29–55.

Laberge, Suzanne and Gillian Sankoff. 1979. "Anything *You* Can Do." In *Discourse and Syntax*, ed. by Talmy Givon, 419–440. New York: Academic Press.

Labov, William and David Fanshel. 1977. *Therapeutic Discourse: Psychotherapy as Conversation*. New York: Academic Press.

Lerner, Gene. 1996. "On the Place of Linguistic Resources in The Organization of Talk-in-Interaction: 'Second Person' Reference in Multi-Party Conversation." *Pragmatics* 6 (3): 281–294.

Lü, Shuxiang. 1985. *Jindai Hanyu Zhidaici* [*Demonstratives and Pronouns in Modern Chinese*], Shanghai: Xuelin Publishing Company.

Rubba, Jo. 1996. "Alternate Grounds in the Interpretation of Deictic Expressions." In *Spaces, Worlds, and Grammar*, ed. by G. Fauconnier and E. Sweetser, 227–261. Chicago: Chicago University Press.

Sacks, Harvey. 1965/1992. Part II, Lecture 6, "'You'." In *Lectures on Conversation* Vol 1, ed. by Gail Jefferson, with an introduction by Emanuel A. Schegloff, 163–168. Cambridge, MA: Blackwell.

Sacks, Harvey. 1966/1992. Part III, Lecture 11, "'You'." In *Lectures on Conversation* Vol. 1, ed. by Gail Jefferson, with an introduction by Emanuel A. Schegloff, 348–353. Cambridge, MA: Blackwell.

Sacks, Harvey. 1969/1992. Part II, Lecture 9, "Sound Shifts; Showing Understanding; Dealing with 'Utterance Completion; Practical Mysticism." In *Lectures on Conversation* Vol. 2 (Winter 1969), ed. by Gail Jefferson, 137–149. Oxford: Blackwell.

Sacks, Harvey. 1975. "Everyone Has to Lie." In *Sociocultural Dimensions of Language Use*, ed. by Ben G. Blount and Mary Sanches, 57–79. New York: Academic Press.

Sacks, H. and Schegloff, E. A. 1979. "Two Preferences in The Organization of Reference to Persons in Conversation And Their Interaction." In *Everyday Language: Studies in Ethnomethodology*, ed. by George Psathas, 15–21. New York: Irvington.

Sacks, Harvey, Emanuel Schegloff, and Gail Jefferson. 1974. "A Simplest Systematics for the Organization of Turn-Taking for Conversation." *Language* 50 (4): 696–735.

Siewierska, Anna. 2004. *Person*. Cambridge: Cambridge University Press.

Song, Zuoyan and Hongyin Tao. 2009. "A Unified Account of Causal Clause Sequences in Mandarin Chinese and Its Implications." *Studies in Language* 33 (1): 69–102.

Sperber, Dan and D. Wilson. 1995. *Relevance: Communication and Cognition* (2nd edition). Oxford: Blackwell.

Stirling, Lesley, and Lenore Manderson. 2011. "About *You*: Empathy, Objectivity and Authority." *Journal of Pragmatics* 43 (6): 1581–1602.

Stivers, Tanya, N. J. Enfield, and Stephen C. Levinson. 2007. "Person Reference in Interaction." In *Person Reference in Interaction: Linguistic, Cultural and Social Perspectives*, ed. by N. J. Enfield and Tanya Stivers, 1–20. Cambridge: Cambridge University Press.

Tao, Hongyin. 1996. *Units in Mandarin Conversation: Prosody, Discourse, and Grammar*. Amsterdam: John Benjamins.

Wales, Katie. 1996. *Personal Pronouns in Present-Day English*. Cambridge: Cambridge University Press.

Xiang, Xuehua. 2019. "Personal Pronouns in Chinese Discourse." In *The Routledge Handbook of Chinese Discourse Analysis*, ed. by Chris Shei, 147–159. London: Routledge.

Appendix A.   Transcription conventions

These transcription conventions are adopted from Du Bois et al. (1993) and Du Bois (2006), with slight modifications.

UNITS	
Intonation unit	{carriage return with a punctuation mark}
Truncated intonation unit	--
Truncated word	–
Speaker identity/turn start	:
Speech overlap	[ ]
UNIT TYPES	
Final	.
Continuing	,
Question	?
Exclamation	!
LENGTHENING	
Lengthening	=
PAUSE	
Long (three tenths or more of a second)	...(.N)
Medium (two tenths of a second)	...
Latching	(0)
PROSODIC PROMINENCE	^
BREATH IN (audible inhalation)	(H)
LAUGHTER	@
CLICK SOUNDS	TSK

TRANSCRIBER'S PERSPECTIVE AND NON-VERBAL ACTIONS

Comment or non-verbal actions	(( ))
Special voice features: Q(quote)	<Q Q>
Uncertain hearing	<X X>
Indecipherable syllable	X

Appendix B.   Glossing conventions

1SG	First person singular
1PL	First person plural
2SG	Second person singular
2PL	Second person plural
3SG	Third person singular
3PL	Third person plural
ASSO	Associative or attributive marker *de*
BA	Object marker *ba*
CLF	Classifier
COMP	Complement
COP	Copula *shì*
INT	Interjection
NEG	Negator
NOM	Nominalization and relative clause marker *de*
PRF	Perfective
PRT	Utterance final particle

Name index

Footnotes are shown by references of the form XnY (footnote Y on page X).

B
Berry, Roger 168
Biq, Yung-O 168, 170N1, 172
Bolinger, Dwight 168
Bruner, Jerome S. 81N1
Bühler, Karl 2, 47–8

C
Chafe, Wallace L. 4–5, 171N3
Chen, Ping 12
Couper-Kuhlen, Elizabeth 132N9, 135N11

D
Davidson, D. 107
de Villiers, Jill 97
Djenar, Dwi Noverini 15
Donnellan, Keith 3
Du Bois, John W. 3–4, 13–14, 143, 171N3, 196, 201

E
Ewing, Michael 7–8, 15–16, 80, 127N4, 136

F
Ford, Cecilia 5
Fox, Barbara 5
Frege, Gottlob 1–2
Fry, John S. 104

G
Givón, Talmy 3–4
Glenn, Philip 163
Goffman, Erving 15, 38, 46
Grice, H. Paul 105–6, 120
Guillaume, Gustave 2

Gundel, Jeanette K. 4

H
Hakulinen, Auli 59
Hanks, William 5, 196
Helasvuo, Marja-Liisa 6–8, 24, 64–5
Hsiao, Chi-Hua 168
Huumo, Tuomas 64

K
Karmiloff-Smith, Annette 83, 97
Kitagawa, Chisato 175–6, 200
Kuno, Susumu 104
Kuo, Sai-Hua 169

L
Laberge, Suzanne 168, 175
Laury, Ritva 6–8, 24, 50, 80
Lehrer, Adrienne 175–6

M
Manns, Howard 14–15
Matsumoto, Yoshiko 7–8, 13, 106N1

N
Nagaya, Naonori 12

O
Ono, Tsuyoshi 6–7, 15, 24, 27, 57, 64, 81, 107, 136, 163N8

P
Plato 1
Prince, Ellen 4
Pustejovsky, James 106N2

Q
Quine, Willard Van Orman 107

R
Russell, Bertrand 1–2

S
Sacks, Harvey 38, 174, 193, 195–6
Sankoff, Gillian 168, 175
Schafer, Robin J. 97
Schegloff, Emanuel A. 6, 196
Seppänen, Eeva-Leena 50
Siewierska, Anna 168
Silverstein, Michael 3
Siro, Paavo 59
Sperber, Dan 196
Strawson, Peter F. 2–3, 7N1
Stukenbrock, Anja 47
Suomalainen, Karita 6–8, 24
Suzuki, Ryoko 7–8, 15, 107, 136, 143, 164

T
Tao, Hongyin 7–8, 136
Thompson, Sandra A. 4, 6–7, 13, 15, 24, 27, 57, 64, 80–1, 132N9, 136, 163N8

V
Vilkuna, Maria 59, 61–2
Vygotsky, Lev 81N1

W
Wilson, D. 196

Subject index

Entries in **bold** denote tables; entries in *italics* denote figures. Footnotes are shown by references of the form XnY (footnote Y on page X).